Garden Route

Brent Naudé-Moseley & Steve Moseley

SUNBIRD
PUBLISHERS

First published in 2010

Sunbird Publishers (Pty) Ltd
www.sunbirdpublishers.co.za

Registration number: 1984/003543/07

Publisher Ceri Prenter
Editor David Bristow
Designers Rob House, Megan Knox and Through the Looking Glass
Proofreader Kathleen Sutton
Cartography John Hall
Index Josephine Bestic

Reproduction by Resolution, Cape Town
Printed by Star Standard (Pte), Singapore

ISBN 978 1 919938 53 0

FRONT COVER: The Knysna turaco, formerly called a lourie – icon of the local
yellowwood forests. INSET IMAGES FROM LEFT TO RIGHT: Beacon Isle hotel; cultivated oysters;
Kynsna Heads. TITLE PAGE: Although these deep woods are often called Knysna, or
yellowwood forest, more correctly they are temperate Afromontane forests.
OPPOSITE: Footprints on an empty beach – you're not alone!

In putting together a book like this, we have been assisted by dozens of people, and although we can't thank all of them individually, we are sincerely grateful for your willingness to help us. Special thanks also go to our sisters who so conveniently live in different towns along the Garden Route: Kelly in Sedgefield, Karen in Knysna, Arlene in Plett; and to Shelley in Wilderness – many thanks for your support. Also to Mark Dixon of the Garden Route Trail, Bev Coetzee from At The Woods guesthouse in Storms River Village, and Ronél Pieterse of Forest Edge at Rheenendal, Knysna – all of whom came back with clear, precise, and prompt answers to our many questions. Thanks go also to the following for their assistance: Marcia at Mossel Bay Tourism, the barefoot writer of Knysna, Martin Hatchuel, Clementine Mbatani of SANParks, and Elke Cable of Knysna Charters. Also to Spike (Steve Pike) of Wavescape, and Marschant of The Swell Guys for info on surfing. As always, we'd also like to thank the great team at Sunbird Publishers!

Brent Naudé-Moseley & Steve Moseley
Loxton, 2009

Contents

INTRODUCTION   7

GETTING STARTED
1 Facts, Figures and Highlights   9
2 Calls to the Wild   15
3 Practical information   25
4 The Big Six Hiking Trails   31

THE PLACES
5 Mossel Bay   41
6 George   65
7 Wilderness   85
8 Sedgefield   97
9 Between Sedgefield and Knysna   109
10 Knysna   131
11 Plettenberg Bay   167
12 Tsitsikamma Region   203

INDEX   223

MAPS
Garden Route   10
Hiking trails   32
Mossel Bay – Regional   42
Mossel Bay – Town   45
George – Regional   66
George – Town   68
Wilderness – Regional   87
Sedgefield – Regional   99
Knysna – Regional   135
Knysna – Town   139
Plettenberg Bay – Regional   169
Plettenberg Bay – Town   171
Tsitsikamma – Regional   205

MAP KEY

- ━━━ National route
- ━━━ Freeway
- gravel tar Main route
- ─── Secondary route
- ····· 4x4 recommended
- ········· Trail
- 🖝 Lodge/accommodation
- 🔺 Camping

- 🍷 Wine Farm
- ✈ Airport/airfield
- ✚ Medical centre/hospital
- 🗿 Memorial/statue
- 🏛 Monument building
- 🅿 Parking
- ✳ Place of interest
- Ⓦ Place of worship

- ✹ Police station
- 🚌 Bus terminus
- ═══ Road, main route
- ▣ Swimming pool
- 📖 Library
- ℹ Information
- 🛏 Accommodation
- -🚂● Train station

The malachite kingfisher is just one the brightly coloured water birds of the Garden route.

HOW TO USE THIS BOOK

This book covers the Garden Route from Gourits River to the Storms River – bookended by the 2 landmark bridges – and is specifically designed to assist independent travellers. However, due to the sheer scale of the activities, attractions, accommodation and eateries that fall into the area, it is by no means a comprehensive guide. What we have aimed to do is to provide you with a guide to the best the area has to offer, rather than everything. With regard to places to stay and things to do, we have listed only our own selection of what we consider to be the best and most representative, across various price categories.

In the first 3 chapters, we provide some background and practical travel information on aspects of the region most relevant to visitors, as well as a brief look at the 'Calls to the Wild' – the plants, animals and landscapes of the area's national parks and reserves; then an overview of what travellers might expect to encounter here.

Chapter 4 covers what are widely regarded as the top 6 hikes in the region, broken down into slackpacking (usually catered trails, where you do not have to carry a full backpack) and full-pack trails.

Then in chapters 5–12 we cover the region in a west-to-east direction (as if coming from the direction of Cape Town and travelling towards Port Elizabeth). Each chapter pertains to a major town along the route and provides information on what there is to see and do, where to stay, where to eat, and other relevant information we hope will assist visitors in planning their itineraries according to their own tastes and preferences.

Notes on the use of Khoi, San and Khoisan

There is no clear understanding of the differences between the people who used to be known as Hottentots and Bushmen. The cultures and the genetics of the 2 groups are complicated and intertwined. In recent times the terms Khoi, San and Khoisan have been used variously to describe these 'first people of Africa'. Simply, when we refer to people who raised sheep, and sometimes cattle, and used pottery, we use the term Khoi; when we speak purely about hunter-gatherers, we call them San; and when we refer to both, or either, Khoisan.

Notes on accommodation categories

Firstly, please note there is a vast range of accommodation we've written about and it is very difficult to pigeon-hole each establishment. We've provided a guideline by separating these into 4 categories based on price/facilities. Prices are for 1 person (/p) or a person sharing (/ps).

◆ SILK – The top pick and one that offers luxurious lodgings, but not necessarily 5-star or silk sheets!

◆ LINEN – Less pricey than silk, but still offering comfort and style, some lean more towards silk and others lean towards calico.

◆ CALICO – Unpretentious and down-to-earth and, in some cases, budget facilities.

◆ CANVAS – camping options.

If you think you have any gems of information that would enhance a future edition of this guide, please contact us at e-mail info@karooimages.co.za.

Enjoy the ride!

Introduction

The Garden Route has been a favourite, almost mystical, destination with locals and visitors from overseas for decades. It is a narrow zone wedged between the Indian Ocean and Cape Folded Mountains that run parallel and close to the coastline, and is a place of great natural beauty. Despite substantial economic growth in recent years, especially around the bigger towns, the area remains South Africa's Garden of Eden, and comprises gloriously long beaches, lush and mysterious forests, rugged coastlines, amber rivers and tranquil lagoons all lorded over by hazy purple mountain ranges. For the purposes of this book, we have covered the area from Gouritsmond, west of Mossel Bay, to Storms River, east of Plettenberg Bay. People will argue over it for ever, but this is and always has been commonly accepted as the extent of the region.

The temperate climate makes it idyllic to visit at almost any time of the year; and, although the beaches are promoted as the main attraction, the forests are equally important. In fact, they are the garden of the Garden Route. Thanks to the varied habitats of forest, fynbos, coastlines, and wetlands, there is a plethora of wildlife, birdlife, and marine life for the nature lover; plus a vast number of activities (adrenalin, adventure, relaxation, or not) and attractions for the visitor. The innumerable accommodation establishments offer everything from 5-star luxury to basic camping facilities; in recent years, the Garden Route has become something of a gourmet route that will satisfy even the most discerning epicure.

There is so much on offer that this book could not possibly be comprehensive, so we have not tried to make it such: we've taken personal experience, cross-referenced it with trusted advice, and added input from local and overseas visitors to the area, and feel the result is an excellent indication of what the Garden Route has to offer across most areas of interest and depth of pockets.

Bear in mind that change in the tourism industry is constant. New places open, existing places close their doors, reputations fluctuate, and management and staff change, so it's possible descriptions in the book may differ to the reality at the time of your visit.

Nothing changes quite as fast as prices: we have given actual current (i.e. 2010) rates for each place that charges a fee, on the understanding that this is the best way to compare places and value-for-money options. From these rates it is easy to compare future prices (and see if anyone is trying to rip you off in the meantime), and extrapolate future prices – at least until the next edition of this guide.

One last note: please tread lightly – this is a very ecologically sensitive area that is being negatively affected by the sheer numbers of people exploring it each year, or chosing to settle here.

By the time Otter trailists reach the beach at Nature's Valley, pain turns to memories.

Facts, Figures, and Highlights 1

Loosely, the definition of a garden is a piece of land usually with a patch of lawn, a few flowerbeds, maybe a veggie patch, some fruit and other trees, and perhaps the odd water feature, all adjoining a private house and used for recreation. In a broad sense the 'garden' in the Garden Route closely fits this description and, most pleasingly, it has all been naturally sculpted. It's just that the 'private house' part – many longstanding visitors feel, and we agree – has gone a bit too far. Its interpretation has been stretched out of proportion to include shockingly designed housing developments, shopping centres, and golf estates. Look beyond these though and focus on everything else that's 'green'. That's where you'll find the real garden attractions and it's where this guide focusses.

Marine reserves along the Garden Route ensure good fishing at places like Gericke's Point.

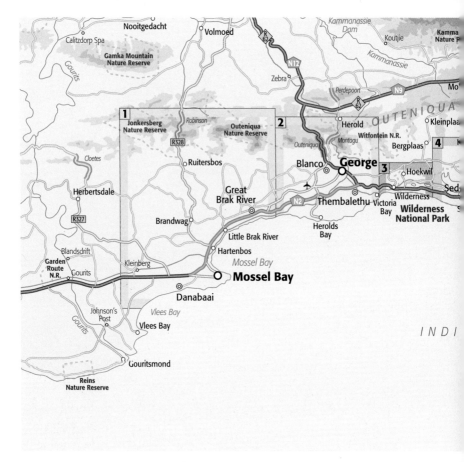

Size

From west to east the Garden Route is roughly 200 km, taking the N2 national road as the spine, and seldom stretches more than 30 km wide between the inland mountain ranges and the coast.

Topography

Undoubtedly the 2 distinguishing features of the Garden Route are mountains and ocean. The coastal plain along which the various routes of the Garden Route meander is really a series of wave-cut platforms formed in the geo-logical past when the sea level here was significantly higher (each level represents an old shoreline). It snuggles up against the Outeniqua and Tsitsikamma mountain ranges to the north while to the south the Indian Ocean unloads onto the alternating rocky and sandy shoreline we see today.

The vegetation is predominantly fynbos (see box on page 107) and Afromontane, or temperate yellow-wood, forest, the latter being remnants of a once vast tract of indigenous trees but which is now interspersed with

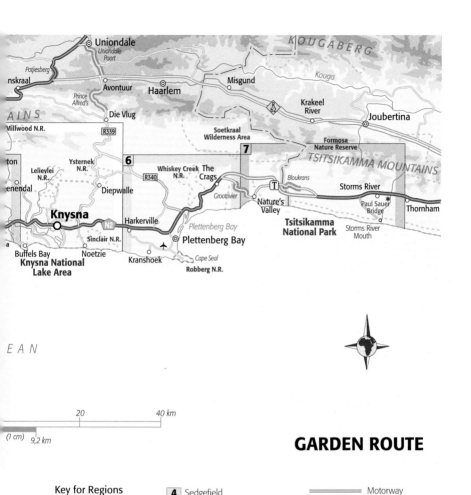

GARDEN ROUTE

Key for Regions

1	Mossel Bay
2	George
3	Wilderness
4	Sedgefield
5	Knysna
6	Plettenberg Bay
7	Tsitsikamma

Motorway
National road
Main road
Secondary road
Route numbers
Provincial boundary

plantations of mainly pine, eucalyptus and blackwood.

The highest peaks in the Outeniqua range push towards 1 500 metres above sea level, while some in the Tsitsikamma range are a little higher at 1 600 metres with pyramidal Formosa Peak being the king at 1 675 metres. Rivers tumbling from the mountain slopes have carved deep gorges and twisting valleys into the landscape, shaded by steep slopes and plunging cliffs. The Keurbooms and Knysna rivers flow into tidal lagoons at Plettenberg Bay and Knysna respectively, while the Sedgefield Lagoon, which is also open to the sea, is fed by water from Swartvlei, the biggest body of water in what is known as South Africa's 'lakes district' (see box on page 89). This chain of five lakes stretches from Wilderness to Sedgefield. Towards the west the forests dwindle to small relict patches in the deeper gorges, and the fynbos takes over.

Climate

A good hint as to what the region's weather has in store for visitors can be taken from the fact that the western gateway town of Mossel Bay is said to have the best climate in the world after Hawaii (and some would argue Johannesburg), with an average of 320 days of sunshine a year. Generally, the entire Garden Route enjoys a temperate climate with average daytime temperatures of around 27°C in summer and around the mid teens in winter. There are exceptions to the rule when summer temperatures can soar into the mid-30s, while in winter snow dusts the higher peaks of the Outeniqua and Tsitsikamma mountains.

The hottest month is February and the coldest July. Berg winds occasionally keep the Garden Route unseasonably warm for brief periods during the winter months. These occur when air moves from a high-pressure (warm) system inland towards a low-pressure (cold) system at the coast, and heats up as it descends (as the air column descends, the pressure increases and – as all scholars of physics will know – this increases molecular energy and repulsion, giving off heat). Rain occurs throughout the year and averages out at somewhere between 550 mm and

1200 mm (the minimum required to sustain forest growth is between 700 and 800 mm, depending on soil and aspect to the sun). May is generally the driest month and October the wettest.

Cities and Towns

Along the full length of the Garden Route there are 5 main urban areas, all on the main N2 arterial, with a scattering of rural settlements, villages and seaside resorts in-between. George is the biggest and only designated city, followed by Mossel Bay, both of which lie in the western quarter of the region. Further east lies the small, but steadily growing town of Sedgefield, and then the popular mid-size tourist towns of Knysna and Plettenberg Bay. East of 'Plett' are only small settlements and resorts including The Crags, Nature's Valley and Storms River village.

Population

There is a cosmopolitan mix of people throughout the Garden Route, the

With its calm lagoon, boats have always been integral to the way of life in Knysna.

The Tsitsikamma coastline is spectacular; with easy access at only a few places, such as here at the Kranshoek view site. The Harkerville Trail traverses below.

majority of whom live in and around the main towns of the region, with a scattering of rural folk on the farms and forestry estates. The total population is somewhere between 400 000 and 500 000 but during the December/January peak season the population of some of the towns multiplies.

Language

Throughout the region, the main languages spoken are English and Afrikaans. In the bigger centres, especially those well frequented by overseas and local tourists, English is widely spoken, with German, Dutch, and French in some of the accommodation establishments. In the few rural towns Afrikaans will usually be the dominant language. Again, in the bigger centres isiXhosa may also be spoken. The first language of just about all the black people of the area is isiXhosa, although most are bi- if not tri-lingual. It was in fact at the eastern extreme of the Garden Route, around the Langkloof, that white colonists from the Cape first encountered Xhosa pastoralists, and not further east at the Great Fish River as many references claim. For centuries, until the first roads were cut in the early 1800s, the dense forests and deep gorges of the area hindered east–west migration.

Tourist Highlights

Whether you are just visiting for a long

weekend or taking the 3 months of accumulated leave that your boss has threatened you will have to 'use it or lose it', the region covered in this book has enough highlights to keep you entertained for the duration. Inevitably there will be favourites you'll want to do more than once, but our bet is you won't mind that, and you may even sneak back a 3rd and 4th time. That's the beauty of the Garden Route; you never really tire of what it has to offer, especially when you discover the heart and soul of the garden.

The most likely place to find this 'real garden' is in the dense, verdant forests that cloak many of the mountains and gorges. Much of this wealth of diversity is protected within the boundaries of national parks and nature reserves (see Calls to the Wild, page 15). These areas offer a host of activities, including mountain biking routes and some of the best hiking trails in the country, abseiling, kloofing, and canopy zipline tours through the forest for the adrenalin addicts, or, for the chilled there are picnic sites for long, lazy lunches.

For water-based activities the long coastline has the whole hog including kite boarding, surfing, boating, fishing, swimming, snorkelling, diving, sun tanning, or just delving into rock pools to see what you can find. There are also ferry trips on some of the rivers and lagoons, sundowner cruises on calm evenings, whale- and dolphin-watching cruises, and shark cage diving at Mossel Bay. A great way to explore the many rivers in the region is by canoe, while for the more adventurous there's also black-water tubing.

A little out of the garden (in that it's on a highway) but nonetheless part of the recreation offered is the highest bungy jump in the world, as well as the bridge walk and zipline at Bloukrans Bridge. For the travelling gourmet there is a profusion of fine restaurants serving cuisine of international standard, plus lots of casual dining eateries, and there is accommodation to suit every preference and budget.

Although the region is not renowned for its bigger wildlife there's plenty here, either in sanctuaries or roaming free. One highlight are the southern right whales that frequent the coastline from around June to November; dolphins are seen carving through the surf all year; and you may even see a wayward penguin waddling along the beach oblivious of the bathers. Remember too, that there are still a few wild elephants gliding through the forests around Knysna, and catching a glimpse of one would possibly be considered the wildlife highlight of anyone's life, so scarce and shy are they.

Taking particular interest in these elephants is self-trained nature man Gareth Patterson (he lived with the Adamsons in Kenya for some time, helping with their lions). Until he started his work in the forests here, taking DNA samples from dung and rubbing posts, it was thought there were maybe only 1 or 2 elies left. However, Patterson believes he has samples from several different individuals and that possibly there are still more. This would be great news indeed (a past attempt to relocate elephants from the Kruger National Park to here failed); however, not everyone agrees with his findings: we can but hope....

Calls to the Wild 2

The Garden Route is not known for its abundance and diversity of big game. However when it comes to mountains, forests, golden beaches and rugged coastlines, it takes some beating.

The sea stretches unbroken all the way from here to the Antarctic. Although it's warm here, huge storms can brew over the Southern Ocean and pound the shoreline in winter.

The Knysna dwarf chameleon is one of 12 dwarf species found in southern Africa – most of them rare and some even endangered.

Where the garden in the Garden Route is at its best is in the mountains and forests that stretch the entire length of the region, and which in places spill from the cloud-bedecked peaks to the wave-washed shores. Large tracts of these 2 regional icons, together with pristine coastal areas and wetlands, are protected within the boundaries of national parks and nature reserves, which offer diverse opportunities for outdoor pursuits and getting close to the spirit of the region.

Many forests conceal life that is secret and secretive, and those on the Garden Route, particularly around Knysna, hide what is probably one of the greatest enigmas of South Africa's natural history – the Knysna forest elephants. Do they still drift among the tall hardwood trees or not, and how many are there really? Their continued exist-ence is an exciting possibility. Sharing their domain are almost 70 smaller mammal species including leopard and honey badger, some 260 bird species and a host of reptiles. Birders and those who enjoy colour in their lives will find therapy in the iridescent hues of the winged creatures that waft amongst the branches of the forests, these include Knysna turaco, Narina trogon, Knysna woodpecker, black-headed oriole, Cape batis, common and swee waxbill, and a number of dazzling sunbirds.

Closer to the sea, coastal dune forest exists between the developments and towns, some of the best examples of which can be seen in the Goukamma Nature Reserve between Sedgefield and Buffalo Bay. Then there's that wealth of floral splendour, fynbos (see box on page 107), which thrives on mountain slopes and coastal dunes. Last but not least the numerous bodies of water in the form of lakes, lagoons and estuaries, plus the Indian Ocean, add an aquatic dimension to the wildlife in the form of common marine mammals such as dolphins, whales, seals, 100-plus species of fish, soft corals ... the list goes on.

In this section we briefly outline the national parks controlled by South African National Parks (SANParks), and the 4 nature reserves controlled by the Western Cape conservation authority, Cape Nature. There are other nature reserves run by botanical societies and municipalities and these are dealt with under the relevant areas.

Buy a Wild Card

To enter many sites and places of interest within the boundaries of the national parks and nature reserves a small fee is charged (from R6 to R25 a person) – this is especially so over the December/January peak season and other school holidays. If these places of natural beauty and tranquillity are high on your holiday agenda these small amounts can add up to a wodge, so it's recommended you purchase a Wild Card, available to South African citizens and foreign visitors (at different rates), which will allow you and your family free entry thereafter. For more information contact the Wild helpline on 086-123-4002 or visit www.wildcard.co.za.

National Parks

For further information on any of the national parks in the Garden Route log on to www.sanparks.org or tel the SANParks Garden Route regional office on 044-302-5600. To book accommodation tel central reservations in Pretoria, 012-428-9111.

Garden Route National Park (GRNP)

The Garden Route is home to the largest complex of indigenous forest in South Africa and, because of its geographical diversity, it ranks extremely highly as a national conservation priority. It was these key factors that were the driving influence in the formation of the Garden Route National Park. The park was proclaimed in March 2009 to incorporate various parcels of private and public lands, which national parks planners began to secretly hobble together in the mid-1990s. It encompasses approximately 121 000 hectares of natural and urban landscape under the management of SANParks.

This huge expanse of land is made up of the existing 68 500 ha within the Wilderness and Tsitsikamma national parks, as well as 52 500 ha of newly

The Afromontane forests are primarily where the 'garden' part of the route is derived.

proclaimed lands. Within the latter figure is 41 538 ha of former state-owned land (mainly afforested 'state forests') scattered along the coastal strip, from the foothills of the Outeniqua and Tsitsikamma mountains to the sea, between George and Kareedouw. The GRNP is unique in that there is no other national park in South Africa that protects marine, coastline, lakes, indigenous forest and mountain catchment environments. As a whole the park is made up of disjointed patches of land and therefore has no fixed beginning and end. Essentially the Wilderness and the Tsitsikamma national parks, and the Knysna National Lakes Area are sections within the greater park. For the purposes of this book we have dealt with each individually.

Wilderness National Park

Situated just east of George, the Wilderness National Park protects patches of indigenous forest and fynbos, long stretches of unspoilt coastline and pristine beaches, coastal dunes, rivers and estuaries, and a series of 5 lakes (see box on page 89) unique in South Africa. Along the coastal plain the park stretches from the Touws River mouth east to Swartvlei and around Sedgefield to incorporate Groenvlei, while inland its patchy boundaries spread east and west along the ridge of the Outeniqua mountains. The park is renowned for its diversity of activities, which include **hiking, canoeing, mountain biking, abseiling** and **kloofing** – for all of these contact Eden Adventures which is based in the park: tel 044-877-0179, e-mail info@eden.co.za or web www.eden.co.za.

Hiking is probably the most popular activity and there is a network of 5 superb walking trails ranging from 4 km to 10 km in length and taking in river, lake and forest scenery – pick up a pocket guide from the parks offices.

The most well trodden of these are the **Half-Collared Kingfisher Trail** through indigenous forest and along the banks of the Touws River to a waterfall, then back along the same route for a total of a little more than 7 km. Another waterfall is reached on the 5 km **Brown Hooded Kingfisher Trail,** between Island Lake and Langvlei. This follows the Duiwe River and then veers off up a tributary, before returning the same way. The **Pied Kingfisher Trail** is the longest of the bunch at 10 km. It starts at the Ebb and Flow campsite, heads off to the coast, along the beach, and then loops back up the Touws River. It then follows the road past Ebb and Flow before turning back to take in some of the Serpentine and finishes where it started – at the time of researching some of the boardwalks still hadn't been repaired after being damaged during floods.

The **Cape Dune Molerat Trail** between Rondevlei and Swartvlei has a 3 km or 6 km route; combining this with a couple of hours in the Rondevlei bird hide before or after the hike makes a nice half-day outing. On the subject of avifauna, with 230 species, bird watching is excellent, especially along the Touws River, Serpentine channel, and the shores of the lakes with their associated reed beds. Part of the park is a designated **RAMSAR site** and there are 3 well-appointed **bird hides:**

besides the aforementioned Rondevlei hide, there's the Malachite hide on Langvlei and, closer to Wilderness town, the Gallinule hide near the Fairy Knowe Hotel (you can get directions from the national parks office at Ebb and Flow rest camp behind the town).

Accommodation, Ebb and Flow rest camp – see under Wilderness on page 94.

Tsitsikamma National Park

Translated, Tsitsikamma means something like 'place of much water' in the language of the Khoisan, the first people known to have inhabited the area. The park was proclaimed in 1964 and is situated in a sparsely populated area of lofty peaks, indigenous forests, private plantations, great swathes of fynbos and unspoilt shores in the western part of the Garden Route. For visitors it's essentially broken down into 2 sections – Storms River Mouth and Nature's Valley. The coastal portion of the park stretches 80 km along the coast and 5 km out to sea protecting not only life in the inter-tidal zone but that of the deep sea too. The inland expanse protects the forests, fynbos and mountain catchment areas.

Walking and hiking is the most popular activity in the park with the multi-day **Otter Trail**, which starts at Storms River Mouth, falling within its boundaries (see Big 6 Hiking Trails on page 33). There are also numerous shorter walks at Storms River Mouth ranging from 1 km to 6 km. Probably the most popular of these is the boardwalk to the **suspension bridge** across the Storms River, or you can walk the first section of the Otter Trail to a **waterfall**.

There's also a **snorkel trail** and **scuba diving** immediately in front of the restaurant, and a **boat trip** up

The Khoi word 'tsitsikamma' refers to the many rivers that tumble from mountain to sea.

the Storms River. At Nature's Valley (see page 204) there're plenty of short walks – ranging from 1 km–6 km and taking in fynbos, forest, and coastline – and **canoeing** on the Groot River and lagoon. Accommodation in the park is either at the spectacular **Storms River mouth rest camp** or in the tranquil **forest campsite** (with raised timber cabins) alongside the Groot River at Nature's Valley.

Storms River mouth is very popular with day visitors and overnighters alike and therefore it has a host of facilities including a shop and large fast food restaurant. There is also a wide choice of accommodation in what many people consider to be the very best, and most scenic, campsite in the country – for details see Tsitsikamma accommodation on page 218.

An African darter suns itself in front of the Malachite bird hide at Langvlei, in the Wilderness National Lake Area.

There is a **SANParks campsite** on the R102 just east of the entrance to the village, named De Vasselot after the first commissioner of forests for the Cape colony, which is in total keeping with the 'nature' theme – all set about under old yellowwoods, with A-frame timber huts and grassy camping sites. If campsites were graded for atmosphere, this one would be 'canvas-with-champagne'. See details under Tsitsikamma accommodation, page 210.

Knysna National Lake Area

While the Knysna National Lake Area isn't a proclaimed national park, it does fall under the auspices of SANParks and encompasses some important conservation areas. This includes the Knysna estuary (lagoon) with its diverse mix of fauna and flora including the endan-gered Knysna seahorse (see box on page 142), and the large tracts of indigenous forest to the north most notably at Diepwalle, and the east around Harkerville and Kranshoek.

Nature Reserves

If you require further information on the following reserves or would like to book a trail or accommodation ahead of time, contact the reservations office on tel 044-802-5310 or log on to www.capenature.co.za.

Outeniqua Nature Reserve

This 38 000 ha reserve encompasses much of the Outeniqua mountain range in the vicinity of George, protecting the flora – mainly spectacular mountain fynbos with some rare endemic species including the George lily – and fauna, and the catchments that supply the region with fresh water. From a motorist's point of view, sections of the reserve are traversed via the Outeniqua and Montagu passes between George and the Little Karoo, and the Robinson Pass on the R328 north of Mossel Bay. However, the reserve is better enjoyed by striking out on foot and will suit those who like a challenge while working their way up in the world. Within its boundaries are some of the highest peaks in the area, with Craddock Peak the highest at 1579m.

There are no facilities in the reserve and it's open only to day visitors who can undertake various **day hikes**, all of which guarantee impressive mountain scenery, beautiful fynbos and the possible sightings of klipspringer and grey rhebuck.

For those of above average fitness the 3 most popular routes start in the vicinity of the reserves office at Witfontein – reached by travelling 4km outside George on the N12 towards the Outeniqua Pass and Oudtshoorn, turning right at the Montagu Pass signboard 800m past the last set of traffic lights at the Engen petrol station. After 500m on this gravel road turn right into the reserve, follow the track to the reserve headquarters, and park in the shade of the old oak trees.

The **Craddock Pass day trail** covers 12,4km and takes around 5 hours to complete. It's a tough climb, following the tracks made by ox wagons in the first half of the 19th century while traversing the mountains on the old Craddock Pass. It ends on the Montagu

Pass 1km from the top and you need someone to pick you up, or there's the 11km, 3-hour walk down Montagu Pass back to the start.

The **George Peak Trail** and the **Craddock Peak Trail** are each around 17km for the round trip and take between 6 and 7 hours to complete. On both summits the hard slog is rewarded with views over George and, in the opposite direction, to the Swartberg mountains on the far, northern side of the Little Karoo. For the really fit the summits can be combined from either trail pushing the total distance to just over 21km (9 hours).

The moderately fit might rather like to attempt the **Pass-to-Pass day walk**, a distance of just over 7km that takes around 3 hours to complete. It starts at the top of the Montagu Pass and travels west to the top of the Outeniqua Pass where the friend who dropped you earlier will hopefully be waiting with some cold refreshments.

There's 1 overnight trail in the reserve and that is the 30km, 2-day **Tierkop Trail**, which starts at the Witfontein forest station, climbs up Tierkop peak where the overnight hut is situated, and then drops down passed the Garden Route Dam behind George.

You need to be well prepared on all trails, carrying your own water and warm clothing as weather conditions on the mountain can change rapidly. For your own safety, please don't forget to fill in the visitors book at the Witfontein office so that if something happens to you a rescue party will have an idea where to look. One of the best times to do these hikes is September and October when the fynbos is in best bloom. To contact the reserve directly and check availability of permits tel 044-870-8323/5. If there is no reply, resort to the Cape Nature number above.

Goukamma Nature Reserve

At 2500 ha the Goukamma reserve between Buffalo Bay and Sedgefield boasts 14 km of beach, some of the highest vegetated dunes in the country, the Goukamma River and estuary and Groenvlei (Lake Pleasant). Because of the diverse habitats, wildlife sightings could include grysbok, bush pig, bush-buck, porcupine, caracal, vervet monkey, honey badger and Cape clawless otter, while bird watchers are in for a treat with around 220 species. It's certainly a reserve for those who enjoy variety in their life.

For overnighting
in Goukamma, see Sedgefield to Knysna page 115.

Day visitors are welcome and the reserve is open daily 08h00–18h00. However, to get the full benefit of what it has to offer it's best to spend a night or 2 in one of their 6 self-catering units. These include 3 thatched rondavels each sleeping 5 people in 2 rooms, overlooking the Goukamma River and estuary near the main entrance close to Buffalo Bay. They're great for a short break with family or group of close friends.

There are 4 hikes in the reserve, ranging from a flat 4 km (1–2 hours) stroll along the southern shore of Groenvlei

(starts near Mvubu and Groenvlei bush camps) – but it's through bush and you don't see much lake – an 8 km (2–3 hour) circular ramble through the fynbos, a beach walk along the 14 km of seashore to Platbank (4 hours), and a 16 km (5 hours) tramp up the dunes and through the milkwood forest to the Groenvlei Bushcamp on the shores of the lake (the latter 3 start at or in the vicinity of the reserves office near Buffalo Bay). The last 2 hikes are both 1-way trails and so return transport needs to be arranged.

At the time of writing the trails were a bit rough around the edges but are great for those who enjoy being out in nature without the crowds. They don't need to be pre-booked but before heading off a permit must first be obtained from the reserve office – here horse rides ranging from 1½–6 hours can also be arranged, canoes hired, and angling licenses bought.

Robberg Nature Reserve

This nature reserve encompasses the entire Robberg (meaning seal mountain) peninsula that juts out to sea 8 km southwest of Plettenberg Bay. Bartholemeu Dias called it Cabo Talhado meaning the steep cape, and with 65 per cent of its surface sloping it's easy to understand why. The 174 ha reserve has a coastline of 16 km and protects not only the indigenous vegetation but also a Cape fur seal colony (the 'robbe'), and the roosting sites of, amongst others, gannets, cormorants, kelp gulls and swift terns. The reserve is open daily 07h00–17h00 with hours extended until 20h00 in December and January.

There are 3 circular hiking routes taking in various aspects of the headland. **The Gap Circuit** is a 2km (40 mins) easy saunter for the whole family to a crevice where the land seems to have tumbled in on itself. In this vicinity some interesting conglomerate rock formations rise above the trail. There is a theory that the Keurbooms River entered the sea through this gap, way back perhaps when Gondwanaland was still intact. **The Witsand Circuit** at 5,5km (2 hours) is best suited to the more regular walker and passes The Gap to skirt the northern rim of Robberg, above a seal colony, before cutting across the centre and dropping to sea level on the far side where a tombolo (for those not familiar with this peculiar word, it's a wide sand spit) leads to a small island. On The Island a breeding colony of kelp gulls can be observed from the encircling boardwalk, before returning to the start via The Gap. For the more experienced hiker, **Point Circuit**, at 9,2km (4 hours), is an extension of the Witsand loop and follows the northern rim to the point, and then curves along the southern shore past The Island and culminates in a climb up the gap and back to the start of the walk.

Situated on the southern shore near the island, the **Fountain Shack** (sleeps 8) is available for those who want to spend a night or more on Robberg's splendid isolation. It's basic and you must take all your own food, drinks and bedding, and be prepared to do without gas, electricity or hot water – you can braai though. The loo has a fantastic view over The Island. There are the barest essentials for cooking and eating,

Robberg beach at Plettenberg Bay is perhaps the best of the entire area, but it is by no means the only one that is beautiful and safe for swimming, surfing, walking, chilling.

and when you set off you're given an overnight kit, which includes 3 kg of compressed grape seeds as braai wood. The shack isn't serviced so you'll need to take out all rubbish and leave the place as you'd like to find it. Rates for the shack out of peak season range from R360 weekdays to R520 weekends for 1–4 people. In peak season the unit goes for R1 040. For more info on Robberg tel 044-533-2125; to book the Fountain Shack tel 021-659-3500.

Keurbooms River Nature Reserve

Approximately 8 km east of Plettenberg Bay the boundaries of the Keurbooms River Nature Reserve embrace 740 ha of indigenous forest along the banks of the Keurbooms River, inland of the N2 highway. There are no official hiking trails, but with the river at the reserve's doorstep a popular activity is hiring a canoe and setting off upstream, beyond the strictly controlled limits for skiers

(3 km) and motorboats (4 km), into the stillness of the forest-draped gorge. Along the way are 3 riverside picnic sites beneath the tangle of forest, the last one across from where Whiskey Creek joins the Keurbooms River. Take your binos and bird book and try not to capsize while panning those streaks of colour.

If that sounds too much and all you want to do is spend the day chilling out next to the water, you can do that too. There's a spacious, shaded picnic site with braai and ablution facilities in the vicinity of the reserve entrance near the bridge over the N2. That's also where you can hire canoes, while under the bridge is the point from which where the Keurbooms Ferry leaves (see Plett chapter for details). For more info tel 044-533-2125.

Vervet or blue monkeys are common residents of all the forests in the region.

DO NOT FEED WILD ANIMALS

Baboons and monkeys that are fed end up dead sooner rather than later. They all too easily become habituated, associating people with food, which leads to the poor sods like us who don't feed them being on the receiving end of their aggression and destructive behaviour. Next time you think that morsel of food you want to hand out (because, *ag shame*, they're so cute) won't make a difference; think again.

Every time you feed a wild animal, you are creating a chain reaction and thereby signing its death warrant: wild primates that become pests end up getting shot. So please don't do it!

Practical Information 3

The Garden Route is no secret destination. In fact it's probably one of the best-publicised and most visited regions in South Africa, and ranks high up on the list of the world's most scenic coastal routes. People from around the globe come here to experience its natural beauty, and over the past decade more and more urbanites have left the cities to settle in this comparative paradise.

Rocky headlands, such as here at Nature's Valley, aid the formation of large bays and wonderful beaches all along the Cape coast – all excellent for healthy pursuits.

With this increase in population, new development may have robbed the landscape here of its 'garden' in places, but it has also ensured the creation of a First World infrastructure in just about all sectors a visitor would be concerned with. However, here are a few subjects you may ponder when planning a trip to the area.

Getting There and Around

Because of its popularity, the Garden Route has a good range of transport options running to regular daily time-tables so you can just sit back and enjoy the ride.

By Air

If your time is limited or you don't want the hassle of a long road trip, there are several airlines flying daily from the major SA centres into George airport. It pays to shop around for the best deals. **Kulula** (www.kulula.com, tel 0861-58-5852) and 1-Time (www.1time.co.za, tel 0861-34-5345) both offer good deals but fly to George only from Johannesburg. **SA Airlink** (www.saairlink.co.za, tel 011-395-3579) and **South African Express** (www.saexpress.co.za, tel 011-978-5577) are generally more pricey but offer an expanded service. They fly from most major centres around the country via Johannesburg and Cape Town.

Once you're through the reception building the hazy Outeniqua mountains give you a soaring welcome and, with that bubble of excitement and anticipation of the lazy days ahead, there are several car hire companies waiting to put you on your way. Two

rental companies at the airport are **Avis Rent A Car** (044-876-9314) and **Budget Car Rental** (044-876-9216).

By Bus

Another option of getting to the region without having to concentrate from behind the steering wheel is to catch a comfortable coach. These also run daily services – some several times a day. From Gauteng and the Free State provinces, coaches take the N1 to Beaufort West and then the N12 via Oudtshoorn to George. Once there you'll need to change coaches to get to other destinations along the route.

The most hassle free coach route is along the coast on the N2 between Cape Town and Port Elizabeth. Coaches stop at Mossel Bay, George, Wilderness, Sedgefield, Knysna, Plettenberg Bay, and Storms River village. The drop-off points are generally at a designated place in each town and further arrangements need to be made to reach your accommodation.

The following companies can be contacted for more specific information: **Greyhound** (083 915-9000, www.greyhound.co.za), **Intercape** (0861-287-287, www.intercape.co.za), and **Translux** (0861-589-282, www.translux.co.za). A trip from Johannesburg takes around 15 hours, while from Cape Town it's a shorter hop of around 7 hours.

For the budget conscious **Baz Bus** runs daily minibus services between Cape Town and Port Elizabeth. This is a good option if you are staying in backpackers' accommodation as they stop at all towns (except Sedgefield) on the Garden Route, pulling up right at the front door of designated establishments. They're not ageist or sexist so, if you feel comfortable mingling with the predominantly young backpacker set, there's no reason not to use this option. Ask about their hop-on, hop-off tickets. Although they take standby passengers it's better to pre-book your seat 48 hours beforehand. For timetables and to book, tel 021-439-2323 or web www.bazbus.co.za.

By Car

For independent travellers who like to do their own thing and not be limited by timetables, all major routes leading to the Garden Route are tarred and in good condition. Between Cape Town to the west (500 km from the Gourits bridge) and Port Elizabeth to the east (260 km from Storms River bridge) the N2 passes either through or nearby all the major towns. From the big centres to the north of the country, take the N1 to Beaufort West and then the N12 via Oudtshoorn to George and then link with the N2.

If you don't possess your own vehicle and want to hire one, try the following companies who have branches in the bigger centres of Cape Town, George or Port Elizabeth: **Avis** Rent A Car (0861-021-111), **Budget** Car Rental (0861-016-622), **Eurocar** car rental (0861-131-000) or **Hertz** Rent A Car (0861-600-136).

Banking/Money

In most cases banks work Monday-Friday 09h00-15h30, and Saturdays 09h00-11h00; most major banks (Absa, Standard, First National) are repre-

The corms of moraea irises were used in traditional medicine to help women conceive.

sented in the towns along the route (Nedbank only in the larger centres).

If you're carrying foreign currency you'll be able to change it at the bigger banks, while bureaux de change offices at most of the tourist hubs stay open until 17h00. If you want to draw money from a hole in the wall to fill the hole in your pocket, ATMs are available in all the towns and credit cards are widely accepted – although some guesthouses work on a cash only basis.

Safety

As with most tourist hotspots around the globe, crime is something to be aware of throughout the Garden Route. Having said that though you'd be very unfortunate to fall victim, and if you did it would probably be of a petty theft nature. To enhance your personal safety take all the usual precautions like locking doors, not leaving valuables exposed, being vigilant when drawing money from ATMs, and checking with

Endless beaches and rock pools, with a little friendship, are the essential ingredients of the perfect childhood holiday that you'll remember for the rest of your life.

your hosts before wandering the streets at night. In recent times there have been a few incidents along some of the beaches and short hiking trails near towns. If you enjoy a stroll, check with some of the locals before heading along deserted beaches, or the local offices of National Parks or Cape Nature depending on the trail you've chosen (see specific towns for contact details).

Fuel

One thing you're unlikely to have a problem with is filling the tank, with all major towns having at least 1 24/7 service station. The distances between towns are shorter than just about anywhere else in the country, so you should have enough to get you to the next town even if the reserve light comes on.

Health

Although the region is malaria-free, be prepared to ward off those annoying, buzzing, biting mosquitoes during the summer months. They're worse in some areas than others, so make sure you always have repellent with you. For things of a more serious nature doctors, dentists and chemists (some open until late), won't be far away. All the main towns have provincial hospitals with casualty and emergency wards and out-patient sections. In general the care and expertise offered is of an above average standard; however, if you have any doubts there are private hospitals in Mossel Bay, George, Knysna and Plett. You will, however, need good medical insurance or cash to pay upfront before you'll be admitted to one of these.

When outdoors, remember: if you are not used to the sun, put plenty of sun block on before lying on the beach to grill and be sure to take sufficient drinking water when heading off on an extended hike.

Roads and Driving

The main artery through the heart of the Garden Route is the N2, starting as a dual carriageway between Mossel Bay and George and then variously narrowing and widening along the rest of its length, with a hard shoulder most of the way. The stretch of road through the Tsitsikamma forest towards Storms River was being upgraded at the time of researching this book and will be a lot safer than the old road – although its upgrade did cause considerable controversy. Heading off the N2 into the forests and mountains, the roads become gravel and many, such as Prince Alfred's Pass to Uniondale, have blind corners and sharp curves and need to be driven with caution. As a general rule speed limits, unless indicated otherwise, are 60 kph in urban areas, 100 kph on rural roads and 120 kph on major routes when travelling through undeveloped areas.

Tourist Seasons (swing high swing low)

The region has several seasons throughout the year, determined by the average number of tourists expected during that time. In general these are: peak season – over summer school holidays, which is generally most of December and halfway through January; high season – the rest of summer until around May; and low season – the winter months July to September. There are also a few book-end seasons, as well as a few spikes when popular festivals are on.

Accommodation

Throughout the region there is accommodation to suit every pocket from budget, through mid-range, to pricey, and expensive. This comes in the form of caravanning and camping, backpacker's lodges, self-catering units, B&Bs, guesthouses, inns, hotels, tented camps, log cabins, forest hideaways, houseboats, and a range of establishments offering unadulterated opulence (see list of recommendations under each town). Whatever your comfort preference, the Garden Route will not disappoint you. Remember though that in the high season, and especially during the December/January school holidays, and Easter weekend, pre-booking is essential.

It should also be remembered that low season is when some establishments close (usually some time in June and July) so that the proprietors have a chance to go on holiday. It is highly unlikely, however, for the entire accommodation fraternity of 1 town to take time off together so you're sure to find a comfortable bed if you didn't pre-book.

Accommodation Prices

Due to the region's popularity, the price of accommodation varies according to season. In many cases the number of seasons borders on the ridiculous, with up to 8 different price brackets over a 12-month period (peak, high, low, mid, mid low … you get the drift). Under the accommodation sections of each town, prices quoted under the respective establishments are an indication of the rate for 1 person sharing, from low to high season. Single supplements of between 25 % and 80 % can be expected on top of these – you should check with the relevant establishment before booking. Prices for a unit are stated as such. Low season rates can often be negotiated and most establishments offer out of season discounts for long stays.

Photography

If you're a keen photographer there's ample opportunity for some stunning holiday shots to show those back home. For camera accessories you'll more often than not find a dedicated camera shop in the main shopping malls and tourist hotspots and many pharmacies keep spare batteries, memory cards, etc. There are also plenty quick-photo shops to get your images put onto disc.

Shops and Shopping

Most shops and businesses are open 08h30–17h00 Mon–Fri and 08h30–13h00 Sat. In the main tourist hubs shops catering to tourists' needs will in all likelihood also be open all day Saturday and Sunday. Large shopping malls will also be open over weekends. This is especially true in the high season. For curios and souvenirs there are plenty of outlets dotted around the more popular tourist hubs.

You'll find most of the large chain stores represented in the bigger towns, with a number of shopping malls throughout the Garden Route: the Garden Route Mall, located on the eastern outskirts of George, is the biggest in the region.

Many towns have at least 1 market, usually on a Saturday morning, where you can purchase fresh produce, artisanal cheeses, home-made soaps, arts and crafts, secondhand books and more. They're good places to go for an outdoor breakfast while mingling with the locals. There are also many lovely farm stalls and other small stores selling interesting wares, as well as informal shopping areas selling mainly African crafts – much of them imported from Zimbabwe and Malawi.

Tree ferns grow along the stream banks at Jubilee Creek, a favourite picnic spot in the forest near Knysna.

The Big 6 Hiking Trails 4

When entering some of the bigger towns in the region visitors can be forgiven for wondering where the hell the garden went. High rises, industry, high-density housing and other developments blur the vision of a verdant Eden. Thankfully, however, outside the urban spread a green-tinted vision is restored.

Like every other good thing in life, a 5-day hiking trail with friends has to have its conclusion. Then again, Nature's Valley is hardly a terrible place to reach trail's end.

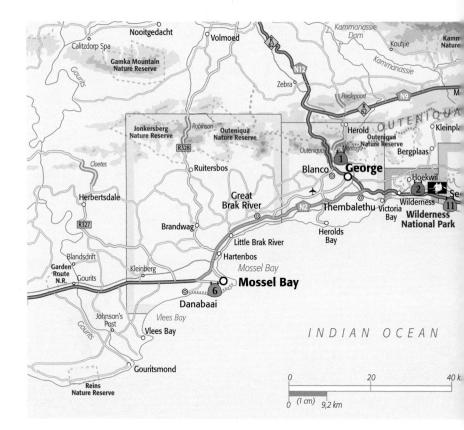

Where land meets sea there are long stretches of glinting beach sand interspersed by rocky outcrops and plunging cliffs. Inland the landscape is blessed with mountain ranges cloaked in fynbos and cool forests of towering trees, feathery ferns and babbling streams. It's in these areas that you'll want to don your hiking boots, strap a backpack snugly over your shoulders and go walkabout to discover the essence of the magnificent Garden Route along some of the best hiking trails anywhere.

Here are 3 popular and well established multi-day, full **backpacking** stamina stretchers, and 3 easy-going **slackpacking** rambles. There is a plethora of shorter hikes and walks in the region and for these please refer to the Calls to the Wild section for trails in the national parks and nature reserves, and the 'out and about' sections under each of the towns.

Full-pack testers

These 3 trails are the real thing – you carry everything you need for several days, barring the roof at night-time. You sweat for the joys of experiencing glorious wilderness all to yourself and your hiking party and at the end you know, in your soul, you've done the

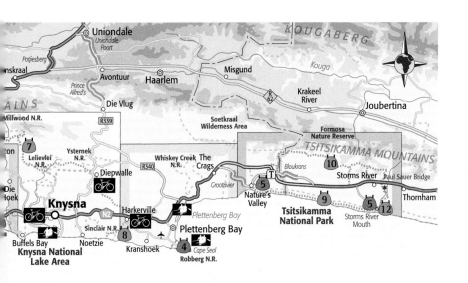

TRAILS

DAY WALKS

1. Outeniqua Nature Reserve
2. Wilderness National Park (Kingfisher)
3. Goukamma
4. Robberg
5. Tsitsikamma National Park

MULTI-DAY HIKES

6. Oystercatcher
7. Outeniqua
8. Harkerville
9. Otter
10. Tsitsikamma

11. Garden Route
12. Dolphin

OTHER TRAILS

Mountain biking

Canoeing/kayaking

good and noble thing; that is, getting as close to nature as you can short of going Stone Age.

Otter Trail

The Otter Trail is probably the best-known hiking trail in South Africa and has had a 12-month waiting list for the best part of 20 years. It starts where the spectacular coastal forests meet the rugged coastline at Storms River mouth within the Tsitsikamma National Park. It follows a narrow but well-beaten path, denoted by blue otter signs, until it ends on the long stretch of gleaming beach at Nature's Valley 5 days and 48km later.

The hike allows a maximum of 12 hikers to traverse forests, fynbos, mountains, beaches, and 11 river and estuary crossings, never straying too far from the coast. The daily distances aren't huge, ranging from 4,8 to 13,8km, but it is a difficult hike and a good level of physical condition is required (rather than 'fitness'). Accommodation is in basic trail huts that provide nothing more than bunk beds with mattresses, rain water collected in tanks, and long-drop toilets (1 with a celebrated view). All else needs to be carried in and it's advisable to plan the contents of your pack carefully so to keep the weight down. A heavy pack can be a real spoiler on the steep sections, of which there are many.

The 1st day is the shortest and is an easy walk, breaking the legs in gently for the steep ascents and descents that lie ahead; spend as much time as you like at the first waterfall and pool. Day 2 is probably the most demanding and day 4 is the longest, but not necessarily the most taxing. It's advisable to take note of tide tables for some of the river crossings (Bloukrans being the tester).

Over the whole distance there's plenty of opportunity for cooling dips, and enough time should be taken to admire the pristine surroundings and hug a few towering yellowwood trees. The river gorges have a mysterious feel to them, and from the heights of the headlands the views are stupendous. You either need to park a vehicle at the Nature's Valley rest camp or arrange a lift for the return trip to Storms River mouth. The 2010 rate is R685/p for the trail. For enquiries about the trail tel 042-281-1629 and to book your place call central reservations on 012-426-5111, e-mail reservations@sanparks.org.

Outeniqua Trail

The Outeniqua Trail is the longest and hardest hike on the Garden Route and is a good endurance challenge for the resilient nature lover. Over the years the trail has changed a lot, once starting near George, but at present setting off from the Beervlei hut at an old forestry station just off the Seven Passes Road inland from Sedgefield.

From there it traverses 108 km of forest and fynbos, covering the slopes and foothills of the Outeniqua mountains to finish 7 days later at Harkerville hut, between Knysna and Plettenberg Bay. For those who feel it's a tad too long, the good news is you don't have to tackle the entire hike but can book shorter sections. If you're going the whole hog, daily distances will vary between 11 and 17 km, which aren't excessively long but some days are tough going and early starts are recommended so you have enough time to absorb the surroundings without having to rush.

The trail varies from steep ascents and descents, through deep gorges bulging with indigenous forest and tree ferns, and across mountain streams chortling over beds of smooth boulders. In places, out on the slopes and plateaus, pine plantations and fynbos exude a different atmosphere. Mountain pools provide opportunities for bracing dips and the views from some of the huts and mountain peaks cannot fail to enchant you.

It's a tough trail, but you don't have to be an athlete to do it. Accommodation is in rudimentary trail huts (some of them old foresters' houses) with bunk beds and basic facilities but all food, cooking and eating utensils, sleeping bags and other necessities must be carried in – this will test your trail packing skills. There are a few luxuries to look forward to like electricity at some huts and hot water showers at Diepwalle.

The trail can accommodate a maximum of 24 hikers a day for each section. If 7 days in the bush isn't enough, then the 27 km, 2-day Harkerville trail can be added – or it can be done as its

Some of the finest trails in South Africa are to be found on the Garden Route, most of them including substantial forest sections, notably the Harkerville and Tsitsikamma hikes.

own mini Otter Trail (see Harkerville, under Plett section, for details). From the Harkerville hut the trail ventures into the Sinclair Nature Reserve for a night and then loops back the following day. If you're into scenic diversity, this is an incredible extension with plenty of rugged coastline and some hairy scrambling up and across rock obstacles. Not recommended if you have a fear of exposure. This section of the trail accommodates only 12 people. 2010 rates are R90/p a night. For reservations and enquiries contact SANParks tel 044-302-5600, e-mail cathyv@sanparks.org or web www.sanparks.org.

Tsitsikamma Trail

At the Nature's Valley rest camp, where the Otter Trails ends, the Tsitsikamma Trail begins. But, unlike the Otter, this 61 km hike heads inland for the slopes of the Tsitsikamma foothills and folds (and some testing passes as well) away from the coast and finishes at either Storms River bridge or Storms River village. MTO Forestry is the custodian of the trail and its ecotourism division is doing a fine job of keeping it and its facilities at a high standard.

The 61 km is covered over 6 days, but for the time-strapped there are 2- to 5-day versions as well. The first and last days are the shortest, with ambles of between 3 and 5 km each, while all other sections clock in at a little more than 13 km. A maximum of 24 hikers is permitted on each section and, as with most trails in the region, nights are spent in simple huts with bunk beds. The facilities at the huts are in general of a higher standard than nor-mally expected and include flush toilets, showers, braai areas with a few cooking utensils, firewood and deep balconies with magnificent views. Everything else must be carried in so pack carefully.

From the outset your days will unfold into a varied wonderland of gorges, tumbling waterfalls, magnificent views, river crossings, indigenous forest, fynbos, rock pools, mountain slopes and high plateaus. The trail is rated moderate to difficult and a good physical condition is required to enjoy the hike. If you're not into challenges and carrying a heavy pack for 6 days, consider doing the portered slackpacking option whereby your luggage will be transported between huts and you can go off as light as a leaf drifting from the forest canopy: the advantages are vast, with improved food options being one. There are also mountain biking and 4x4 or 4x2 options on sections of the trail, but only where they don't clash with hikers. The 2010 rate is

Butterflies are the fairies of the forest, although the name comes from a myth about them feeding from milk pails.

R100/p a night. For more details contact MTO Ecotourism reservation office on tel 042-281-1712 or e-mail ivy@cyber-perk.co.za. They have a decent website www.mtoecotourism.co.za.

Slackpack beauties

For those who are not familiar with the term or concept of slackpacking, it basically means the trails are guided, portered and catered. You take only what you need while walking and they take a weight off your mind as well as your shoulders.

Garden Route Trail

This trail is the brainchild of Mark Dixon who is also the guide and imparter of all sorts of interesting information about the region and what lives there, and a big drawcard here is the diversity of activities and habitats it covers. It's also a trail where, for the most part, you can bag your shoes and feel the sand spill between your toes as you amble in a dream-time, drinking in the land and sea with just something to eat and drink weighing gently on your back. Shoes need donning really only for the jaunts through the forested areas around Wilderness and Goukamma.

The 65-km hike is enjoyed over 5 days. It begins near the town of Wilderness (see page 85) at the Ebb and Flow rest camp in Wilderness National Park on the Touws River, and ending at Brenton on Sea. The distance has been broken down into easily manageable sections, with emphasis on unhurried days and a leisurely pace – morning starts are around 09h00.

This isn't a hike where walking is all you do: Mark has cleverly incorporated canoeing and some of the main attractions in the area into the 5 days. Accommodation for the 4 nights has been carefully selected at Wilderness, Sedgefield and the Goukamma Nature Reserve, and evening meals vary from a restaurant meal on night 2 to Mark's own culinary wizardry.

The first day starts at Ebb and Flow in Wilderness National Park with a canoe trip of 5 km up the Touws River, dark coloured by tannins leached from forest debris but perfectly clean, and then a 5 km walk along the Giant Kingfisher Trail through indigenous forest, and up a few ladders to a waterfall. The afternoon is then spent wending your way along the Serpentine channel where bird watching is at a premium. The night is spent in accommodation at the Ebb and Flow resort and the next morning the N2 highway is breached – and that's the last you'll see of rushing traffic until the end of the trail.

From there, the days unfold like a perfectly choreographed stage show with the possibility of seeing whales and dolphins on the swells and looking out for endangered African black oystercatchers. Day 2 comprises a 20 km beach walk to Sedgefield with perhaps a dip in some of the tempting rock pools at Gericke's Point. Day 3 from Sedgefield to Goukamma (14 km) is along a stretch of beach for 9 km before veering up into the coastal dunes covered in dense forests and then out into the fynbos. Day 4 starts with a canoe trip on the lazy, dark waters of the Goukamma River and then an 8 km dune and beach walk in Goukamma.

Day 5 starts with a walk to the Lagoon mouth in Goukamma Nature Reserve and then a beach walk to Brenton on Sea (9 km). Then, *ag shame*, it's all over bar the memories, which last for a very long time.

The 2010 price of R4 600–R5 800/p – depends on group size, minimum 4 and maximum 12 – includes park fees, accommodation, activities and all meals except supper on day 2. There are shorter versions of the hike and Mark is happy to tailor an itinerary to suit. There're also 2 popular night hikes: the moonlight meander at full moon, and the starlight stroll at new moon. These take place from Swartvlei parking area to Gericke's Point and last 3 hours (19h00–22h00), and are guided by Mark's sprightly mom, Judy, and cost R60/p.

Apart from comfortable hiking clothes, walking shoes or trainers are preferable to boots because of the mostly soft conditions underfoot, take sandals for the beach sections if you don't want to walk barefoot, a wide-brimmed hat, sunglasses and water-proof sunblock – barefoot walkers need to take special care not to get the tops of your feet sun burned. To book your place call Mark Dixon on 082-213-5931, e-mail beachwalk@gardenroutetrail.co.za, web www.gardenroutetrail.co.za.

The Oystercatcher Trail

The African black oystercatcher is an endangered shore wader with jet black feathers and brilliant red bill, eyes and legs that apparently mates until 'death do them part'. The majority are happy to call South Africa's coastline their home.

During the closing decades of the C20 their numbers dropped alarmingly to the point where they were declared an endangered species. However, with the banning of beach driving and other conservation measures, there are places where numbers have stablised and are even growing: one of these is the coast-line along which the Oystercatcher Trail runs.

Trail founder Fred Orban has a soft spot for most things natural, and in particular this feathered friend. He lives among a cluster of restored fishers' cottages at Boggom's Bay, 30 km west of Mossel Bay (see accommodation on page 59), and in order to share his coastal paradise with others he set up this trail with lots of thought given to the frills that take the sweat out of hiking. A few hours spent with Fred and Willie Komani, his main guide, will instil a new respect for the coastal region and give you plenty of stories to tell your mates back home. The trail is reputed to be among the top 5 hikes in the country and has been listed by the BBC as one of 30 hikes to do before you die.

The trail starts at St Blaize Cave in Mossel Bay and travels west along the coastline to Gourits River mouth, a total distance of 48 km; daily sections are no longer than 15 km. The days that follow are filled with interesting titbits freely offered by your willing guide; there's plenty of time to play beachcomber while sifting through shells and an array of other objects spilled ashore by the waves. Or just mould your rear end into the squeaky clean sand and let the sea breeze tug at your hair while you watch frothy fingers of surf stroke the shore.

The African black oystercatcher actually eats mostly mussels found on rocky shorelines.

The route seldom veers far from the pristine coastline and interesting stops along the way include caves of the first inhabitants of the area, the Khoisan, who were hunter-gatherers, their fish traps constructed using rocks, and their shell middens. Weather permitting, there's also time to explore rock pools with mask and snorkel. Amongst all the natural sights, sounds and smells that will be caressing your senses during the hike don't forget to keep a personal tally of the beautiful black-feathered birds, the oystercatchers. If 5 days is just too much to be out in the sun, there's a 3-day option from Boggom's Bay to Gourits River mouth, a total of 25 km.

Accommodation for the first 3 nights is usually at Boggom's Bay in one of the Sandpiper Cottages. These are Fred's self-designed fisher's cottages, which boast stylish décor and furnishings that could easily entice you to forego the hike and stay firmly planted in their comfortable embrace. Hikers are picked up at the end of each day's section and brought back here for fireside suppers. Alternatively accommodation can be arranged in Mossel Bay. On the 4th night, another of Fred's designs awaits in the form of Kanon Cottage at Cape Vacca.

Rates for 2010 are R6 550/p for the 5-dayer, and R3 600/p for the shorter option, and include accommodation and all meals from supper on the day of arrival to the hearty champagne brunch on the day of departure. As with the longer trail option, don't forget sunscreen, a wide-brimmed hat, sunglasses, and sandals as well as boots. The preferred minimum group size is 6 and maximum 12 and ages from 8 upwards – the oldest person to have completed the trail is 86. For inside information tel 044-699-1204 or cell 082-550-4788, e-mail stay@sandpipersafaris.co.za.

Dolphin Trail

This is a green flag trail, which means the trail owners acknowledge their responsibility to the environment and maintain a high level of user satisfaction and a value-for-money experience.

As with the Otter Trail, this scenic saunter starts at **Storms River mouth** (see page 220) but instead of heading west, it takes off in the opposite direction, across the suspension bridge spanning the river and winds eastwards along the rocky coast. Participants on this hike have the edge over the Otter trailers in that they're not weighed down by a backpack bulging with everything they'll need for the duration; and instead of rustic huts for overnight stops they slumber in 4-star (hiking) luxury. The scenery, however, is no less spectacular. The 17 km trail is completed over 2 days and knowledgeable guides will ensure you get the most out of the region.

While the distances may be short – and smirked at by some hardcore hikers – don't think you can go from being a couch potato to lacing up a new pair of boots and hitting the trail. While anyone older than 12 years of age is welcome to give it a go, the rugged terrain requires that participants are used to an active lifestyle and maintain a reasonable level of fitness.

Use the afternoon of your arrival to loosen up your legs on some of the short routes in the park or even a small section of the Otter Trail, but more tempting is just chilling in the splendour of the area. That evening you get to meet your trail hosts over supper and from then its memory making on a grand scale. The first day, providing the weather wizard has cast a calm spell, a short boat trip into the Storms River gorge sets the scene. The route

then follows a sine-wave profile, rising to magnificent views and plunging to mountain streams and rocky coastline with lots of time to rest and no need to rush. The trail passes caves, lookouts, bays, rock pools, and through indigenous forests strung with old man's beard lichen. Should all be calm on the rugged seashore snorkelling, or just a cooling dip, is a possibility at rock pools along the way.

The 2010 rates are R4 200/ps and a little more than R5 000 for a single. This includes 3 nights' accommodation, at Tsitsikamma National Park, Misty Mountain Reserve and The Fernery respectively, all meals from supper on the day of arrival to breakfast on day of departure, guides, transportation of luggage, and a tour through the old Storms River pass. To reserve your 2 days of pampered perambulation, contact The Fernery on tel 042-280-3588 or e-mail info@dolphintrail.co.za.

Leave your worries behind: the first tentative steps on the Otter Trail begin at the western extreme of the campsite at Storms River mouth.

Mossel Bay 5

Literally translated, Mossel Bay means 'mussel bay', which should not be confused with Muscle Bay, although you will see shiny, bronzed, well-defined triceps, biceps, and pectorals, displayed by wearers of why-bother tangos and mine's-bigger-than-yours Speedos. Although it's not unheard of to see such sights on the long glistening beaches around the town, the mussel that gives the town its name is of the shellfish kind and its plump body is enjoyed on a plate as a starter or part of a seafood platter.

The Point at Mossel Bay is a favourite place to park off. While bathing is much better further along the bay, the Point is a hot spot for surfers.

Mossel Bay is the first town travellers encounter when entering the Garden Route from the Cape Town side, which is the direction we are using for the purposes of this book. One of the first things to catch your attention when nearing

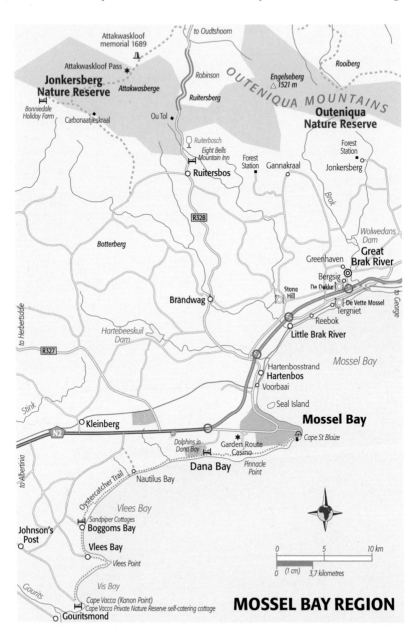

MOSSEL BAY REGION

the town along the N2 is the jumble of pipes, flues and buildings that make up Petro SA – formerly known as Mossgas. This industrial monster came into being in 1987 to produce synthetic fuels and by-products from off-shore gas deposits. It was considered a necessity to reduce South Africa's dependence on imported oil during the apartheid era. A little further and you enter the outskirts of the town: to be truthful, most people just take the N2 bypass and avoid the place altogether, zooming past its equally industrial-looking backyard. However, it does have attractions, not least of which is one of the best beaches in the region.

This was the general location of the first meeting between European explorers and the indigenous Khoi 'strandlopers' (beachcombers) of the southern Cape. It all came about in February 1488 when Portuguese sailor Bartolomeu Dias and his crew landed hereabouts in 2 100-ton caravels while searching for the end of Africa and a possible sea route to the spice lands in the East. The Khoi, who followed a partially pastoralist lifestyle, were sighted in the area with their cattle and Dias initially called the landfall Baia dos Vaqueiros (Bay of the Cowherds). It wasn't until 1601, when Dutch Admiral van Caerden found a plentiful supply of mussels to feed his crew that it became known as Mosselbaai, or Mossel Bay.

Human habitation of the area goes way back, around 80 000 years or more, when the indigenous people of South Africa lived here in close association with nature. Their home over the millennia were caves along the seashore including the one situated at Cape St Blaize to the south of the town, which can still be visited today. In fact with ongoing archaeological research being carried out, the area is being referred to as the first known home of modern humans, *Homo sapiens*.

The town saw rapid growth during the property boom years of the 1990s and early 2000s and it has expanded enormously. Unfortunately, from an aesthetics point of view, there's more in-your-face industry and commerce than the pretty

WHY VISIT

For the great weather. This almost guarantees halcyon days on which to enjoy its various activities, especially the beaches and the surf.

WHAT'S WACKY

The fact that not only is there a company offering the public the opportunity to get into a cage and be submerged in the sea amongst great white sharks … but that there are those of us who actually choose to do this. For fun!

TOURIST INFORMATION

Mossel Bay Tourism is on the corner of Market and Church Street and has plenty of brochures, info and details on accommodation, adventures, tours and attractions in town and the surrounds. It's open Mon–Fri 08h00–18h00, Sat–Sun 09h00–16h00; tel 044-691-2202, e-mail admin@visitmosselbay.co.za or web www.visitmosselbay.co.za.

seaside town it once was. However, if you venture off the N2 where the more modern suburbs are located, and head to the older part of the town towards The Point, things begin to look a lot better. Delve a little deeper still and the town and surrounds actually has the potential to entice the visitor with lots of sunshine, beaches and waves, with a few other fun things on the side.

On that note Mossel Bay and its surrounding coastline has some of the best swimming spots along the southern Cape coast – 24 km of beaches in total – and some of the best weather in the world. It's no wonder people come here for beach and surf fun. There's also whale-watching (June–October), it's 1 of 2 places in the country offering shark cage diving, and we have it on good authority from the dudes with boards strapped to their ankles that the surfing is excellent. There are also plenty of hiking and walking options along the coast and inland. Should you tire of all the outdoors stuff, the maritime museum is well worth a visit, and in the grounds an ancient milkwood tree stands as the first post office in South Africa.

So, if you travel not just to see, but also to explore and discover, you'll find something that'll have made the stopover worthwhile. Also consider that the town gets jammed packed with holidaymakers during the December summer break to such an extent that you can hardly squeeze a mussel between the muscles.

Out and About in Mossel Bay

Although the town seems to be a sprawl of modern constructions, there are still architectural gems and sandstone buildings of historic significance dotted around the old town. These can be seen on a **historical self-guided walking tour**. The historic maritime museum and a row of Welsh cottages in the old quarter are notable. A detailed map and easy-to-use brochure is available from the tourist office.

Swim and laze on the beach

If you're a beach enthusiast, you'll love Mossel Bay. It has a wide arc of golden beach offering safe swimming, fishing, surfing, scuba diving and a host of other water-based activities.

Central beaches

The Point has a walkway along the rocks so is ideal if you don't like sand but want to swim in natural rock pools. It's also for those who don't like the tug and spill of breakers, as there's a pleasant tidal pool that's ideal for children on the left as you enter The Point parking strip; and a second natural tidal pool among the rocks is directly in front of the upmarket The Point Hotel. In the vicinity you'll find a number of casual places to eat and drink.

Of the swimming beaches **Santos Beach** is the closest to the old town and is the only north-, or sun-facing beach. It's popular with families because of its large, gently sloping beach and its protected and mostly calm waters. There are public ablutions, a large parking area, and restaurants overlooking the bay nearby.

Next along this large bay is **De Bakke Beach**, which has small swimming areas in between rock outcrops and a big parking area, ablutions and grassed

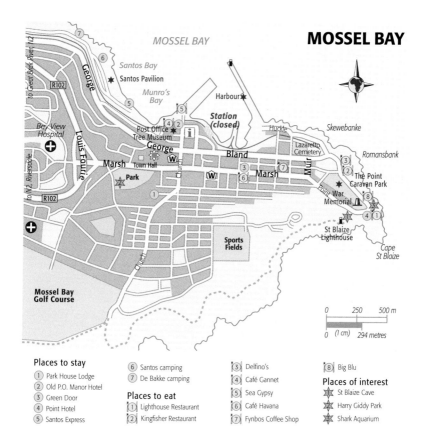

MOSSEL BAY

to Great Brak River, N2
to George, N2
R102
Santos Bay
Santos Pavilion
Munro's Bay
Harbour
Station (closed)
Bay View Hospital
Post Office
Tree Museum
Skewebanke
Huckle
Lazaretto Cemetery
George
Bland
Romansbank
Marsh
Town Hall
Marsh
The Point Caravan Park
Park
War Memorial
Louis Fourie
to N2, Riverside
R102
St Blaize Lighthouse
Sports Fields
Cape St Blaize
Mossel Bay Golf Course
Church

0   250   500 m
0 (1 cm) 294 metres

Places to stay
1. Park House Lodge
2. Old P.O. Manor Hotel
3. Green Door
4. Point Hotel
5. Santos Express

6. Santos camping
7. De Bakke camping

Places to eat
1. Lighthouse Restaurant
2. Kingfisher Restaurant

3. Delfino's
4. Café Gannet
5. Sea Gypsy
6. Café Havana
7. Fynbos Coffee Shop

8. Big Blu

Places of interest
- St Blaize Cave
- Harry Giddy Park
- Shark Aquarium

banks with braai places for the use of day visitors, plus a restaurant nearby.

Further around the bay, below the high-rise holiday flats and hotels, **Dias Beach** stretches for 3 km and has 2 good swimming areas, ablutions, a water park for the kids and a large convenience market nearby – if you left your reading material behind there's a book store here. It's also good for fishing and long evening strolls. The main Dias Beach parking is next to the high-rise, luxury Diaz Strand Hotel and there's a big, tiered parking garage behind the hotel if it's really busy; the

area has a couple of restaurants and places for a drink.

Eastern beaches

There's really no reason to look further than central Mossel Bay for nice beaches, but if you want a change of scenery try some of these. **Hartenbos Beach** is a 20-min drive northeast of town and has some good swimming places and 6 km of beach, plus ablution facilities. A further 5-min drive **Little Brak River** is popular for its long beach and river mouth, and there're ablutions and a big parking area. **Reebok Beach** is yet a little further east

You don't have to brave the waves or crowds to find a nice swimming or tanning beach, like this one near the mouth of the Little Brak river estuary.

and is known for its great tidal pool and around 8km of beach that is not really good for swimming because of a shallow rock ledge running along the coast – it is good, though, for rock-pooling at low tide. Then comes **Eiland Beach** at Great Brak River, which is a bit scruffy, and then **Glentana Beach** about halfway between Mossel Bay and George has 4km of beach and a shipwreck to walk to at low tide.

For some underwater adrenaline head out to sea with **White Shark Africa**, which offers one of the ultimate adrenaline rushes, **cage diving** with great whites. Sharks are wild animals, so there's never a guarantee they'll respond to the bait trail the boat lays in order to lure them closer. However, for this very reason it's exciting just being on the water, knowing they're out there

somewhere and there's a good chance you'll get up close and personal with them. Although it's not as well known as Gansbaai as a shark diving destination, here you won't be surrounded by boatloads of other adrenaline junkies, and if these big fish aren't playing along there are always the seals on Seal Island to keep you entertained. They're based on the commercial slipway at the Mossel Bay harbour. Tel 044-691-3796 or check out www.sharkafrica.co.za.

Go fishing either from a boat, or the shore. The latter offers long beaches with some deep gullies and rocky outcrops to the east and west of town. You may catch elf (shad), steenbras, baardman, kob (kabeljou), leervis (garrick), musselcracker and possibly even the now-rare galjoen depending on the area of coast you choose. Several outfits offer deep-sea trips including **Deep Sea Adventures**. Their boat, *Dreamcatcher*, can take up to 10 passengers and they do 2 trips a day each lasting 5–6 hours, supply tackle and bait, and kids are welcome. They target bottom-feeders so expect kabeljou, red roman, silverfish and geelbek (Cape salmon) to be included in your haul and as long as your catch is above minimum size you can take it away with you. They operate from the commercial slipway down at the harbour. For more details tel 044-696-5123 or cell 072-454-2988, e-mail deepseaadventures@etime.co.za or web www.deepseaadventures.co.za.

Early sea birds will enjoy sitting at **The Point**, watching fishers and surfers plying their trade as the sun rises. Mothers play with children on the beach, and dogs trot happily, with tongues lolling, behind their owners. This is the time to get inspired and join the joggers, speed walkers, and not-so-speedy walkers.

Surfer dudes find Mossel Bay really gets them amped. There are several good, and some great, **surf spots** near town, like The Point, near the caravan park. This is where you'll find the **Inner Pool**, said to be overrated, and the **Outer Pool** that's known as the main wave at Mossel Bay. When there are no rip currents or sharks, it's said to be gnarly (surfspeak for excellent). On the northern side of the peninsula, there's surfing at **Santos Reef**, and although it lacks raw power, it can be good fun. Moving along the bay towards Hartenbos, **Ding Dang** comes next and is best in SW to west winds; then Dias beach, which is dependent on sand-

banks to work; and there could be good waves at Hartenbos as well, particularly in a light northwest to west wind with a clean southeast to east swell. For latest updates, check out www.wavescape.co.za/spots-by-region/garden-route.

Scuba diving conditions vary so it's best to hook up with A E Diving, based at the Dias beach parking. It's owner-run by young brothers Daniel and Séan Rogers, a couple of guys with a zest for life and adventure, and a love of the ocean. They offer shore and boat dives (minimum group sizes may apply) to the best dive sites around Mossel Bay including colourful reefs at a depth of just 7 m – reefs include Mitch's, Santos, Stingray and Dolosse, plus one at Klein Brak River Mouth, and Windvogel for experienced divers. The waters here are generally warm with an average viz of around 6 m. They offer PADI courses, do

The bilingual Outeniqua Choo-Tjoe waits for departure at Mossel Bay station.

Nitrox-mix dives, hire out equipment if you don't have your own, and also do abseiling and rock climbing trips for groups of 4 and more. To find out more give them a call on tel 044-692-0313 or cell 082-621-8619, e-mail info@adventuresedge.co.za or web www.adventuresedge.co.za.

There are a host of other hedonistic water-based activities including **kayaking**, **parasailing** and **jetski rentals** and most of the operators have offices and ticket kiosks at the harbour – turn sharp left as you enter harbour gate.

There are several operators offering **sea trips**, either for sight-seeing or fishing and one of the ways to find out more is to visit the harbour on an evening when all boats are parked in a row on the left, facing Santos beach. Their contact details are on the boats, and there are also info booths and booking offices down there that can be visited during the day.

Seal Island is a blip in the bay about 2 km from the harbour where around 5 000 seals live. Various companies run trips, including Romonza, which has been run by the same family for some 30 years. Trips leave the harbour every hour on the hour from 10h00 and cost around R100/p, and are discounted for children. Call Charmaine on 044-690-3101. **Seven Seas Charter** is another option, tel 044-691-3371. Each year from June to October, **southern right whales** visit the country's coast to calve. Mossel Bay and surrounds host various pods of whales, many of which hang out in Boggoms Bay. The best places for land-based whale-watching are at The Point; from Cape St Blaize light-house; any of the beaches, although the whales will be beyond the breakers; the cliff tops south of town. To have closer sightings, join one of Romonza's **whale-watching cruises**.

An icon of the Garden Route is the renowned steam engine, the **Outeniqua Choo-Tjoe** (see under George on page 68) for details and a description of the George–Mossel Bay trip.

> Warning: If you're arranging your own dive group it's not advisable to venture anywhere near Seal Island as that is where the great white sharks hunt seals.

The maritime history of Mossel Bay can be explored at the **Dias Museum Complex** where you can board a replica of Dias' caravel in the **Maritime Museum**. This ship was sailed from Portugal and arrived in Mossel Bay in 1988, to commemorate the 500th anniversary of Dias's landing here. Standing on the deck of this 23,5-m-long boat, it's hard to imagine how 30 crew spent 6 months on calm and stormy seas with little to protect them from the elements. Check out the display of **navigational instruments**, and put yourself in the early European explorers' shoes. They had no idea where or indeed if land was, and yet bravely sailed into terra incognita in blind faith that they would find land and fresh supplies. There's also a **collection of ancient maps** from those days and a good shipwreck display.

One of the most humbling experiences at the complex is to stand beneath the 600+-year-old **Post Office Tree** and stroke its bark, knowing you are literally touching history. Although it cannot be irrefutably substantiated that this is the exact tree sailors used as a depot for leaving and collecting letters in an old boot, it's very likely to be the one. A great memento is to post a letter here in the boot-shaped letterbox, as it'll be postmarked 'Old Post Office Tree'. The museum complex also houses **The Fountain**, a freshwater spring used by Dias that still flows; a **Shell Museum**, said to be the largest in the country, shows the ecology of the mollusc plus a systematic display of shells from all over the world; and aquarium; **a culture display**; **granary**; **padrão** (stone cross); a **Ethno-Botanical Garden and Braille Trail**; and **Munro Cottage** built around 1830. The complex is open 09h00–16h45 Mon–Fri, and 09h00–15h45 on weekends and public holidays. For further info visit www.diasmuseum.co.za.

There's a **shark aquarium** at The Point, beneath the Dros steakhouse and Big Blu pub, which has a display of small sharks.

Alongside Tourism lies the **Craft Art Workshops** where artists, such as the talented **Matthews** (Mthetheleli Malambile) create, and where you can buy some lovely holiday mementoes and gifts. Matthews's signature artworks are his colourful township scenes depicted in cards and collages.

For something different, do a **Backroad Safari** 'Meet the People' tour with Jauckie Viljoen. You head towards the mountains, and meet up with local crafts people who are the small entrepreneurs of the area. Some skills have been handed down over generations: depending on when you go, you could

The cave at Cape St Blaize, the point of Mossel Bay, was one of many similar shelters along the Cape coast used by Khoisan strandlopers since 'before the flood'.

meet Alfred the brick-maker, Tannie Millie the bread and jam-maker, and Janneman the leather bag maker. Then there's Baruch, who roasts coffee beans and sells heavenly Baruch's coffee in the area, and Hans Munro, 7th generation oyster fundi. His family began harvesting coastal oysters in 1716. To book this cultural experience, tel Jauckie on 083-262-2307, email: info@backroadsafaris.com, web www.backroadsafaris.co.za or www.meet-the-people.co.za. The Back-road Safari also visits tucked-away Ruiterbos Valley about 35 km inland from Mossel Bay on the R328.

Park House Lodge is one of many lovely old sandstone houses in Mossel bay old town.

If you can afford the R550/p fee for a 60-minute **ride on an elephant**, head out to upper Little Brak River where **Botlierskop Private Game Reserve** has a day-visitor centre and restaurant. It's a 3 000 ha luxury game farm with 20 species of game, which you might spot on 1 of their 3-hour game drives. They have a host of activities to keep you busy for the best part of a day. Tel 044-696-6055, e-mail botlier@mweb.co.za, web www.botlierskop.co.za.

Another wild experience can be had at **Jukani Wildlife Predator Park**. It's 1 km off the N2, 5 km from town and offers viewings of wild animals and a farmyard playground. Guided tours are at 10h00 (best for viewing), 12h00 and 14h00 and last about 40 minutes, but the 16h00 feeding tour is the one you really want to be on. Entrance is R95/p for the day so you can do a tour, go to the beach, and come back for more. Open daily 09h00–17h00.

The big cats include white lions, tigers, jaguars and pumas. To contact them tel 044-698-2004, e-mail info@

jukani.co.za or web www.jukani.co.za.

Act the old sea dog and visit the 20,5 m high **St Blaize Lighthouse**, which was erected in 1864 as a beacon for sailors and is 1 of only a few still manned lighthouses. It offers panoramic views over the peninsula and bay, towards the Outeniqua mountains. It's open for tours from 10h00–15h00 Mon–Fri from May–Sept, or daily during the summer months. Adults are charged R16, children R8 each. For further details call 044-690-3015 or visit www.transnetnationalportsauthority.net.

Cape St Blaize Cave, at Mossel Bay's Point, has revealed artefacts from the Khoi people, dating back 80 000 years, some of which are housed in the Culture Museum. A boardwalk leads into the shallow shelter. To find it, drive around the point, and just past the hotel is a parking area and signs.

The **St Blaize Trail** starts at the cave and winds 13,5 km along a contoured cliff-top path to Dana Bay, west of Mossel Bay. It offers incredible scenery and views

The view across from Bonnievale Guest Farm to the Attakwaskloof mountains, among the most rugged and inaccessible places in the Cape Folded Mountains – unless you have a 4x4.

of the coastline. Spot coastal birds and dolphins year-round, and whales from June–Oct. The trail can be walked in the other direction, and either way you must arrange to be collected unless you're happy to retrace your footsteps. No permit, map or directions needed.

It's also here, near The Point Hotel, where you can view the **war memorial**. It was erected in 1924 in remembrance of the people of Mossel Bay who died during WWI, and in 1954 another panel was added for WWII.

For a stroll in the park head for **Harry Giddy Park**, which has bowling greens, tennis courts and lots of old stonework. It hosts occasional arts and crafts fairs.

Mall rats or anyone wanting to do some real shopping will be pleased to know that the relatively new, and large, **Langeberg Mall** between town and Hartenbos, on the R102 has over 100 shops to browse.

If the waves aren't up to providing the kind of ride you're looking for, swap your surfboard for a **sandboard** on Dragon Dune near Vleesbaai. It costs R350/p for 3 hours of sand-spitting fun. Speak to Leon on 044-691-3811 or 082-971-1405, e-mail info@billeon.com or web www.billeon.com.

Not to be outdone on the **golfing** front, Mossel Bay now has an 18-hole championship course at nearby **Pinnacle Point** course (some hookers and slicers say it's one of the finest links in the world). Here golfers may be enticed to chase that ball around the 1 000-acre resort, which sports superb holes perched on the cliff tops above the pounding Indian Ocean. Unfortunately, on the other side are the environmentalists who say it should never have been built right on the sea edge. For further details tel 044-693-3438, e-mail golf@pprgolf.co.za or web www.pinnaclepointgroup.co.za.

Nightlife comes in the form of several establishments offering a **pub, dancing and live entertainment**, but the main game in town is the **Garden**

Hitting the lip at Mossel Bay Point. You have to be a committed surfer to chance these waters that, further out at Seal Island, is patrolled by the 'men in grey suits'.

Route Casino. The casino has 370 slot machines, gaming tables, a kids entertainment centre and crèche, and famous 120-dish buffet restaurant. To get there, take the R102 west towards Cape Town and the turn-off is well signposted on this road. Nocturnal jols in town include **Café Havanna** in Marsh Street that has live music on some nights, and for the young at heart **Stones** in Bland Street hosts DJs, comedians, entertainers and bands and is sure to have you spinning around the dance floors.

Overnight in Mossel Bay

Be aware that in season, especially over Christmas and New Year, the town and surrounds is packed so *propvol* that, even if you're gregarious, there's a good chance that at some stage you'll want to put the oke next door's purple chihuahua on your braai.

Central
SILK

The **Old Post Office Tree Manor Hotel** is situated in an old stone building, dating back to 1846, right across the road from the tourist info office and a gannet's hop away from the harbour. It offers 3-star en-suite double rooms as well as 4-star self-catering Harbour Suites (sleep 4); all units have modern décor and the usual mod cons like air-conditioning or fans, DStv, and tea/coffee stations. There's a well positioned swimming pool, the Blue Oyster Bar is the place to be for sundowners overlooking Munro Bay, and their Café Gannet Restaurant (see under where to eat) is open 7 days a week. Their Harbour Suites cost around R1 510 for 2 and the en-suite doubles are from R1 160 for 2. Rates exclude breakfast, which is optional at the **Café Gannet**

Restaurant at R115 a person (yes, R115 for breakfast). For full details tel 044-691-3738, e-mail book@oldposttree.co.za or web www.oldposttree.co.za.

The Point Hotel is 4-star graded and in a great location looking onto the rugged coastline at The Point. The 52 double, twin and queen double en-suite rooms occupy 5 floors and each has sea views, DStv, fans/heaters, tea/coffee station and a private balcony. There's a ladies bar serving cocktails and other drinks and The Lighthouse Restaurant (see under where to eat and drink) is one of the better eateries in Mossel Bay. Rates are around R600/ps and breakfast costs R85. For more details tel 044-691-3512, e-mail the point@pointhotel.co.za or click on www.pointhotel.co.za.

LINEN

The 3-star **Green Door** at 49 Marsh Street has a good range of accommodation including a dorm, en-suite B&B doubles and family rooms and a self-catering flat in a Victorian house. The décor is modern, and rooms, including the dorm, have MNet and percale linen. Some rooms are sea facing and have private balconies that offer views of the harbour and mountains. The flat is fully equipped for self-catering, and has 1 double room and a room with a double bunk, open-plan lounge and full kitchen – great for a family. B&B rates are from R250–R390/ps depending on season. Out of season, a family room sleeping 4 costs R850, and the self-catering flat is R900. The dorm beds are available for R250/p. For full details tel 044-691-3820 or e-mail greendoorbb@mweb.co.za.

CALICO

Park House Lodge and Travel Centre is a combined 3-star guesthouse and 4-star backpackers in a grand 1860s double-storey sandstone house with wrap-around wooden balcony, wrought-iron pillars and plenty of fretwork. They're conveniently situated above the old town at 121 High Street where it becomes a cul-de-sac at Harry Giddy Park. The soothing background *thwok* of ball on racket-strings from the courts next door could easily entice guests to voice the invitation, 'Anyone for tennis?' Backpackers have never had it so good, with dorms on the top floor of the old house opening onto the balcony overlooking the garden, while downstairs is the TV lounge, breakfast room and communal kitchen.

The modern double-storey annex houses en-suite doubles and singles with shared bathrooms and there are more dorms above the reception and travel centre. There's a tea/coffee station available throughout the day, tables, chairs, hammocks, and swing-chairs in the tranquil gardens, which shelter beneath shade trees and ivy-covered stonework. Candles and paraffin lanterns add atmosphere in the evenings, and there's an overall relaxed vibe. Even if you're only slightly gregarious we can recommend this to any traveller through all age groups. The owner, Durr Meyer, has built it up over 12 years. And while his craggy features and laid-back manner appear more suited to someone who spends their days waiting for that perfect wave, he's an interesting character and host. There's a braai for the use of visitors and breakfast and supper can be pre-ordered at reception. Rates for dorms are R120/p, and en-suite doubles R170–220/ps, tel 044-691-1937, e-mail info@parkhouse.co.za or web www.parkhouse.co.za.

For backpackers and budget conscious travellers, lodgings with a difference come in the form of the **Santos Express Train Lodge**. It's a few carriages hooked together and permanently parked off Santos Beach so, instead of drifting off to clickety-clack, it'll be to lappety-lap. They offer singles, twins and 1 double in standard coupés and compartments so all you get is a bed, and ablutions (a shower and 2 toilets) are at the ends of each carriage. There's a casual restaurant and 'happening' bar with a deck overlooking the bay and mountains; it's near the harbour and museum complex and just a short stroll to the town centre. Rates are R120–180/ps; tel 044-691-1995, e-mail beds@santosexpress.co.za or web www.santos-express.co.za.

CANVAS

The Point Caravan Park is the pick of the bunch and ideally located overlooking the sea at The Point, and within walking distance of the tidal pool, the St Blaize Cave and a few good restaurants; tel 044-690-3501. **De Bakke Caravan Park** and **Santos Caravan Park** are situated on the thin coastal strip between the R102 and the shore when heading towards the old town from the Dias Beach side. They're within easy walking distance of good swimming beaches and have lovely views across the bay. De Bakke also has self-catering 1-, 2- and 3-bedroomed chalets; tel 044-691-

2915. All 3 are municipal sites. Rates for camping, depend on the position of the site, and are roughly R110–R310 a site for up to 6 people and 1 vehicle in low/high season. **De Bakke chalets** cost R330 for a 1-bedroomed unit, to R950 for 3 bedrooms. Pensioners' discounts apply in low and mid seasons.

Eating Out in Mossel Bay

All coastal towns offer good opportunities to indulge in the local fare and Mossel Bay is particularly known for its mussels and sole.

The **Lighthouse Restaurant** at the 4-star **Point Hotel** has a fabulous setting right on the edge of the sea, and although it's highly desirable to dine outdoors during fair weather, it's really exciting during the odd storm when the waves are crashing on the rocks, spraying white froth into the blackened sky. As one would expect of a luxury hotel, the restaurant is aimed at those who wish for a touch of fine dining in a quiet atmosphere with attentive service.

Looking down on the Point Hotel from the St Blaize lighthouse.

The replica of Bartolomeu Dias's caravel, sailed from Portugal to Mossel Bay to mark the 500th anniversary of that mariner's 'voyage of discovery' and now in the Maritime Museum.

The menu is innovative and varied, and the extensive wine list ensures plenty of choice. While waiting for your starter, enjoy good home-made bread and, if you're lucky, a pod of dolphins might be seen from your table. Open from 07h00, for buffet breakfast, to 22h00. For further info tel 044-691-3512, e-mail the point@pointhotel.co.za or web www. pointhotel.co.za.

Delfino's Espresso Bar and Pizzeria is a casual lunch spot and is also at The Point, overlooking the surfing spot, and they specialise in the usual coffees and espressos but also serve lungos and ristrettos – go find out for yourself what these are. The view is fabulous, you can eat in or outdoors, and the menu includes light eats, pizza and pasta. They're open daily from 07h00–23h00; tel 044-690-5247.

Above Delfino's is the glass-fronted **Kingfisher Restaurant**, and yup, it has the same gorgeous views. As dusk settles on the ocean, sip a cocktail and watch the last few water babies playing in the tidal pool below while surfers catch the last waves in the dying light. Then get stuck into the menu, which has fish as the main theme, great fish in big portions – don't miss the butterfish or angelfish. They often have sushi specials, the wine list is good, the salads are excellent, and they have liqueurs for after dinner enjoyment as you watch the night sky reflected in the ocean and, time depending, the moon rising over the sea. It's a vibey eatery, great for families and offers good value for money. Open daily 11h00–23h30; tel 044-690-6390.

The Sea Gypsy Café at the working harbour has a atmospheric, even romantic location right on the water. In fact, if you felt like feeding the fish or seagulls, you need only toss your plate over your shoulder and you'd hit one on the head. This is one of those rustic wooden harbour cafés with lots of seafaring spirit, a wonky bar, and you might even see the ocean lapping beneath your feet if you look through the cracks in the floor. The patio area outside is a great place to relax over a beer or tuck into some oysters. Open daily 09h00–23h30; tel 044-690-5496.

Café **Havana** in an old double-storey house on Marsh Street is probably more suited to the younger crowd, but it has a few interesting dishes. The menu is Cuban-based and is good for a night cap when they have live music; go early to get a seat. It's open for lunch and supper either inside or out, and has a really laid-back vibe. If you're feeling chilled, you're bound to join the patrons who will be – sorry, but we have to say it – havana great time. Open daily 12h00–23h30 for food and even later for cocktails; tel 044-690-4640.

Locals say Café **Gannet**, located in the Old Post Tree Manor Hotel complex, is still a favourite for seafood. It's trendy and aims at the discerning palate, but these days that could mean you're rubbing shoulders with an ancient surfer dude or a nouveau riche investor. Enjoy a pre-dinner drink on the patio overlooking the bay. Open 7 days a week for breakfasts, light meals, lunches and suppers from 07h00–23h00. To book in season tel 044-691-1885, e-mail gannet@oldposttree.co.za or web www.oldposttree.co.za.

A good place for breakfast or tea is **Fynbos Coffee Shop** in Marsh Street opposite the old stone church. You walk through a large gift shop that's packed with stock, and eat in a big conservancy that has classic country décor. Open 08h30–16h45. Look out for their specials.

If you're into handcrafted artisanal breads, head to the Langeberg Shopping Mall near Dias Beach where **La Baguette's** fare will sort you out for the day. They do light breakfasts, lunches, pizzas, and a crazy variety of artisan breads baked in the wood-fired oven, and they keep cold beer and wine in the fridge. You'll find them in the banking section of the mall. Open Mon–Fri 07h30–17h30 and Sat 07h30–16h00.

Big Blu, alongside the Point Hotel, looks out across the rocks and is a casual place for a drink outside on a nice day. They serve food all day and their tapas bar is popular for light meals. It's a good place for easy-going folks and operates every day from 09h00 until late. Tel 044-691-2010 or web www.bigblu.co.za.

North and East of Mossel Bay
Hartenbos

This very Afrikaans-flavoured village has a quaint homeliness about it. The beachfront is taken up by the ATKV (Afrikaner cultural association) Hartenbos Beach Resort, which is divided in 2 by a shopping centre. During December and Easter school holidays it's abuzz with holidaymakers, many from the farms of the Karoo who have holiday homes there, and because of this it's fondly referred to as the 'Karoo by the sea'. Many side streets even carry names from this great semi-desert of the interior. During festive times there's an atmosphere of one big extended family gathering. If you want to catch share in the buzz, there are large beachfront parking areas for the general public to the east and west of the resort.

The beach at Hartenbos lends itself

to long strolls either on the near end-less soft and gently sloping beach or on the paved walkway just above the beach. Quaint seaside cottages snugly line the narrow side streets leading off the coastal road. These give way to more modern houses towards Mossel Bay. Behind the ATKV offices, in Kaap De Goede Hoop Ave, the Hartenbos Museum is worth a visit and preserves the historic Afrikaans culture, with the main theme detailing the Great Trek – that great Cape-Dutch diaspora of the 1830s. Open Mon–Fri 09h00–16h00 (closed for lunch) and Sat 09h00–12h30. Entrance fee is R5/p.

Ruiterbos Valley and Robinson Pass

Just north of Mossel Bay the R328 heads inland to the rural area of Ruiterbos, a scenic valley of farms and small holdings worked by friendly country folk, B&Bs, and some crafty

oulets at the base of the Outeniqua mountains. It is small enough to drive around and explore without getting lost. Past Ruiterbos the road winds over the Robinson Pass, which traverses the Outeniqua mountains and leads to the semi-arid Little Karoo and the ostrich centre of Oudtshoorn. The historic pass was constructed by Thomas Bain (see box page 70) between 1867 and 1869 and was realligned and tarred in the 1950s. Taking this road makes a nice day drive and there are a few very nice places to stay and lots of things to do. Visit website www.ruiterbos.co.za to find out what's offered.

Overnight in Ruiteberbos Valley
LINEN

The 4-star **Eight Bells Mountain Inn**, alongside the R328, with its magnificent 200-year old oak tree, has a long history as a place to lay a weary head.

Trail guide Willie Komani (right) takes hikers on the Oystercatcher Trail through their paces along Boggoms Bay, one of 5 overnight stops on the trail.

In recent decades it has reaffirmed itself as a legendary place to stay. Its 25 units range from double rooms and rondavels to family suites and wooden chalets set at different locations in the peaceful gardens. Some of the original old lodging rooms have been incorporated into the reception buildings of today, adding even more character to this wonderful country retreat. All units have TV, under-floor heating, fans and air-conditioning.

There's a large and cosy communal lounge in the main lodge with fireplace, games and mini library and a billiard room, bar and restaurant serving breakfast, lunch and supper from a good menu, so there's really no reason to do anything but relax. If that's a little too mundane there's a pool, horse riding, walking trails, squash and tennis, and a recreation room and jungle gym to keep the kids amused. Day visitors are welcome to enjoy a meal or tea and cakes beneath brollies on the *stoep* or in the garden while being entertained by the vervet monkeys swinging in the big shade trees. It's serene and quaint and ideal for couples and families who enjoy a rural feel and mountain views. B&B rates range from R420–R550/ps throughout the year except over school holidays when they are R500–R630/ps. To book tel 044-631-0000, e-mail info@eightbells.co.za or web www.eightbells.co.za.

CALICO & CANVAS

For outdoor enthusiasts **Bonniedale Holiday Farm** tucked deep into the mountains next to the Attakwaskloof Nature Reserve offers a range of accommodation, from B&B rooms in the old farmhouse to camping. Outdoor activities are the name of the game here with horse riding, hiking, mountain biking, dips in refreshing rock pools and some mean 4x4 trails – rated among the top 10 in South Africa. Day visitors are welcome. To get there take the R328 for around 25 km until you reach a school on the left, before you reach Eight Bells Mountain Inn. Turn left here, 8 km further turn right and a further 18 km will bring you to their doorstep. B&B rates are R280/ps, self-catering chalet from R140/ps, tented camp R95/p and camping with your own tent R65/p. For a full list of activity rates contact Nico and Danette on tel 044-695-3175, e-mail bonniedale@mweb.co.za or web www.bonniedale.com.

West of Mossel Bay
Overnight in Dana Bay
LINEN

Dana Bay, about 7 km west of Mossel Bay, is for the most part a neat-trimmed residential area whose roads incorporate a network of crescents and cul-de-sacs. It has 2 swimming beaches with ablutions and a lookout point for whale and dolphin spotting. Be careful if you want to swim here, as there are serious currents at play.

If you're keen to stay over, the proprietors of **Dolphins Hill** in Brenton on Sea, Knysna, have a place near First Beach called **Dolphins in Dana Bay**. The wooden house is on a green belt and just a short walk from the beach. The large upstairs flat sleeps 6 (2 en-suite doubles and 2 single beds in the loft) with open-plan lounge/dining room/kitchen and a fireplace. Downstairs sleeps 4 to 8. They

The cross at Cape Vacca is a replica of one of the old Portuguese crosses that marked that nation's progress to the East.

each have TV, private verandas with sea views, built-in braais and are comfortable for families or groups of friends.

Rates are R1 000–R3 500 an apartment a night and they offer great winter specials. For more info tel 044-381-0527, e-mail dolphins@mweb.co.za or visit www.dolphinshill.co.za.

LINEN

About 30 km west of Mossel Bay the small conservancy of **Boggoms Bay** has become well known as the home of Fred Orban's slackpacking **Oyster-catcher Trail** (see hiking trail section page 38) but it's not only hikers who venture here. There's a 1 km beach and 2 swimming areas, but no ablution facilities. It's a great place to escape to, and a few days spent here wandering the nearby beaches and rocky outcrops

will instil a pleasing sense of peace in visitors. Whether you're a romantic couple or a family a real treat is a few nights in Fred's 4-star self-catering **Sandpiper Cottages** (sleep 2–6), but book well in advance as they're popular and are used by the trail blazers. These Cape cottage-styled thatched units are furnished in keeping with the old days but are fully equipped right down to CD player and laundry facilities. Self-catering rates are R450–R650/ps and the minimum-2-night-stay rule applies. Breakfast is an optional extra, as is dinner, but meals must be ordered in advance. Guests have free use of Fred's sports and wellness centre, so if you're building up those holiday love-handles, this is the chance to work them off; or just pamper yourself in the spa. For more details call 044-699-1204, e-mail stay@sandpipersafaris.co.za or web www.sandpiper.co.za.

The next bay along is **Vlees Bay**, which is an area of private holiday houses that has virtually no public access to the beach. There is only a very small public parking area on a steep hill, so a long hot walk uphill back to the car after a day on the beach, if you've managed to find the beach – there's a security boom at the entrance to Vlees Bay so ask the chaps there for directions. What is interesting is that it was named during the days when Portuguese and Dutch sailors traded goods for meat with local indigenous inhabitants, 'vlees' and 'vleis' being the Dutch or Afrikaans word for meat.

Gouritsmond is about 50 km west of Mossel Bay and is the mouth of the

Gourits (or Gouritz as it is sometimes spelt) river. It's a popular fishing spot, and also an area of mostly residential houses. The 1 side of the river falls under Mossel Bay and the other under the Albertinia municipality. On the western bank of the mouth stands a cluster of modern and semi-modern houses. The boats parked on the lawns of many of these homes are testament to this being a popular fishing area.

LINEN

Cape Vacca is on the eastern bank of the Gourits River, reached via about 10km of good gravel road, and is a private nature reserve. You'll find an isolated and delightful 4-star self-catering cottage here that's in the same style as Fred's Sandpiper Cottages at Boggoms Bay. It stands in a dramatic setting, surrounded by fynbos, sand and sea that's great for fishing, long lonely strolls on the rugged coastline, or just sitting back and doing nothing. It offers 5 single beds in a loft; and 1 single and 2 doubles downstairs. Each level has its own bathroom and there's a separate toilet. There's an open-plan lounge and kitchen, and separate dining area with 10-seater table that's ideal for large families or groups. Rates R1 500–R2 200 low/high season for the cottage. To book, tel Daan van Rensburg on 083-647-5279 or 044-699-1327. Nearby is a wooden cross that stands as a reminder that Cape Vacca was once an important navigational headland.

Around 30km west of Mossel Bay, where the N2 crosses the Gourits River, **the country's first bungy site** was opened way back in 1989. Sadly, at the time of writing, it was closed due to what sounds like a lot of red tape and politicking. **Face Adrenaline** who operated the bungy and a bridge swing had to close down and some 20 people lost their jobs. It's unlikely they'll open here again soon, but thankfully their mega-bungy at Bloukrans River between Plettenberg Bay and Storms River (see page 212) is still scaring the daylights out of the crowds. Check out web www.faceadrenalin.com for further info.

En Route to George

There are several resort-like settlements between Mossel Bay and the George area and they all have safe (but always take precautions, like not swimming alone), clean beaches with few rocks, which are bliss out of peak holiday periods. Over the Dec–Jan season, lifesavers are present. Some of the better known of these are, from west to east, Little Brak, Great Brak and Glentana.

Christmas time at Little Brak, but for much of the year beaches like this one will be deserted.

Little Brak River

Just 10 minutes' drive from Mossel Bay lies this tiny coastal village on the banks of the river that gives it its name. Its position at the river mouth makes it a popular watersports and angling destination. It has possibly the best swimming beach in the area, outside Mossel Bay, with surf for a bit of rough and tumble and the calm waters of the river for the placid types and kids. There's a huge parking area and ablutions. If you need a reason to visit Little Brak River other than for the great beach then make it a culinary one.

Eating Out in Little Brak

Vaaljapie Restaurant is situated on Little Brak station and is open for breakfast, lunch and suppers or just coffee and cake, or cocktails Tues–Sat 09h00 'til late and Sundays 09h00–15h00. It's situated in the old corrugated-iron waiting room and other station buildings with some tables on the platform; it's very quaint, and has a dedicated following. Try it, it's different; tel 044-696-5878.

Stone Hill Restaurant is a highly recommended country restaurant offering a broad gastronomic experience. The wine cellar has a decent stock of quality wines and offers a tasting facility and sales, while the restaurant itself, as proprietor Alan Robertson says, 'offers fun dining during the day, and an evening fine-dining experience.' It's popular with locals and serves mostly organic food, including vegetables, herbs, flowers and salad ingredients from the restaurant's own garden; most dishes come with a delicious twist. To get there from Mossel Bay take the N2 and after 6 km take the Little Brak River, Rhebok/Fraaiuitsig turn-off. Turn left at the stop and it's located on the left 500 m further. Open Mon–Sat 10h00–23h00 and Sundays from 12h00–15h00. To book a table tel 044-696-6501.

If fresh oysters get you swooning then continue past Stone Hill, turn left at the first junction and continue until you reach the little **general dealer's** store in **Riverside**, an outlying extension that was the original settlement of Little Brak River. At the general dealer's and the rather unassuming building across the road, you can pick up **fresh wild oysters** harvested that day from the rocks around Mossel Bay – provided they haven't run out – for less than half the price you'd pay anywhere else. It belongs to the 7th-generation Munros whose great ancestors were the first commercial fishermen and hunters of whales and seals in Mossel Bay, and who started harvesting oysters here in the early 1700s. They were the owners of the first bar in Mossel Bay and built the original Munro cottages, replicas of which stand in the grounds of the Maritime Museum. To check availability, tel 044-696-6140.

De Vette Mossel is fast becoming a culinary attraction. It's housed in a temporary structure erected on the sand dunes between Klein Brak and Great Brak – follow the signboards on the R102, which runs on the sea side of the N2. Patrons indulge in a 9-course menu accompanied by pot bread, farm butter and homemade jam, and you can eat as much as like of each course. It's a 3-hour dining experience best enjoyed in bare feet and casual wear. Most courses are cooked on open fires, and the restaurant is almost a Bedouin affair with reeds and canvas and the 'dining room' beneath an open-sided tent. It operates from beginning December to end April every year (and may soon operate from 1st September) with 2 daily sessions during school holidays. Lunch is served from 12h00–15h00 and supper from 18h30–late. Put it at the top of your list because, oh man it's *lekker*. There's a set price for the menu and take your own cooler box with drinks. Booking is absolutely essential so call 079-339-0170.

Overnight in Little Brak
CALICO & CANVAS

On the banks of the Little Brak River, 6km inland from the coast, **Riverside Holiday Resort** offers 6 2-bedroomed (sleep 4), fully equipped self catering chalets with TV and braai areas. They also have caravan and camping sites with clean ablutions, a small kiosk for basic supplies, the usual sea-side fun things to do to keep the kids happy, and a restaurant open only during the high season. There's good fishing and, with the river navigable for 20km, hiring one of their canoes for nice long paddling sessions is recommended. Rates for the chalets are R480–R800 a unit low/high season, and campsites are R55–R100/p low/high season. To find out more tel 044-696-6061, e-mail info@riverside-resort.co.za or web www.riverside-resort.co.za.

Great Brak River

The town of Great Brak River is situated a further 7km towards George and is made up of a few disjointed suburbs lying on both sides of the N2. As with Little Brak River this town gets its name from the river along the banks of which it is built. The main town centre lies inland of the N2 and was built around the Searle family manor (built by the founder next to the old bridge, of which he was toll keeper) and their enterprises, which included their boot and shoe factory. It was because of this business that Great Brak River became the first town in the southern Cape to have electricity when the Searle sons built a hydroelectric power station to run the machinery. Today shoes are still an important product of the town with the Watson shoe factory shop, located near the bridge, selling quality products at bargain prices.

Tree huggers should not miss the huge Chilean pepper tree behind Chris Spies' **art gallery** in Station Road – it's reputedly the biggest in South Africa. Chris loves to chat about it so feel free to visit his gallery and ask questions. **Eiland Beach** is Great Brak's main stretch of sand and is near the mouth of the lagoon on the edge of a suburb known as Southern Cross. It requires a walk over the dunes from the car park. Again because of the sea and river combination Great Brak is popular for water-based activities; there's also the 3km Wolvedans walking trail, which follows a route along the river to a lookout point at Wolvedans Dam.

Tourist Information

There is a **regional tourist office** in Amy Searle Street, which has a few rooms of interesting displays concerning the local history. Open 09h00–16h00

All celebrated gardens need rain, which keeps not only the forests of the Garden Route growing, but also the coastal fynbos near Gourits River mouth.

Mon–Fri and 09h30–12h00 Saturday. Contact Ina Stofberg tel 044-620-3338 or e-mail gbrtourism@intekom.co.za.

Eating Out in Great Brak

Ouma Bettie se Winkel in Charles Street is a quaint *winkeltjie* that sells traditional products like jams, sweets and dried fruits, and if the atmosphere of the place grabs you there's a tea garden outside for *lekkergoed* and light lunches.

De Dekke, alongside the N2 at the Great Brak River off-ramp, is a large timber establishment built around ponds with fish and water birds. It has an antique shop that, they claim, is the largest collection of antiques and collectables in South Africa. Alongside, the De Dekke restaurant and bar is a popular gathering place for the locals, especially on Friday and Saturday nights when there's live music, and serves honest portions of good food. It's a pleasant spot to stretch your legs, grab a bite in a country atmosphere, and pick up that Oregon pine dresser you've been wanting. The restaurant is open 11h00–22h00 Mon–Sat; tel 044-620-2531 or e-mail dedekke@telkomsa.co.za.

Overnight in Great Brak
LINEN

If you want to be near the sea, **At the Seaside** offers 2 semi self-catering (with only a microwave and fridge) studios – 1 sea-facing and 1 looking towards the mountains – and a fully equipped self-catering 2-bedroomed flat in the upmarket sea-front area of Hersham. Located just behind the fynbos fringing the beach you can sit and watch the waves from your private patio or deck. All units have TV. Rates are reasonable at R160–R200/ps low/high season. For more info tel 044-620-3221 or 082-374-6466, e-mail stay@theseaside.co.za, or web www.theseaside.co.za.

If you prefer to be away from the incessant drumming of the waves, the 4-star **Ilita Lodge** is big and bold on the hillside overlooking the Great Brak River valley. They offer 10 en-suite double rooms all with balconies to enjoy the

A wooden walkway down to Dana Bay beach protects the delicate dune vegetation.

views, DStv, air-conditioning, tea/coffee stations and mini bar. There are also 3 fully equipped self-catering apartments (each sleeping 4 to 6). There's a separate swimming pool for guests, secure parking, and use of a spa bath and gym. B&B rates are R350–R575/ps low/high season and the self-catering apartments cost R1400 a unit a day for up to 4 people and R2100 sleeping 6. Tel 044-620-4143 or 083-460-1059, e-mail info@ilitalodge.co.za or web www.ilitalodge.co.za.

CALICO & CANVAS

Caravanners and campers can head to **Pine Creek Private Holiday Resort**, which has 120 grassed and shady sites, and a range of facilities directly on the banks of the Great Brak River just past the tourist information office. There are the usual fun things for kids to do during the holidays, and it's nice and quiet out of season. They also offer 2 fully equipped self-catering chalets each sleeping 6 people. Rates for camping R130–R320 a site for 4 people low/high season, and the

chalets are R500–R700 a night for the unit low/high season. For bookings and enquiries tel 044-620-2434.

CANVAS

The beach at **Glentana**, 30km east of Mossel Bay, has several access points some with no facilities and some with rudimentary ablutions. On the eastern side of the village, near where a rocky headland plunges into the sea, is the main swimming beach with more modern ablutions and a café with outside tables and brollies behind the large car park – open only in high season. Around this headland is the wreck of the Port Natal floating dock that ran aground in 1902. The remains can be seen on a walk around the headland at low tide. Near this beach is the 3-star **Glentana Caravan Park**, which has around 50 shady and sheltered sites below the rolling hills. It's just a hop, skip and jump from the soft, sea-stroked sand. For more info, tel 044-879-1536.

WANT TO KNOW WHAT THE REGION OFFERS?

Take any letter of the alphabet, let's say L: lovely long beaches; lush forests; languid lagoons; landscapes; legends; lip-smacking linefish; luxurious lodgings; lingering lunches; lazy lakes; lobsters; lilies; lusty lagers; looping lichen; luminescent leaves; leopards; leapfrogs; languorous lolling; latitude; longitude; louries – okay, so technically they're now called turacos; and finally … laissez faire … live and let live.

George 6

This, the 6th oldest town in South Africa, is located on what was once the site of a woodcutter's outpost, established by the Dutch East India Company in the late 1700s. It was the 1st town founded under British rule at the Cape and was originally known as Georgetown, after the ruling British monarch of the day, King George III.

One of the main arteries through the regional centre of George, largest town on the Garden Route, is York Street. The town was named in honour of English King George III.

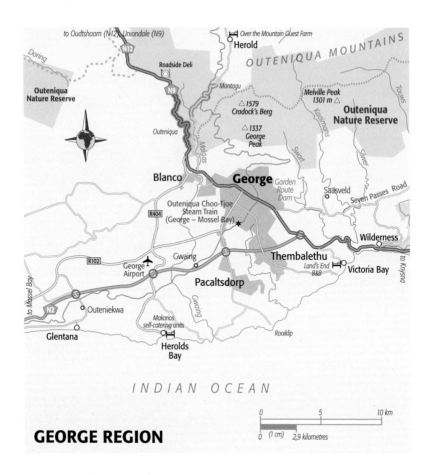

to Oudtshoorn (N12), Uniondale (N9)

Over the Mountain Guest Farm
Herold

Doring

N12

Roadside Deli

OUTENIQUA MOUNTAINS

Outeniqua
Nature Reserve

N9

Montagu

△1579
Cradock's Berg

Melville Peak
1301 m △

Outeniqua
Nature Reserve

Outeniqua

△1337
George
Peak

Kaaimans

Swart

Touws

Silver

Blanco

George

Garden
Route
Dam

Saasveld

Seven Passes Road

Outeniqua Choo-Tjoe
Steam Train
(George – Mossel Bay)

R404

Wilderness

Gwaing

Thembalethu

R102

George
Airport

Land's End
B&B

Victoria Bay

to Mossel Bay

Pacaltsdorp

to Knysna

N2

Outeniekwa

Gwaing

Makarios
self-catering units

Rooiklip

Glentana

Herolds
Bay

INDIAN OCEAN

0   5   10 km

0   (1 cm)   2,9 kilometres

GEORGE REGION

Although George is the biggest centre and the main business hub on the Garden Route, it's also the only major town that doesn't lie on the coast, its closest beach being 9 km to the south-east at Victoria Bay.

Over the past decade it has seen rapid growth and expansion in population, with people from the bigger centres up north setting down roots here in search of a quieter, less stressful lifestyle. This town has both a busy and a country vibe, with tree lined avenues and pockets of preserved heritage

among its more modern sprawl. Even though it's the main gateway to the region and has many visitors flying into its airport daily, from a visitor's point of view it's a case of biggest isn't best and George finds itself way down the list in terms of reasons to visit. Par for the course, it does have some excellent golfing opportunities on some of the finest courses South Africa has to offer, the best known of which is Fancourt (see details under Out and About) – although some people claim the local municipal course is among the 10 best in the country. It's also well situated for people who like to stay in 1 place and don't mind doing day trips to access the masses of nearby attractions, while having the convenience that this small city offers, including lots of formal shopping opportunities.

George's spectacular location at the base of the Outeniqua mountains has to be considered favourably with the highest peaks, Craddock (1579 m) and George Peak (1337 m), standing sentinel over the bustle below and always visible from just about anywhere in the vicinity. On the slopes below these lofty landmarks, and within the protected confines of the Outeniqua Nature Reserve, are a number of hiking trails that will elevate outdoor enthusiasts to some of the finest views in the area (see Out and About section).

Out and About in George

George is renowned as the golfing mecca of the southern Cape, and considered by some to be South Africa's premier golfing destination. Choices include several golf courses in and around the city, plus driving ranges and a world-class golf academy. There are also different short golf courses in the area. **Golfers** with large wallets can putt their stuff at the world-famous **Fancourt Hotel and Country Club** Estate, or if that's out of your range, 'scuse the pun, then there are short and mini-golf courses such as the **Three Chameleons Short Golf Course**, and

---

WHY VISIT

♦ If you're a shopaholic, it has the largest shopping mall on the Garden Route – The Garden Route Mall on the eastern edge of the city before descending Kaaimans Pass.

♦ Golfing opportunities

♦ Train museum and Choo-Tjoe trip to Mossel Bay

WHAT'S WACKY

The Power Van trip up the Outeniqua mountains

TOURIST INFORMATION

George Tourist Office is located beneath a magnificent old oak tree in a historic building at 124 York Street, near the traffic circle where the N9/N12 joins Courtney St as you enter George CBD from the west. It's open Mon–Fri 08h00–17h00, Sat 09h00–13h00; tel 044-801-9295, web www.visitgeorge.co.za or www.georgetourism.co.za.

INTERCITY BUSES

The Intercape and Translux coach services pick up and drop off passengers at the George railway station, while the Greyhound service has its terminal at St Mark's Square closer to the city centre.

FLYING INTO GEORGE

George's airport is situated 16 km to the southwest of the city centre and receives a steady stream of scheduled flights from most other major centres in South Africa. Most of the bigger car rental companies have depots at the airport.

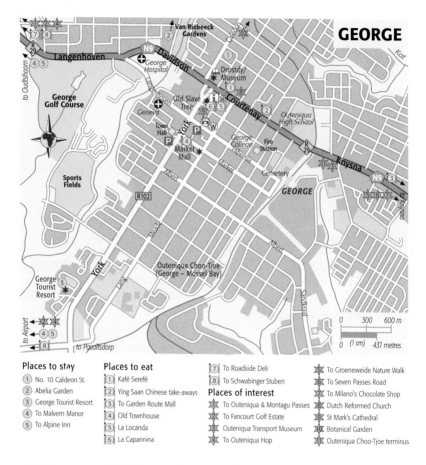

GEORGE

Places to stay
1. No. 10 Caldeon St.
2. Abelia Garden
3. George Tourist Resort
4. To Malvern Manor
5. To Alpine Inn

Places to eat
1. Kafé Serefé
2. Ying Saan Chinese take-aways
3. To Garden Route Mall
4. Old Townhouse
5. La Locanda
6. La Capannina

7. To Roadside Deli
8. To Schwabinger Stuben

Places of interest
1. To Outeniqua & Montagu Passes
2. To Fancourt Golf Estate
3. Outeniqua Transport Museum
4. To Outeniqua Hop

To Groeneweide Nature Walk
To Seven Passes Road
To Milano's Chocolate Shop
Dutch Reformed Church
St Mark's Cathedral
Botanical Garden
Outeniqua Choo-Tjoe terminus

a driving range at Windymere Farm
in the same area. To walk in the footsteps of many of the world's top golfers
at Fancourt you have to either be a
member, a guest of a member, or be a
hotel guest.

Either way it's going to set you back
R500–R1500 to play 18 holes on 1
of the 3 courses, The Montagu, The
Outeniqua, or The Links. To find out
more call 044-804-0000 or log onto
www.fancourt.com.

The **Outeniqua Transport Museum**,
the only one of its kind in the country,
is housed in a cavernous shed alongside the railway bridge in Courtenay
Street. The unexpectedly large display
includes locomotives, coaches and a
replica of an old station, plus other
vehicles and animal-drawn transport.
There's a model train room and miniature train, and a restaurant for refreshments. This is also the departure point
for the **Outeniqua Choo-Tjoe trip**
between George and Mossel Bay, which
is the last scheduled-departure, short-
haul stream train journey in South
Africa. However, it's important to note

here that when the risk of veld fires is high, the steam engine is replaced with a vintage diesel locomotive.

The train runs every day, except Sundays and Christmas Day. It leaves George at 10h00, arriving in Mossel Bay by noon, then departing Mossel Bay at 14h15 to return to George by 16h30. The wood-panelled carriages, which are usually alive with excited chatter, have mock-leather padded seats and offer a comfy ride. The route winds out of George, passes farmlands with the Outeniqua mountains in the background, and crosses 2 large rivers, the Gwaiing and the Malgate. It offers views over the Indian Ocean, passes through a tunnel, crosses 5 bridges, the highest of which is 120 metres, and chugs across the Great and Little Brak River lagoons.

Just outside Mossel Bay it passes Hartenbos, and then it enters Mossel Bay via the Voorbaai yards, which are the largest steam locomotive maintenance workshops in the country. Its last puff of steam escapes as it comes to a stop at the bottom of the Dias Museum complex near Santos Beach. Entry to the museum is at a largely discounted rate if you have train tickets. This is a non-smoking train. To book this experience, tel 044-801-8288, e-mail debbiec@transnet.co.za or web www.transnetheritagefoundation.co.za. Sadly, at the time of researching there were rumours that this steam experience may close down. In fact, the train used to run between Knysna and Mossel Bay, until huge storms in the mid 2000s caused the collapse of the line around the historic arched Kaaiman's bridge and the engine was marooned on the western side of that river.

The **Outeniqua Power Van** is a wee rail bus that trundles up the Outeniqua mountains along old tracks, to the top of the historic **Montagu Pass**. En route, you can view 4 different passes, waterfalls, forest, 6 tunnels and glorious fynbos-covered mountain scenery. There's a guide on board who'll fill you in on interesting things. It departs from the Transport Museum and trips last 2½ hours. As a general rule, a minimum group size of 14 is required and it's best to book your place the day before you want the ride. They are fairly flexible and have several itineraries they undertake for groups, including a trip to Great Brak River.

For **mountain bikers** who like the downhill bit, they'll take your wheels to the top of Montagu Pass so that you can cycle the exhilarating 15 km back down the winding, historic pass route to George. You don't need to be a fitness fanatic to manage it and they rent out bikes if you don't have your own. It operates Mon–Fri departing at 11h00 in winter, and 09h00 and 15h00 in summer, and they can do up to 3 trips a day in December. To reserve your place call Nico on tel 044-801-8239 or 082-490-5627, or e-mail opv@mweb.co.za.

Veteran car lovers will be pleased to note George hosts the second largest **motor show** in the country, held on the 2nd weekend of February each year in the grounds of the PW Botha College. The focus is on veteran and classic cars and tractors up to 1970. It can attract over 900 entrants. For more motoring news contact Chris van Staaden on tel 082-491-5254.

With George's close proximity to

the slopes and peaks of the Outeniqua mountains there are a number of good **hiking trails** varying in duration from rambles of a few hours to multi-day tramps. Many of the hikes are within the **Outeniqua Nature Reserve**, and most offer great opportunities for viewing proteas, restios, ericas and other types of fynbos, for which the area is reknowned (it forms part of the Cape Floral Region World Heritage Site). For more detailed descriptions of these hikes see Calls to the Wild on page 15.

For **walks in the forest** head to the Groenkop Farleigh Indigenous Forest, which falls under SANParks. It cloaks the mountains around the Nelson Mandela Metropolitan University and the Saasveld campus. To get there turn onto the road to Saasveld – signposted from the N2 at the first traffic lights after Pick 'n Pay when leaving the eastern side of town (the start of the Seven Passes historic road). Here you can do the **Groeneweide Nature Walk**, which is a network of 3 routes of 9 km, 11 km and 13 km each. They are all relatively easy and make a nice day's outing. A pair of binoculars is essential to spot forest birds including Knysna turacos and Narina trogons, and you may have close encounters with bushbuck, baboons, vervet monkeys and bushpigs. On the longest route there's a big **Outeniqua yellowwood tree**, or kalander, to stand in awe of, and a place to cool off in the Silver River. To get to the start of the trails, turn into the campus grounds, park near the tennis courts and cricket pitch, and look for a copse of pine trees near which the green signboard denoting the start can be seen. You must complete the self-issue permit before starting off and there are maps there too. For further information contact Farleigh Indigenous Forest office on tel 044-356-9021, or SANParks on 044-302-5606. The forest is open to visitors 06h00–18h00.

THE MANY MOUNTAIN PASSES OF THOMAS BAIN

During the latter half of the 19th century Thomas Bain earned himself the title of South Africa's master road builder. His reputation surpassed that of all his peers due to his incredible skill and craftsmanship (including that of his father, Royal Engineer road builder Andrew Geddes, from whom he learnt the craft). He built a total of 24 mountain passes in South Africa, many of them through rugged and seemingly impenetrable terrain.

Virtually all these passes are still in use today, little changed, following the same line and using the original supporting dry-stonework and even some of the original bridges. Many of the passes in the Garden Route were built by Thomas Bain including Prince Alfred's Pass near Knysna; Grootrivier, Bloukrans, Storms River passes between Plett and Tsitsikamma; and the 7 winding, dipping, climbing routes on Seven Passes road between George and Knysna (see box on page 73).

Bain, 'the man with the theodolite eye', is not to be confused with the contemporary explorer and artist Thomas Baines.

Looking down into Craddock Kloof where the Montagu Pass, built by Henry Fancourt White, follows a natural weakness in the Outeniqua mountains.

There are a number of **scenic half or whole day drives** from George. If you arrived in George along the coast you'll not have experienced the spectacular **Outeniqua Pass**, which traverses the Outeniqua mountains from the Little Karoo to the coastal plain. If you have time, it's worth the drive and there are a few pull-off places from where you can enjoy the view. The distance to the other side of the mountain is about 20 km, and you can stop here at the **Roadside Deli** (see Eating Out section) for a bite or cup of coffee and then turn around and do it again – on the return trip you don't have to cross the busy road to access the viewsites. The most interesting stop is the **Four Passes lookout** from where you can observe the Outeniqua Pass (that you're on) begun in 1943 using Italian POWs and completed in 1951; the Montagu Pass down below, which was completed in 1847 and is 1 of the few passes in the region not built by Thomas Bain (the man in charge was Henry Fancourt White, whose imposing house now stands within the Fancourt golfing estate); the railway line completed in 1913; and the Voortrekker Pass – more commonly known as the Craddock Pass – a tortuous ox wagon road used between 1812 and 1847.

An alternative and much more exciting route over the mountains is via the gravel **Montagu Pass**, a scenic road winding over the mountains, initially starting much lower than the Outeniqua Pass, following the Malgas River gorge, and climbing gradually until cresting the main ridge of the Outeniquas and dropping down to the tiny hamlet of **Herold** (see end of this chapter). The pass was built by White, a road engineer from Australia, but was named after John Montagu, the colo-

An historic bridge on the Seven Passes road near Saasveld; one of only a few of the original bridges still standing on this road engineered by master road builder Thomas Bain.

nial secretary of the Cape at the time. Grab something to eat or drink at the little store in Herold; from there you can either retrace your steps or travel along the N9 to loop back down the Outeniqua Pass.

The **Seven Passes Road** (see box below) is a pleasant day drive, or an alternative to the N2 between George and Knysna, that meanders among the foothills, forests and farms. From George, turn onto the road to Saasveld – signposted from the N2 at the first traffic lights after Pick 'n Pay when leaving the eastern side of town. When you reach the Nelson Mandela Metropolitan University campus (the old Saasveld forestry college) a road sign announces the **'Old George-Knysna Road'** and along its entire length, the road alternates between tar and gravel, and winds up and down 7 different passes, from which its name derives. There's a **big tree** – an 800-year-old Outeniqua yellowwood – and picnic site at Woodville Forest a short distance past the Touws River Pass. This road can be accessed from George, Wilderness, Sedgefield or Knysna, so if time's limited you can choose a shorter loop. If it is garden you wish to see, with a 'G', this route is a must-do for all travellers.

One of George's best tourist attractions is the **Outeniqua Country Hop** – a play on words because the route offers a hop, skip and a jump between attractions, and is just a hop, skip and a jump away from George, and it also falls into hop (as in the herb used to brew beer) country. It's centred around the rural areas of Blanco and Geelhoutboom, southwest of the city, but includes attractions scattered as far off as those in amongst the peaks of the Outeniqua mountains, including the high hamlet of Herold where the hops are actually grown. The Hop offers everything from farm fresh produce and good cheese to outdoor activities, agritourism, accommodation

---

THE SEVEN PASSES ROAD

The historic Seven Passes Road, a national monument, covers roughly 75 km and was completed in 1883 after 16 years of toil. It was constructed by South Africa's road building maestro Thomas Bain (see box on page 70) and his brother-in-law Adam de Smidt, until they had a falling out over the route the road should take – higher up and more tortuous but with shorter bridges, or lower down and with longer spans across the deep gorges. They never spoke again. It was started from the George side and for 70 years after completion served as the main link between George and Knysna – until the N2 nudged it aside in 1952. Essentially the Seven Passes are, from west to east Kaaimans River Pass, Silver River Pass, Touws River Pass, Dieprivier Pass, Hoogekraalrivier Pass, Karatara Pass and Homtini Pass. Some include the Phantom Pass, which links it to Knysna from Rheenendal. This below-standard road was completed in 1862, but was later upgraded, making it 8 passes if you choose to drive, or ride, it.

and places to eat. Take a look at their website www.outeniquacountryhop. co.za, which has an excellent map, or get the map from tourism.

To give you an idea of what the Outeniqua Country Hop offers, we've detailed 3 of its attractions: a cheese farm, a berry farm, and an animal sanctuary. If you really like cheese, head to **Silver Lily Dutch Cheese Farm** where cheesemaker Marianne Schroëder produces a boerenkaas that's so more-ish it'll make your body dance with joy even if you don't have a Dutch gene in your DNA. If you like the strong stuff, her Silver Blue is fabulous. Apart from cheese tasting, sales and an explanation of the cheese-making process, phone ahead and order cheese platters or fondues that can be enjoyed in the tea garden. Open Mon–Sat 10h00–16h00, closed on Sundays, tel 044-870 7424.

Redberry Farm is a working berry farm where you can pick your own strawberries in season, which is more or less in summertime. They offer a guided tour of the farm and have an outdoor tea garden and children's playground that's perfect for both weary parents and their over-zealous kidlets. On your way out you can buy super gifts and fresh produce – including strawberries, naturally – from their farm stall. Open Tues–Sat and public holidays from 10h00–16h00.

The **Barnyard Donkey Sanctuary** is a worthy cause if you think of how many beleaguered donkeys one sees around. At the southern end of York Street there's a turn-off onto the R102 to George airport, and along here you'll find this sanctuary. It's a private animal welfare

organisation that offers hands-on experiences with rescued donkeys, and if you have children, they're welcome to bring apples and carrots to feed the donks.

Botany enthusiasts and plant lovers will appreciate the **Audrey Moriarty Environmental Centre**, which houses a prestigious botanical collection. Alongside it is the **Garden Route Botanical Garden**, which is open daily and hosts a wild flower show in September/October. To check up on dates, and for more information tel 044-874-1558.

The **George Museum**, which you'll find behind the library, is housed in the Old Drostdy (courthouse), built in 1811. You can see the building at the traffic circle at the top of York Street. The main emphasis is understandably on the timber industry. Displays include a reconstructed woodcutter's cottage and labelled indigenous trees, and there's a cross-section of an Outeniqua yellowwood tree that is estimated to have lived from 1220 to 1977, making it 757 years old when cut. The museum is open Mon–Fri 09h00–16h30 and 09h00–12h30 on Saturdays.

While on the subject of things old, there are a few historic churches, such as St Peter and St Paul, the oldest Roman Catholic church in the country. The stone St Mark's Cathedral in Cathedral Street just off York Street, was consecrated in 1850 and is reputedly the smallest cathedral in the southern hemisphere. The Dutch Reformed Church standing tall in Courtenay Street just past the museum, was completed in the early 1840s and has a neo-classical façade, Greek cross plan, and rich yellowwood finishes.

The Four Passes lookout on the Outeniqua Pass stands on the newest of the passes that traverse Craddock Kloof and its flanks between lush George and Oudtshoorn in the arid Little Karoo.

Chocoholics will love **Milano's chocolate shop**, just off the N2 east of George (there is some strip development here) near the turn off to Victoria Bay. It's open Mon–Fri 08h00–16h45, and over weekends during season, and has been making chocolates for more than 10 years. They sell home-made Italian nougat, Belgian chocolates and truffles. The theory is you can buy at factory prices. For further enticement, tel 044-889-0390.

Overnight in George
Central
LINEN

There are a number of good lodgings in the vicinity of the George Museum between Caledon Street and Arbour Road. Our first choice is **No. 10 Caledon Street**, a popular 4-star double-storey guesthouse. Rooms are en-suite and have TV, and either a balcony or terrace with mountain views, or they open onto the large manicured garden. There's also a self-catering cottage with 2 en-suite bedrooms. Breakfast is either full English or continental, and there's secure off-street parking. The hosts, Horst and Gerdi Schiebe, speak English, Afrikaans, German and Dutch and will recommend restaurants and things to do. B&B rates are R375/ps. Tel 044-873-4983, e-mail 10caledon@mweb.co.za or visit www.10caledon.co.za.

CALICO

Another good option is **Abelia Garden** in a quiet location in Plane Road off Arbour Road. Here Pieter and Alta Scholtz will make you feel at home in good clean accommodation at very affordable rates. They have 1 en-suite double and 2 doubles sharing a bathroom. All have private entrances, TV, tea/coffee tray, fridge and soft self-catering facilities. Rates are R160 to R200/ps with discounts for longer stays. Give Alta a call on tel 044-874-6209 or 083-462-8822, or check out www.wheretostay.co.za/abeliagarden.

CANVAS

George Tourist Resort is at the southern end of York Street and is popular with those on a budget. It has recently been privatised and is undergoing upgrading. Choose from en-suite chalets that sleep 4 or 8 people, or rondavels that sleep 4, all of which are equipped for self-catering and have a TV and braai facilities (you must, however, provide your own towels and dish clothes). For campers and caravanners there are more than 150 sites spread over pleasant grounds. Facilities include a swimming pool and play park for the younger set, and guests may use the gym, indoor pool and sauna for a fee. Chalets cost R410–R950 for 2–8 people in low season, and R900–R1 300 in high season; rondavels cost R310–R430 for 2–4 people in low season, and R710 a unit in high season; camping costs R170–R300 a site for 4 people in low/high season. Tel 044-874-5205, e-mail reservations@george-tourist-resort.co.za, or visit www.george-tourist-resort.co.za.

George west (Blanco, Geelhoutboom and Outeniqua Hop areas)
LINEN

Malvern Manor lies just 1km off the R404, at the end of a good gravel road

Today you can drive it or you can bike it (we're talking mountain bike heaven here), but 100 years ago the only way over Montagu Pass was by horse cart or ox wagon.

that passes lush paddocks and low-ing cows before taking you up their red-brick driveway. It is owner-run by Sandra and Michael Cook who fell so in love with this tranquil area they moved here from England and set about converting the farm's Cape Dutch-style country house into a **4-star guest-house**. The Cooks concentrate on their visitors and leave the dairy to a lessee farmer. Rooms are stylish, comfortable and spacious, and facilities include private patios and a heated pool. A dam on the property offers bluegill and big-mouth bass fishing, and peace reigns supreme – as long as the bass is the only one with a big mouth. This is an idyllic setting for anyone wanting the peace of the countryside within proximity of the city. Breakfast is a delight and includes Sandra's home-baked seed loaf that's so divine you'll have to leave the room to stop eating it. Rates are from R600/p sharing. Tel 044-870-8788 or 084-867-6470, e-mail info@malvernmanor.co.za, or web www.malvernmanor.co.za.

CALICO

Alpine Inn is a German-styled country inn at 3 Montagu Street, opposite Fancourt and offers reasonably priced lodging and wholesome breakfasts. They have 1- and 2-bedroomed en-suite units and cottages where you can stay on either a self-catering or B&B basis. Each has a private patio, TV, tea/coffee station, sound system and fans. Rates are from R450 for 2, to R700 for 4 people in the larger suites. Big breakfasts cost just R40/p. They have specials during winter. Attached to the Alpine Inn is their **Schwabinger Stuben restaurant**, bar and beer garden that serves up hearty German-style dishes, with eisbein being their speciality. The murals in the pub and restaurant come from the brush of a very talented artist. They're open for breakfast, lunch and supper Mon–Sat, and breakfasts and lunch on Sunday. Tel 044-870-7643, 073-231-5549, or e-mail info@alpineinn.co.za, web www. alpineinn.co.za.

Eating Out in George

With George being a small city, it has dozens of places to dine out, including all the popular chain restaurants. There are also several places that have become institutions; one not to be missed if you like a taste of far-flung cultures is the **Chinese take-away** called **Ying Saan** on the corner of Courteney and Mitchell streets. It's been owner-run by Eddie and Mary-Ann Ying for 27 years and is still serving up consistently good quality food. They're open Mon–Sat from 11h30–14h30 and 16h30–20h00; if you want to phone in an order, tel 044-873-3567.

For mall maniacs who get peckish while purchasing and perusing, the food court at the **Garden Route Mall** has a choice of eateries to suit most easy-eating preferences, as well as fast-food outlets positioned at strategic places throughout. However, for those who take their dining experience a little more seriously the following restaurants should be on your list:

Our first choice is **Kafé Serefé**, a popular **Turkish**-South African eatery that has exotic ambience thanks to wall murals, gleaming copper dishes, Turkish mementos and a meze counter.

The Garden Route is exotic in many more ways than you might at first imagine; as seen here at Kafé Serefé, a popular eatery in George with a strong Turkish flavour.

The name is pronounced sherr-a-fay and means 'to good health'. On arrival you're welcomed with a spray of rose water for your hands, and a piece of Turkish delight, served by waitresses who jingle between tables thanks to hip-scarves embroidered with fake coins. Although Turkish dishes are the main part of the menu, there is much more on offer, such as well-aged steaks and kebabs.

The restaurant belongs to the Van Rensburg family who own the award-winning butchery downstairs and supply the 'approved safe meat'. Their breakfast menu includes schwarmas and a Turkish option; for lunch or dinner try the pork neck steaks with goat's cheese and brandy-fig sauce. There's also a kids menu. Traditional Turkish dishes include Sultan's Stew,

and Shish Kebab, and all options offer good value for money. Wednesday and Friday night's diners are joined by belly dancers jiggling their wobbly bits. Their wine list has won awards while the smoker's room has hookah pipes and cigars. They're open during the day from 10h00–16h30 Mon–Fri, and for dinner 19h00 until late Mon–Sat. You'll find them at 60 Courtenay Street; to book tel 044-884-1012, e-mail vrfoods@mweb.co.za or web www. vanrensburgsfoods.com.

The **Old Townhouse** in Market Street, just off York, is situated in an atmospheric old building and has been going 8 years. It's owner-run by Bryan Hockly and Janet Loopstra, who serve upper-class country food with lots of vegetables. The menu is varied but they're well known for superb steaks, the wine list is extensive and carefully selected, and they cater to discerning diners. Keep an eye out for their weekly specials. Open for lunch 12h00–15h00 Mon–Fri and dinner 18h00 until late Mon–Sat. To reserve a table tel 044-874-3663.

La Locanda, behind George Tourism in York Street, is a family run Italian restaurant where chefs Dario Soresi and Matteo Battaini have created an extensive menu. They're well known for their home-cured cold meats and traditional dishes made just like their grandmothers taught them. This is a relaxed, comfortable and wholly Italian eatery. Open lunch Mon–Fri, dinner Mon–Sat; tel 044-874-7803.

Alternatively, the atmospheric **La Capannina** next to George Tourism is popular and serves lunch Mon–Fri 12h00–15h00, and dinner Mon–Sat from 18h00 until late tel 044-874-5313.

See **Schwabinger Stuben** at the Alpine Inn under George west.

Fancourt offers 5-star dining in 5 on-site restaurants: Italian, fresh seafood and sushi, Pacific Rim cuisine, light organic meals and flavours from Africa; tel 044-804-000 or visit www.fancourt.com.

If you're self-catering or able to stock up en route home, **Van Rensburg's Foods** is a very worthwhile stop. It opened in 1940, and has been in the same family ever since. They've won the 2007 and 2008 Platinum Cleaver Award (for best butchery with 4 or more outlets in the Western Cape); and guarantee their meat. For further info visit www.vanrensburgsfoods.com.

Make a bit of an outing and take a leisurely 20 km drive over the Outeniqua Pass to the increasingly popular **Roadside Deli** situated on the N9/N12, across the road from hop-trellised fields. It's casual and friendly and a place to breathe in the mountain air. They're famous for their pizzas, which can be bought whole or by the slice; and the lasagne can be eaten in or taken home frozen. Make sure you buy at least 1 loaf of their rye bread that's also baked in the pizza oven. Tables are outdoors overlooking the hops fields across the road, and a large jungle gym will keep the kids happy for a while. If you're in a rush, get your coffee-to-go. Alongside is a well-stocked wine shop and farm stall. Open Tues–Sat from 08h30–17h00, and Sundays from 09h00–16h00; tel 073-258-4818.

Near George
Herold's Bay

Herold's Bay lies on the coast 18 km southwest of George. It's a small resort consisting of just a few streets and set beneath imposing cliffs where (mainly holiday) houses surround a little bay. It comprises 2 headlands – Vöelklip and Slaapklip; both are popular with anglers, and there is also a **beach** and **rock pools** including two **tidal pools**. Part of the residential area sits high above the bay on the hill, and there are a few places to eat. The old-beach-cottage authenticity has been breached by some monstrous modern houses, but if these are kept to a minimum the bay will remain a gem. It's also a **popular surfing spot** with one of the most consistent breaks in the country, but can be surfed only in small to medium swell. The **Dutton's**

Herold's Bay is one of the smaller, lesser-known fun holes near George, but locals pride it for its seclusion, its fine beach and even finer part-natural tidal pool.

Cove trail is a pleasant 4 km meander overlooking the sea.

LINEN

We recently discovered a tremendous place to stay, the upmarket self-catering units at **Makarios**. This is a large and modern purpose-built guesthouse mere steps away from the beach, which means you have only a narrow strip of tarred road between the front door and the sand. The name is Greek, clearly, and means to be blessed, which owners, Louis and Antoinette Holtzhausen, certainly are. The 5 units are light and airy, and each has a sea view (to a greater or lesser degree) and patio with braai.

Depending on which unit you're in, you can dine al fresco overlooking the ocean. Facilities include TV (take your own smartcard or pay an additional fee for DStv), safe and personal alarm system. The bathrooms are underfloor heated, rooms have fans, and kitchens are fully equipped, which includes stove with oven, large fridge/freezer, microwave and dishwasher. Units are also serviced daily. There is a lift in the building for those who can't handle the stairs or have a lot of luggage. Rates are reasonable at R525 a night for 2 people in low season, to R2 875 for 6 people in high season. Tel 044-872-9019 or 084-554-1231, e-mail info@makariosonsea.co.za or web www.makariosonsea.co.za.

Locals recommend the **restaurant** at **The Herold's Bay Hotel** near the

If you're a surfer you'll know all about 'Vic Bay' – a narrow inlet with one of the most reliable breaks on the entire southern Cape coast. Accommodation is limited but highly desirable.

entrance to town, and there's an eatery at Dutton's Cove up on the hill. From Herold's Bay, take a drive east up the N2 to **Kwelanga Country Retreat**, which has lovely views and a restaurant that's open daily for breakfast, lunch and dinner.

Victoria Bay

It's said that Vic Bay, as it's fondly referred to, is the most charming bay on the southern Cape coast, and we'd agree. Its topography of magnificent cliffs sheltering a narrow cove has thankfully saved it from development, and today there are only 20-odd waterfront cottages and houses giving it the atmosphere of a lovely old coastal holiday village. It lies 3 km off the N2, and

a total of 9 km from George city centre, so it's popular with those wanting the mod cons and shopping opportunities plus a seaside break.

In summer and on fine-weather Sundays the small bay can be packed to capacity with sun worshippers and hedonists. There's a lot of parking at the bottom of the hill as you approach the bay, and a locked gate allows vehicle access to residents only. Above the beach there's a large grassed area and ablution facilities; and above this, at the top of a steep bank, is a caravan park with fabulous views of the bay and ocean beyond. Also near the entrance is a beach-chow restaurant where you can sit in the shade of brollies or get take-aways.

The centrepiece of most older towns in South Africa is a Dutch Reformed Church, each with a distinct spire, built by settlers of mainly Dutch origin: this 1840s one is in the centre of George.

The bay offers some of the safest beach swimming in the region; it has a jetty and tidal pool on the western shoreline in front of the houses. However, it's probably most famous as an idyllic **surfing spot**. Surfers come here for the near perfect waves – which become even closer to perfect in winter months – that offer a gloriously long ride. They also dig it for the *lank* **dolphins**, and in season **whales** can also be seen offshore. During our most recent visit, we watched a pod of dolphins approach from the east and pass within metres of a line of surfers. If you don't have your surfboard with you, Land's End B&B **hires out boards** for R200 a day, body boards for R100, wetsuits for R100, fins for R30 a time; or half the price for half the day.

Overnight in Vic Bay
LINEN

A great advantage of staying at Vic Bay is the lack of passing traffic. This is especially the case if you're staying at **Land's End**, which is the last house on the cul-de-sac. Owners Rod and Shanell Hossack reckon theirs is the closest B&B to the sea in Africa, and with the waves breaking over the rocks just across the narrow brick-paved road, we're not going to argue.

The guesthouse entrance is via a gorgeous Javanese door that's inlaid with mother-of-pearl, and is just one of many Indonesian touches throughout. The front veranda, where breakfast is served in summer, overlooks the ocean. There are 2 double rooms off this veranda, 1 of which can be made into a family room. Upstairs is a honeymoon suite and a luxury double room.

The guest lounge has books to browse through and, if you don't want to eat out, you can prepare your own meal in the communal kitchen. It's easy to spend hours watching the surfers, who wait for waves just off the rocks right in front of Land's End, and black oystercatchers hunting for food nearby. Rod is surf mad and he'll fill you in on all aspects of the sport, including obscure surf spots around Indonesia. B&B rates are R320–R620/ps, depending on season, room and length of stay. Tel 044-889-0123, e-mail rod@vicbay.com or web www.vicbay.com.

CALICO

For those who like doing their own thing, **Seabreeze Cabanas** is a self-catering complex where the choice varies between modern 2-storey holiday flats sleeping 4, 6 or 8, and 2-bedroomed wooden chalets. All are fully equipped, except for towels, have TV with MNet and braai facilities, and there's a communal swimming pool. They're situated alongside the entrance road to Vic Bay about 300 m from the beach. Rates for the wooden chalets are R380–R900 a unit low/high season for 2 people; and the duplex flats cost from R420 for 2 to R1 600 for 8 low/high season. Tel 044-889-0098 or web www.seabreezecabanas.co.za.

CANVAS

Victoria Park Caravan Park enjoys an elevated, if somewhat exposed, position on the hillside overlooking the sea and is a relatively small park with only 38 sites, some with their own individual ablutions.

Victoria Bay has just a single row of houses, and a small campsite. At the end of the road is Land's End Guesthouse – but don't expect to find a bed unless you booked well ahead.

For more details tel 044-889-0081.

Overnight in Herold
CALICO

Herold, not to be confused with Herold's Bay, is a quiet hamlet in the foothills to the north of the Outeniqua mountains that's reached direct from George via the gravel Montagu Pass, or from the Oudtshoorn side via the Outeniqua Pass and along the N9 towards Uniondale. It's here you'll find **Over the Mountain Guest Farm**, which provides accommodation, a pub and restaurant in renovated buildings that were once the post office, police station and a house of sin in the early 20th century. Accommodation costs from R330/p B&B, and self-catering cottages sleeping 4–6 cost R600–R825. Dinner is by arrangement and will set you back around R120/p. There are various walking and mountain biking trails, and good bird watching. In season, you can tour the operating hop farm nearby. Tel Dave and Gail on 044-888-1700 or 073-170-7120, e-mail at overthemt@polka.co.za or web www.overthemountain.co.za.

Herold Wines is nearby. They grow, make and bottle the juice at the winery and they offer cellar tours, tasting and sales. Their flagship is pinot noir, and their range includes sauvignon blanc, red and white blends, and a sweet desert wine. They are open Mon–Sat 09h00–16h00. Call Vivien Harpur on 072-833-8223.

Wilderness 7

Legend has it that Wilderness got its name because of the request of
a woman in the mid 1800s: she sang to her true love, beseeching him
to sweep her away and make her a home in 'the wilderness'.

The coast from Mossel Bay to Wilderness (seen here) reputedly has the mildest weather in the
country and just about the whole world; that makes it a favourite site for learning to paraglide.

As you glide down the winding Kaaimans River pass take it slowly, not only so you can enjoy the wonderful natural surroundings, but also to avoid being forwarded a speeding ticket from at least 2 permanent cameras along the way. Where the road flattens out at sea level you'll enter the town of Wilderness, which spreads out (but not very far) on both sides of the N2. The main village is the small bubble of activity around where the N2 highway just touches the shoreline, while on the coastal side a narrow fringe of seaside homes runs along the beach front.

But to pick up the legend of the naming of the place .... Being the soppy romantic type, the suitor did just that, and his choice of location of where the fairytale couple would settle was where Wilderness stands today. The less romantic version is that, in 1877, a chap by the name of George Bennett purchased a portion of land on which to farm, near the Touws River mouth. This farm he called Wilderness, which was a pretty apt description of the place back then, and the name stuck. Whatever the true reason, if you can turn a deaf ear to the traffic along the N2, Wilderness is still a fair description for the place. One of the better known people to have resided here was ex-South African president, the late P W Botha, whose most infamous piece of verbal literature was his Rubicon speech, which turned out to be one of the main reasons for him ending up as just a voice in the wilderness (this was part of his constituency, centered in George).

The town and the area surround-ing it are relatively unspoilt, although residential properties stretch along both sides of the N2 for a good few kilometres. Developments have been kept to a minimum and there is more natural environment visible than brick and mortar. This is largely thanks to the proclamation of the Wilderness National Park back in 1987 that put limits on permissible development of the area.

There are 2 main reasons to visit here: the beaches and Wilderness National Park, which together give outdoor enthusiasts a varied choice of activities all in close proximity to each other. Wilderness is probably best known for its bodies of water, not least of which is the Touws River estuary. This narrow

WHY VISIT

For its great forest walks, bird watching on the glinting lakes and Serpentine channel, canoeing on the Touws River and Serpentine, and the glorious 7,5 km beach.

WHAT'S WACKY

Doing a tandem paraglide from high above the N2 and over the crashing surf.

TOURIST INFORMATION

The Wilderness tourism office is in Milkwood Village at the main N2 junction. They're open Mon–Fri 08h00–17h00 and Sat 09h00–13h00, tel 044-877-0045, e-mail weta@wildernessinfo.co.za or visit www.visitgeorge.co.za.

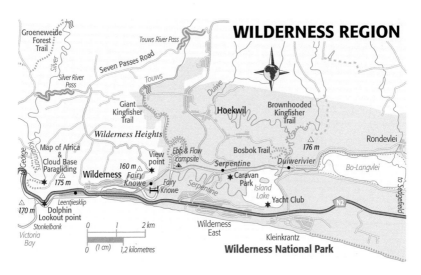

WILDERNESS REGION

Groeneweide Forest Trail

Touws River Pass

Silver River Pass

Seven Passes Road

Touws

Duiwe

Giant Kingfisher Trail

Hoekwil

Brownhooded Kingfisher Trail

Wilderness Heights

Rondevlei

Map of Africa & Cloud Base Paragliding

Wilderness

160 m

View point

Ebb & Flow campsite

Bosbok Trail

176 m

175 m

Fairy Knowe

Serpentine

Serpentine

Duiwerivier

Bo-Langvlei

Fairy Knowe

Caravan Park

Island Lake

Yacht Club

to Sedgefield

Leentjiesklip

170 m

Dolphin Lookout point

Stonkelbank

Wilderness East

N2

Victoria Bay

0   1   2 km

0   (1 cm)   1,2 kilometres

Kleinkrantz

Wilderness National Park

stretch of tranquil water is central to the town's leafy neighbourhoods, which are distributed along the base of the forest-veiled foothills flanking it to the north. It's also the western gateway to the Lakes District (see box on page 89), which stretches eastwards to beyond Sedgefield. Because of the combination of sea, lagoon, river and lake, the variety of watersports here is particularly varied. The abundance of water and the wetlands that flank it support a large percentage of water bird species. So, if you're crazy about the great outdoors, Wilderness is definitely a destination to consider (see Wilderness National Park under Calls to the Wild section, page 15).

Out and About in Wilderness

Swimming is obviously the number 1 activity here, what with long, glorious beaches to be relished. Be aware though that currents can be strong when the surf is pounding and the sea can be treacherous. The 3 most popular

swimming beaches are **Leentjiesklip** at the western extreme of the long strip of Wilderness coastline, tucked below Dolphin Point and easily identifiable by the finger of rock that points into the sea. It's also a popular fishing spot and has ablution facilities and parking, although the latter is quite small.

Paddling is one of the main attractions on the Touws River near Wilderness.

The Touws River flows through Ebb and Flow campsite, which is the main SANParks facility of the Wilderness lakes recreational park.

Touws River Mouth beach is reached via the parking area next to the NSRI on the sea side of the N2, east of the bridge over the Touws River. A little further afield is **Vic Bay** (see under George on page 81). There are a few other beaches to the east, which are popular mainly with fishers. The board-walk on 6th Avenue is in Wilderness East and leads down to **Flat Rock**, which is a good place to try for that big one that doesn't get away. Travelling east towards Sedgefield on the N2, turn right at the Caltex fuel station, then left into South St at the circle, 1st right into 5th St, then right again into 6th St and follow the road to the parking area. **The Fisherman's Walk** on 8th Avenue is also in Wilderness East and reached the same way except, instead of turning into 6th St, continue until 8th St. This is

a particularly steep walk to the beach and best left to the locals. **Kleinkrantz Beach** is 3 km further east along the N2 from the Wilderness Beach Hotel turn-off and is a good fishing spot and easily accessible.

While **surfing** is possible along the beaches of Wilderness when conditions are right, those in the know prefer to leap into their beach buggies and head up the Kaaimans Pass to Vic Bay (see under George on page 81).

Other than the beaches, **Wilderness National Park** is the town's biggest asset and has plenty of outdoor activities including **bird watching** and **hiking trails** – see Calls to the Wild section on page 15.

Other hiking trails can be undertaken in the Farleigh Forest Estate on the Seven Passes Road towards George

– see Groeneweide Nature Walk under the George section (page 70).

With the string of lakes and the Serpentine channel on your doorstep, there are plenty of opportunities to drag a **canoe** to the water's edge and set yourself adrift for a few hours. Some popular routes include along the Serpentine to Island Lake and back – great birding in the reed beds – down to the mouth of the Touws River. Also, instead of walking all the way along the 7 km Half Collared Kingfisher Trail, canoe the first 2,5 km there, and the same back. To hire canoes and find out more information about guided **canoe tours contact** Eden Adventures – see details below.

Eden Adventures is situated in the day visitor's area next to the Ebb and Flow campsite in Wilderness National Park. They have been in the adventure business here for 13 years and offer a range of activities including an abseil alongside a waterfall; kloofing – you might find yourself in a 1 m-wide gorge that reaches 80 m into the big blue, and half and whole day tours taking in a combination of activities. They also hire out canoes. Give Chris Leggatt and his crew a call; tel 044-877-0179 or 083-628-8547, e-mail info@eden.co.za or web www.eden.co.za.

Dolphin Point on Kaaimans Pass is a good lookout point from which to spot whales and dolphins. It faces east across Wilderness, down to the mouth of the Kaaimans River and the bridge across which the Outeniqua Choo-Tjoe used to run before nature put paid to that. A short path leads from the viewpoint parking to a thatched parasol where you can sit and watch the sea and waves rolling into the river mouth while the traffic rushes past above. You can't turn

---

THE LAKES OF THE WILDERNESS NATIONAL PARK

Between Wilderness and the Goukamma River just east of Sedgefield, lies a series of coastal lakes and lagoons that are very special in the hearts of the locals. Separated from the coast by a chain of tall, thickly vegetated dunes this 'Lakes District' is protected within the boundaries of the Wilderness National Park (the Touws River and Serpentine to the west, as well as Knysna estuary a little way east of Goukamma, are generally seen to be part of the Lakes District).

From west to east the lakes are Island Lake (the island is known as Dromedaris Island), Bo-Langvlei, Rondevlei, Swartvlei and Groenvlei, and while some are linked by narrow channels, others stand alone. Swartvlei is the only 1 of the coastal lakes that has an outlet to the sea through the Sedgefield Lagoon and, because it is partly tidal, is the most saline of the 5 lakes. On the other hand Groenvlei has alkaline water and has no influence from saltwater at all. The Serpentine channel, with its many switchbacks through thick reed beds, drains Island Lake into the Touws River. The lakes and associated wetlands are important breeding and roosting grounds for many aquatic birds.

into Dolphin Point if you're approaching from the George side, but just past it there's a small parking on the left, and from here a walkway passes under the N2 and comes out where the parasol is situated. You might be entertained by the animal-skin-adorned self-appointed dancing impi guide who makes this spot his own. It's worth the small tip.

Another stunning lookout point is the **Map of Africa**. From the N2, pass through Wilderness village and at the T-junction just past the Protea Hotel turn left into Heights Road. The road winds up a steep hill for 2,2 km and just past the small Bundu Superette turn left and follow a dirt road for 2,5 km to the site, across from which is the paragliding launch site. If you're there when the inflatable wing chutes are coming and going it can make for a couple of interesting hours.

Cloudbase Paragliding offers tandem flights from one of the coun-

try's safest launch sites, high above Wilderness near the Map of Africa viewsite. They have a policy of flying only when conditions are good and it's possible to fly for a minimum of 15 minutes, guaranteeing value-for-money flights. Keep in mind the best flying time is around 10h00 and booking is essential. Jan and Khobi are full-time professional instructors who offer a 1-day intro course as well as basic licence courses. A tandem flight costs around R500, an intro course R1 000, and it's R7 500 for the basic licence course. To get their drift tel 044-877-1414 or 082-777-8474, e-mail jan@cloudbase-paragliding.co.za or visit www.cloudbase-paragliding.co.za.

The **Seven Passes Road** between George and Knysna can be accessed from Wilderness by driving up Heights Road and onto White's Road (see box on page 73). Alongside the Seven Passes Road,

Craft and food fairs are a popular attraction for both locavores and visitors who want to get a taste of the local produce, like here at the Wilderness Friday night market.

Ancient milkwood trees beside the Touws River lagoon at Moontide Guest Lodge provide an idyllic canopy under which to enjoy a lazy breakfast.

about 15 km from Wilderness, is the **Big Tree** and **Woodville Forest Walk**. The 800-year-old Outeniqua yellowwood marks the start of a pleasant 1-hour amble through dank indigenous forest. Pack a picnic and make a morning of it.

There are various **markets** held in Wilderness. The **Friday market** is open from 16h00–21h00 in the Milkwood Village, which is on your left as you turn off the N2 into Wilderness. Buy some nibbles, like samoosas, and enjoy the live music. On Sunday mornings there are markets that may include old cars, a dog festival, sports event, outdoor expo, nursery expo, or the normal market. The **Craft Market** is organised by the Honourable Rangers and held on the last Sunday of the month, the **Village Market** every second Sunday of the month, and the **Ngamathuba Market** on the first and third Sunday of the

month. It's best to get exact dates and times, either from tourism, or from Mr Alewijn Dippenaar on 082-457-5656.

Overnight in Wilderness
SILK

The owner-run 4-star **Moontide Guest Lodge** is on the edge of the Touws River Lagoon in Southside Road, at the end of a cul-de-sac; you're guaranteed a peaceful stay in very comfortable and atmospheric surroundings. The 9 units range from double rooms to suites sleeping 4 and are furnished with carefully selected antiques, paintings and rugs. They all have DStv, bar fridge and tea/coffee station. The treetop sanctuary is a real treat, especially for honeymooners. A bountiful breakfast is enjoyed under centuries-old milkwood trees on wooden decks overlooking the Touws River lagoon, or in the thatched dining-cum-lounge area. The birdlife in and around the garden is incredible, there's a splash pool to float in, and seductive sun loungers on which to while away the hours. This place has a magical ambience. B&B rates vary depending on the unit and season from R320–R860/ps. To book, call Maureen Mansfield on tel 044-877-0361, e-mail moontide@intekom.co.za or web www.moontide.co.za.

The elegant **Dune Guest Lodge** is right on the sand dunes and only 85 steps on a wooden walkway from the long, long Wilderness beach. They offer 4 en-suite B&B rooms, and a self-catering apartment. The seaside décor is in keeping with the sound of the surf pounding below, and each room has a private deck or patio with sea views, bar fridge, TV with MNet, under-floor heating and tea and coffee facilities. They have 1 disabled-friendly unit. Rates for the B&B units are R650–725/ps, and the apartment costs R1 600 for 2 people including breakfast. Give Gary and Melisa a call on tel 044-877-0298 or 083-941-1149, e-mail info@thedune.co.za or web www.thedune.co.za.

LINEN

The 3-star **Fairy Knowe Hotel** has been around for many years and is an icon of the Wilderness area. It's a large family-friendly establishment situated on a horse-shoe island on the Touws River. This riverside property offers 42 en-suite rooms, some of which are river-facing, others garden-facing, and there are rondawels. Facilities include a restaurant that's open to the public and has a reasonably priced menu, ladies

bar, swimming pool, bicycle hire, flood-lit tennis court and boating facilities (rowing boats, canoes, paddle-boats for hire). B&B rates are R350–R440/ps. They often have good weekday and weekend specials for stays of 2 nights or more. To find out more tel 044-877-1100, e-mail fairyk@mweb.co.za or web www.fairyknowe.co.za.

Cloverleigh Guest House is a 4-star, AA-recommended **B&B and self-catering** establishment across the road from the Touws River lagoon within walking distance of Wilderness village. The owners, Johan and Annatjie Kruger, have thatched cottages, a honeymoon suite, and a 2-bedroom 2-bathroom family unit. All have a microwave and fridge, ceiling fans, TV and kettle braais. It's a peaceful spot on the edge of the forest and the garden has lots of birdlife. The visiting Knysna turacos and bushbuck delight guests when they come to feed. B&B rates are R250–350/ps depending on season. Give them a call on tel 044-877-1327 or 082-897-3324, e-mail cloverleigh@lantic.net or web www.cloverleigh.co.za.

CALICO

Beach House Backpackers is tucked into a grove of ancient milkwood trees about 100 m above the expansive beach at Leentjiesklip. When the beach gets too hot, the bar with pool table and terrace will have you hooked into staying far longer than planned as you sip a bevvy and watch the sunset turning the sea into liquid silver. Dorms cost R125/p, doubles R300–R460 a unit. It has DStv, and is a Baz Bus stop. Coming from George, take the first right as you're

You should never be in too much of a hurry when travelling along the Garden Route to have time to stop at places like the lookout above Wilderness Beach, or you'll miss its soul.

descending into Wilderness and keep right. To find out what's the buzz tel 044-877-0549 or 082-828-0714, e-mail info@wildernessbeachhouse.com or web www.wildernessbeachhouse.com.

CANVAS

Accommodation at the **Ebb and Flow rest camp** on the banks of the Touws River is split into 2 sections; **Ebb and Flow North** is for those who like to be closer to nature than luxury; it has a sweeping grassed camping section along the river bank with no electricity, budget 2-bed rondavels, some with en-suite bathroom and others that share the ablutions of the campsite.

Across the road is **Ebb and Flow South**, where the park offices are situated, and which has electrified camp and caravan sites and self-contained 4-bed cottages with DStv and partially equipped kitchens, and 2- and 4-bed cabins, some with partially equipped kitchens and others that make use of communal cooking facilities. Some accommodation is disabled friendly. Rates for camping are R140–R220 a site for 2 people depending on position and availability of electricity, the rondavels at Ebb and Flow North are R240–R270 for 2, and at Ebb and Flow South the cabins are R450 for 2 and the cottages are around R900 for 4 people. To contact the park directly tel 044-877-1197.

Eating Out in Wilderness

There are something like 20 restaurants in and around Wilderness village and you can walk from one to the other checking out the menus until you find something that stimulates your taste

There is a pleasant mix of nature and and built environment at Wilderness. The Touws River here marks the western extreme of the Lakes District, which runs east towards Knysna.

buds. You'll find everything from pizza to fresh fish and a menu d'gustation.

Pomodoro, in George Road, is a relaxed Italian restaurant serving good pizzas and pasta and other dishes throughout the day. It's open every day from 08h00–23h00 so you can always bank on it for a meal; tel 044-877-1403.

The Girls, named after the passionate owner-managers Roxanne Blum and Cheri Sheridan, is highly recommended by the locals and has an African theme and warm atmosphere. They serve consistently good food, and their varied menu includes some interesting combinations such as Moroccan-style ostrich fillet, or peppered beef with chilli-chocolate sauce as a main course. They're particular about the produce they use, so oysters are wild, and all fish they serve is coded green on the SASSI sustainable seafood list. (To check the status of the fish you plan to eat – green, yes; orange, maybe; red, no – SMS the name of the fish to 079-499-8795.) Their prawns are also good, and they're happy to do a tasting menu. The restaurant is fully licensed and you'll find them next to the garage at the junction with the N2. Open Tues–Sun 18h00 until late, tel 044-877-1648, e-mail wildmagic@mweb.co.za or visit www.dining-out.co.za/goto/thegirls.

If you enjoy fine dining and want to experience one of the country's top eateries, book (it's essential) at **Serendipity Restaurant**. It offers a memorable evening of gourmet food prepared by chef and co-owner Lizelle Stolze who's won numerous awards, and has lectured at one of the leading culinary schools in the country. The res-

Luckily there are not really 'kaaimans' (crocodiles) at the end of the Kaaimans River abseil.

taurant's been voted as one of the Top 100 in SA for years, and has qualified for various awards. A 5-course table d'hôte menu costs from R249/p. Tel 044-877-0433 or 082-709-1922, e-mail info@serendipitywilderness.com or web www.serendipitywilderness.com.

Track 29 is situated in the old station building, and offers a menu d'gustation and silver service for the discerning diner. Each day brings new delights, and every dish is prepared fresh. Each of the 5 courses is paired with a glass of local wine, and taken leisurely so at the end of the meal you won't need a wheelbarrow to get you to your car. Owners, Robert and Sandra Drummond – he front of house and she in the kitchen – assure you of a delightful dining experience.

The lookout above Wilderness gives a vantage of where the Touws River forms a very distinctive shape; it's also the jump-off site for local paraglider pilots.

Booking is essential, and the set price of R350/p covers all courses and the wines. This fine dining experience is open Mon–Sat 19h00–22h00. To book tel 044-877-1503 or 082-783-4894.

Between Wilderness & Sedgefield

Timberlake Organic Village is a cluster of wooden cabins, set in a clearing below a forest of pine trees, on the left of the N2 when heading towards Sedgefield. Many of them house specialist foods, plus there are arts and crafts, a fairy garden, health store and coffee shop. It's here you'll find **Zucchini Restaurant**, which serves organic country food like fresh fish, pasta, soup and their speciality, called cigars, which are giant spring rolls filled with all sorts of interesting combinations. Emphasis is on quality and flavour, and the owners, Stephan Henning and Zelidé Breedt, are passionate about what they do. Dishes are made only when you order, portions are generous, and wherever possible they use produce from the village's own vegetable garden. They're eco-friendly and adherents of the slow food movement. Special touches are evident, right down to the carafe of water that comes with lemon wedges and herbs. Fridays are pizza nights, there's a deck for summer dining, and a fireplace warms the restaurant in winter. They're open Tues–Sun, closed Mondays. To book, tel 044-882-1240, e-mail info@zucchini.co.za and for more info web www.zucchini.co.za.

Timberlake Village is open Tues–Sun from 09h00–17h00, and they host a **Friday Night Market** from 16h00–21h00. Closed on Mondays.

Sedgefield 8

If you're not keen on the commercial centres of Knysna or Plettenberg Bay, the small town of Sedgefield provides a pleasant alternative that's still within easy access of all the popular tourist attractions of the area. This is an attractive area; the Swartvlei lake flows into the Sedgefield lagoon, which in turn flows into the Indian Ocean between fynbos covered dunes, and in the distant north lie the Outeniqua mountains.

The tranquil lagoon at Sedgefield is not a real river mouth but the outlet of Swartvlei lake, itself a river valley drowned in times past by the build-up of coastal dunes.

The town was established in 1928 as a halfway stop along the newly completed railway line between George and Knysna, and its name referred to the abundant areas of sedge grass growing around the lakes in the area. Brent recalls: 'I remember Sedgefield in the 1970s, when it was a scattering of houses along sand roads. Hardly a tree lined the single strip of tar that was the N2, until my father instigated a tree-planting project to improve the main entrance. Residential roads were lined with gum trees, beneath which we'd search for the footprints of fairies and elves as we walked hand in hand with our grandparents.'

Today, many of these gum trees remain, exhibiting brilliant red flowers in summer, and there is a central business district along two slip roads that run parallel to the N2. It's here you'll find shops, services and facilities for your immediate needs.

Approaching the town from Wilderness, you pass through the lovely main lakes area, crossing Swartvlei a little way before you reach Sedgefield: the face it shows to N2 traffic does not do the rest of it justice, lying as it does on a lovely waterway and with an equally attractive beach. On the town perimeter, the highway splits into two lanes separated by a vegetated traffic island, and there is one set of traffic lights indicating the main Sedgefield entrance. Turn right here and follow the road to, and along, the Sedgefield lagoon, through a residential area more charming than the highway side suggests, and ultimately to the parking high above the beach at the lagoon mouth. Sedgefield's greatest appeal lies in its undeveloped beaches and coastline, thanks to the large sand dunes that lie between the town and the sea.

The **Lakes Festival** is held each March–April and hosts leisure and sports events, including yachting, fishing, cycling, and running.

Out and About in Sedgefield

OK, let's tackle the **horse fence** first, because we're sure you're most intrigued by this. This is a boundary wall com-

WHY VISIT
To enjoy its beaches.

WHAT'S WACKY
The horse fence — look out for it on the left after you've passed the traffic lights when heading east; it's become a bit of an ironic 'national monument' in the area.

TOURIST INFORMATION
Sedgefield Tourism office is at 30 Main Road. From Wilderness, turn right off the N2 at the only traffic light and immediately right again into Main Road, which runs parallel to the N2. It's a little way down on the left. Operating hours are Mon–Fri 08h00–17h00, Sat 08h30–13h00. Open on public holidays from 09h00–13h00, except Christmas and New Year's Day. Tel 044-343-2658/2007, e-mail Sedgefield@knysna-info.co.za or web www.tourismsedgefield.co.za.

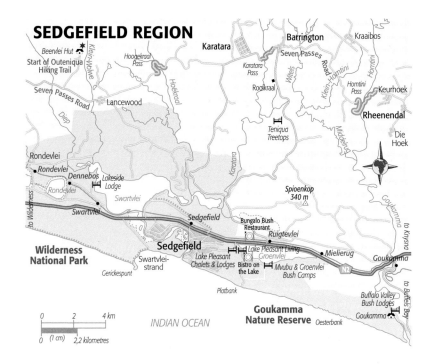

SEDGEFIELD REGION

Beervlei Hut
Start of Outeniqua
Hiking Trail
Klein-Wolwe
Hoogekraal
Pass
Seven Passes Road
Diep
Hoëkraal
Lancewood
Rondevlei
Rondevlei
Dennebos
Lakeside
Lodge
Rondevlei
to Wilderness
Swartvlei
Swartvlei
Wilderness
National Park
Gerickespunt
Swartvlei-
strand
Platbank

Karatara
Barrington
Seven Passes
Karatara
Pass
Rooikraal
Whets
Klein-Homtini
Kraaibos
Homtini
Road
Homtini
Pass
Keurhoek
Rheenendal
Teniqua
Treetops
Middelrug
Die
Hoek
Karatara
Spioenkop
340 m
Sedgefield
Bungalo Bush
Restaurant
Ruigtevlei
Sedgefield
Lake Pleasant Living
Groenvlei
Mielierug
Goukamma
Lake Pleasant
Chalets & Lodges
Bistro on
the Lake
Mvubu & Groenvlei
Bush Camps
N2
to Knysna
Goukamma
Buffalo Valley
Bush Lodges
to Buffels Bay
Goukamma
Goukamma
Nature Reserve
Oesterbank

INDIAN OCEAN

0   2   4 km
0   (1 cm)   2,2 kilometres

prising cement horses complete with a gate of 2 horses rampant. It was built in 1971 by Petrus Neethling in front of his modest home; each came complete with red car reflectors for eyes! We wonder whether the man had any idea that nearly 40 years later it'd still be a talking point? Brent: 'As a child, I remember the amusement with which this fence was greeted; many thought it hideously kitsch, and others admired Mr Neethling's determination to retain his wall in spite of local criticism. My mother could not bring herself to look at it she found it so appalling; whereas my sister and I loved to count the horses as they sped past.'

The fence recently underwent a marvellous upgrade when a vet bought the property and invited local artists to take

the bit between their teeth, harness their talents, and tackle each horse, with a wonderfully colourful result. Go see for yourself.

Absorbing UV rays and travelling across the water in some way or another are the highlights here. There are **5 beaches** to choose from, and accessible spots where the kids can paddle in the **lagoon's** shallow water. **Sedgefield Beach** is at the lagoon mouth and is accessed from Upper Kingfisher Drive. There's a fairly steep walk down to the beach, but it's made a lot easier thanks to a boardwalk. **Myoli Beach** is just east of Sedgefield Beach and is at the end of Galjoen Road, while **Cola Beach** is even further east. It's a small town, so you'll soon find your way to the various access points. **Swartvlei**

Beach lies west of the town and you'll have to take the N2 towards George, cross the bridge over Swartvlei, turn next left as signposted and the road ends at the beach.

Platbank Beach is reached by taking the N2 still further east to Groenvlei, turn right to Lake Pleasant, follow the road past **Lake Pleasant Living** (hotel) and up over the dune until it ends in a small parking area. It's 3,3 km from the N2 to Platbank parking. There are no facilities except for a boardwalk down to the sea. But what is that rusty winch on the beach? Evidently, back in the 60s, a forestry manager with a passion for fishing set up a winch system to enable him to reach his preferred fishing rock 60 m into the surf. A basket was operated by his staff and used to transport him to the rock; also to return fish to the shore and dispatch beers to quench his thirst.

If you want to wet your pants there are various **watersports** that can be enjoyed, such as canoeing, windsurfing, waterskiing and yachting on the Sedgefield lagoon and at Swartvlei, but remember that this is an estuary and as such it is environmentally sensitive so please respect it. North of the N2, **Swartvlei Lake** is by far the largest of the various lakes that lie between Knysna and Wilderness. It's popular for wind sports with generally good offshore winds and limited interference from motorboats – unless the water skiers are out in force. This body of water is well stocked with fish such as garrick (leervis) and elf (shad).

Gericke's Point is a shale headland west of Swartvlei Beach, and at high tide it almost becomes an island. To get there, head west out of town, cross the bridge over Swartvlei and turn next left off the N2. Leave your car at the beach parking area (there's a car guard there most of the time) and walk west – see detailed hiking trails. This is a very popular **fishing** spot; as is Platbank Beach;

To catch fish you've got to use good bait, says an old Blues song. A fisher casts his throw-net in the Sedgefield estuary for mullet fry that he'll use to catch something tastier from the sea.

however, you'll come across anglers hypnotised by the sea all over this part of the coast so just chat to them about what's biting and where. Remember to get the necessary permits and stick to bag limitations.

Surfing can be good at Gericke's, but get tips from the locals because the waves can easily get out of control; there are rock slabs, a jagged reef, and the area can be 'sharky'. Depending on the sandbanks, there can be good surf in front of the car park, plus various areas to hit the water: if you walk 20+ minutes west along the beach (at low tide so you can climb over the rocks) there's a spot that works in a northeast, onshore wind.

Sedgefield is also quite popular with **kite surfers**, and the best people to speak to are Neels and Adri who own Bungalô Bush Restaurant (see page 112). They have a shop, offer lessons, rent gear and sell second-hand gear, and this is also the place to get info on scuba diving, as well as stand-up paddling. Tel 044-343-3118, e-mail info@bungalo.co.za or web www.bungalo.co.za.

If you want to spot some **birds** that are not in bikinis, there is an abundance in the area (over 250 species) that includes estuarine, marine and forest species. Sedgefield borders the Goukamma Nature Reserve to the east, which is a hotspot for marine birds; and there are 3 public bird hides on the lakes to the west (see Wilderness National Park under Calls to the Wild on page 15), 2 of which are close to Sedgefield. Here you might see the blue-mantled flycatcher or secretive

A chorister robin-chat, one of the many colourful but secretive forest birds.

white-starred robin; and some have even been fortunate enough to glimpse a Victorin's warbler or African finfoot, the latter being an extremely secretive 'skulker' and very sought after in birding circles. Swartvlei lake is often alive with waterfowl, and is occasionally visited by flamingos. For further info, or to do a guided tour, visit web www.gardenroutebirding.co.za.

There are numerous **walking and hiking trails** in the area; some are specifically designed to allow the public access to the different ecosystems with bird watching in mind. **Sedgefield Circular Walk** is 11 km and goes from Myoli Beach to Platbank, then inland; it's best to start on a low tide so you can pass around the rocks at Lagoon Mouth. The **Oysterbank Walk** is from Myoli Beach to Platbank (3,4 km), then a further 6,5 km to the oyster beds, and back. You could drive to the Platbank parking

The small town of Sedgefield surrounds a lagoon that flows out into the Indian Ocean. From the N2 arterial you see only the 'back' working side of this otherwise delightful place.

and just do the second leg of this walk if time is an issue. Highlights include spectacular fossil dunes, secluded bays, lots of oystercatchers, a colony of Cape cormorants nesting on the cliffs, and lots of rock pools to investigate. **Gericke's Point Walk** should be done at low tide if you want to circumnavigate the rocky peninsula and explore the fabulous rock pools, which are popular with snorkelers. There are fossilised dunes and roosting kelp gulls. There's always the chance of spotting dolphins, and in season whales also frequent these waters. Hikers can also do the **Cloud Nine Circuit** detailed under cycling, below. To do any of these walks as a guided trail, or for further info you can visit web www.gardenroutetrail.co.za. For trails in Goukamma Nature Reserve,

see Calls to the Wild on page 15.

Cyclists can do several circular routes starting and ending in Sedgefield. **Cloud Nine Circuit** is 11,4 km and climbs up the steep hill behind town, passes the paragliding take-off site with its great views, and descends behind the hill towards Swartvlei, then returns via the N2. The 43,5 km **Hoogekraal Circuit** covers rural landscapes and roads; it climbs and descends hills, takes in wetland scenery as it traverses the Ruigtevlei Road and then climbs a long hill to the Hoogekraal plateau, returning to Sedgefield via Rondevlei. **The Lakes roads** are also worth exploring; get a map from the local tourism office and, if you're a birder as well, you can make a day of it and spend some time at one of the hides along the way.

The best-known icon of Sedgefield must be the **Wild Oats Farmers Market** that's held each Saturday from 07h30–11h30 in summer, and 08h00–11h30 in winter. You'll find it on the left just off the N2, about 1 km west of town (before, if coming from the Cape Town side) between Swartvlei and the town's landmark traffic lights. Get there early to ensure the best selection from the 60-odd stall holders that include those purveyors of foods that are organic, innovative, healthy, pure or otherwise unhealthy-but-oh-so-delicious. It's renowned for its tight quality control and variety of produce, most of which is edible or quaffable. This is also a great place for breakfast (see Eating Out).

Alongside the Wild Oats market, **Scarab Village** is a group of permanent stalls and shops. If you're into the 'dung thing', it's here you'll find the famous Scarab Paper that's made from elephant dung. It's named after the scarab or dung beetle. This market also has various craftspeople; and for those of you who like mouse-food, the Cheeseman shop stocks an unmissable selection. There are also a few makers of rustic furniture, using mostly indigenous woods.

If you have children, treat them to a visit to **Utopia Fairy Garden** where they can explore paths, walkways and secret corners on their hunt for fairies. The garden has aviaries with birds, and an integrated nursery specialising in orchids, clivias and daylilies. There's also a magical little shop displaying thousands of fairies, and a shady few tables where you can enjoy tea and cake in warmer months. The nursery, fairy

Every Saturday morning the locals and tourists flock to Sedgefield's Wild Oats market. Among the many pickings are organically farmed cheeses and some of the best artisanal bread you'll find.

garden and shop are open Mon–Sat from 09h00–17h00, and the tea garden operates from Sept–April. For further info, tel Carrie Kruger on 044-343-2183 or 083-343-1288.

The bigger children may enjoy **paragliding**, which Sedgefield is known for (mainly ridge soaring along the sea-facing fossil dune face). Even if you don't want to take to the air, drive up to Cloud 9 (get directions from tourism) to watch the paragliders in action and take in the sweeping view of the town and estuary below, and coastline in the distance. Tandem flights and instruction are offered, tel Hannes on 082-413-3007 or Elize 082-499-0855, e-mail info@coastalparagliding.co.za, web www.coastalparagliding.co.za or alternatively www.cloudbase-paragliding.co.za.

There's a **horse riding** centre that's operated in Sedgefield since 1982, called **Cherie's Riding Centre**, from where they offer forest rides, tuition, and kids' day-camps. They also offer a range of other products, and provide helmets, well-trained horses and professional guides. Booking is essential, tel 082-962-3233.

Old car enthusiasts will love **Sedgefield Classic Cars**. It's visible from and on the left of the N2 when heading towards Knysna, and is packed with veteran, vintage, post-vintage and post '45 vehicles. Worth a browse just to appreciate the classic lines and solidity of cars in those days.

Since part of the aim of this guidebook is to promote various local products and their makers, we can't leave out **Kelly's hand-painted T-shirts** –

The feeling of community in places like Sedgefield extends to decorating the public amenities.

they are nothing like the ordinary fabric painted wares you usually get. Call Kelly on tel 082-306-1713.

Overnight in Sedgefield

NB: For accommodation near – but not in – Sedgefield, see chapter 9, Between Sedgefield and Knysna, on page 109.

Although there is a selection of accommodation right near the beach, there is none right 'on' the beach, because of the large sand dunes that separate residences from the coastline. We've chosen a couple further from the beach, which offer value for money.

CALICO

The Goose is owner run by Pat and Dave Hanton who are as down to earth as you can get. They offer 2 spacious self-catering apartments in their A-frame house at 6 Makou Street. The downstairs unit sleeps 4 in a double, and a sleeper couch in the small lounge, and the bougainvillaea-fringed stoep looks onto the garden, while the upstairs unit sleeps 6 in a double and 2 twins and has a balcony. Both units have a cool and pleasant atmosphere, SABC and MNet TV, and there's a braai area under some towering wild strelitzias. The place is pet friendly, and breakfasts can be pre-ordered. Best of all the rates are wallet friendly at R180–R300/p sharing low/high season. Tel 044-343-3194 or 072-345-8983, e-mail info@the-goose.co.za or web www.the-goose.co.za.

LINEN
Just around the corner at 43 Pelican Lane is the 3-star **Pelican Lodge**. All rooms are en-suite B&B and fully equipped self-catering TV with MNet, swimming pool and braai facilities. It has a reputation for being expertly run. For further info tel 044-343-3283 or 076-263-3542, e-mail info@pelicanlodge.net or web www.pelicanlodge.net.

LINEN
Lakeside Lodge is an exclusive eco-retreat located on the edge of Swartvlei lake in the Wilderness National Park. To get there, head west, cross Swartvlei, turn right off the N2 to Swartvlei, and follow the signs. It's **4-star** graded and has en-suite B&B or luxury self-catering units facing the water. Facilities include a pool, tennis court, full-sized snooker table, 9-hole chipping course, use of mountain bikes, and 24-hour internet. Old pine trees hung with weaver's nests shade the large manicured grounds and the surrounds are rich in birdlife. It'll suit those who enjoy extended periods of soporific bliss and moments mesmerised by the shimmering glint of the sunlight across the extensive

The 'horse fence' has been a feature of Sedgefield's main drag for decades. Its current owner is a veterinarian who has jazzed up the once-ailing cement steeds.

Between Knysna and Sedgefield lies Groenvlei, the most easterly of 5 large open water bodies that constitute the Lakes District. You can canoe there, or you can just stand and stare.

Fynbos is the most important element of the Cape Floristic Region (a World Heritage Site) and is endemic to the southwestern areas of South Africa, as well as the higher, Afro-alpine mountain areas. It is most commonly found in the winter rainfall region – in fact it can be biologically defined as a Mediterranean floral type. It's characterised by drought-resistant plants that grow in poor soils and, as its name suggests, this evergreen shrubland vegetation has very fine (*fyn*, from the Dutch *fijn*) leaves.

Of the incredible 8 000+ flowering species, which is said to be more than is found in the entire northern hemisphere, the better known species are proteas, ericas, and restios; but it also has a wealth of bulbous species (Liliacaea), many of which are endemic. Fynbos has a complex life cycle, and fire is a necessary part of the regeneration of many species (it is the smoke, rather than the heat, that triggers seed growth). Nearly 400 species of fynbos are very rare, upwards of 200 on the verge of extinction, and nearly 40 of those recorded are in fact extinct. In terms of area covered, the fynbos biome represents by far the world's smallest floral kingdom and, in terms of biodiversity, is considered the world's highest priority floral type.

waters. Low to high season rates are R295–R350/ps for a standard B&B room, R370–R550/ps for executive and luxury B&B rooms and self-catering is R330–R495/ps. Speak to Jean about their great winter specials. Tel 044-343-1844, e-mail stay@lakesidelodge.co.za or web www.lakesidelodge.co.za.

Goukamma Nature Reserve has great and well-priced bush camps (see Calls to the Wild on page 15).

Eating Out in Sedgefield

It's good to know that old staples like an authentic Italian restaurant are still out there. **Trattoria Da Vinci** is so traditional the owners, Steve and Leah Baleta, make fresh pasta every day – you'll see it drying above the counter. The restaurant has been around a long time, so is well aged, as are the murals depicting trattoria-type scenes.

Dishes are all prepared fresh daily and served in generous portions at candlelit tables. To complement the atmosphere, there's a wood-fired pizza oven in front of which Steve weaves his magic; and when they have their fabulous paella on special it's finished off in here. Don't miss Leah's flavoursome marinated vegetables; they're scrumptious. You'll find the trattoria tucked into a corner of Woodpecker Mall in Main Road; pass the Spar supermarket heading west, and they're just a little further along. They're open every night from 18h00 until late, but as they're famous for their pizza, it's best to book. Tel 044-343-1867.

Sedgefield's **Wild Oats Market** is the place to head for breakfast, which is enjoyed in a convivial atmosphere under the trees. Choices are many and include filled vetkoek, and the whole cholesterol-laden full house cooked over open coals. Yum. They also sell food to take home, either in frozen form or fresh. This is healthy, home-made 'fast food'. Open 07h30–11h30 in summer, 08h00–11h30 in winter.

The **Whistle Stop Café** is owned by the friendly Joe and Louisa Groenewald who are famous for their fresh home-baked pies; in fact they've made such a good name for themselves much of their business comes from out-of-towners making a point of stocking up on their way through. They serve light eats and have a Wednesday lunch special of boerekos to eat in or take home at a cost of R35 a plate. You'll find them near the main N2 intersec-tion in the old railway station, just turn inland at the traffic lights and you can't miss them. Pop in between Tues and Fri 08h00–15h00, Sat 08h00–13h00, and Sundays 09h00–12h00.

There are also various standard basic coffee shops in town; they seem to come and go, but **Fijnbos Café**, along-side the tourist office, has been around for a while and you can sit outside under brolleys, or indoors in winter. They serve good iced coffee.

La Piazza is very much a local's drinking hole and hangout. You'll find it at the circle between the traffic lights on the N2 and the lagoon. It's a laid-back place serving pizza and pasta, and the pub is the place to meet and have a few sundowners on the deck. Open 12h00–22h00.

Sedgefield is not famous as a gourmet centre, but at Trattoria Da Vinci you can enjoy freshly made pasta and blessedly thin-base pizzas. Just don't miss the wholesome marinated veggies.

Between Sedgefield and Knysna 9

As the lives of many people become increasingly urbanised and ruled by technology, rural areas like this one become immensely appealing to us. There's a peaceful, seemingly slow-paced way of life where horses graze lazily on long grass, cows are herded sedately from one field to another and bees buzz over vegetable patches. Betwixt and between lie quiet roads waiting to be explored, atmospheric accommodation and opportunities to forget the glitz and glamour as you get back to nature.

It is 7 km from the 'castle rocks' at Brenton on Sea to Walker Point at the far western end of Buffalo Bay; you certainly won't regret 1 step of the walk.

Moving from west to east from Sedgefield to Knysna, there are a whole string of rural areas that are well worth being investigated.

This chapter covers:
- Groenvlei & Lake Pleasant
- Ruigtevlei & Karatara
- Buffalo Bay & Goukamma
- Rheenendal
- The Western Head & Phantom Pass areas (White Bridge; Belvidere, Lake Brenton and Brenton on Sea)

Groenvlei & Lake Pleasant

Groenvlei is a spring-fed lake brimming with an abundance of bass 'n birds. It's the only body of completely fresh water of all the lakes between Wilderness and Sedgefield and is quite unique in that it is not fed by any river. The resulting clear water is ideal for large- and small-mouth black bass, so this is a favourite hunting ground for fishers who try their luck from the shore or from boats, with electric motors or paddles (no petrol motorboats allowed). The lake has only 1 natural fish species, a 2 cm estuarine herring. Bass were introduced in 1933, with introductions of bluegill and kurper (tilapia) following in later years. The sand dunes fringing the southern edge of Groenvlei are 201 m above sea level, making them among the highest vegetated dunes in South Africa (those at Cape Vidal in northern KwaZulu-Natal reputedly being the highest in the world); and milkwood trees in the thicket on the southern side are thought to be more than 800 years old. These dunes, lake and pristine coastline form part of the Goukamma Nature Reserve and offer great birding. The annual 2-day bass fishing competition, which has been held for more than 20 years, is hosted by Lake Pleasant Chalets and Lodges, and held at the beginning of May. For info tel 044-343-1985.

Overnight in Groenvlei & Lake Pleasant
SILK

A long-time landmark a few kilometres east of Sedgefield on the shore of **Lake Pleasant** (Groenvlei) is the upmarket

---

WHY VISIT
To experience rural tranquillity.

WHAT'S WACKY
Phantom Pass is not named after a ghost. The story behind the rusty winch on Platbank beach. Tenquia Treetops houses tucked into the trees. (We'll leave it at that cos looking at the proof, you won't fit much more in.)

TOURIST INFORMATION
Sedgefield Tourism, 30 Main Street, tel 044-343-2658/2007, e-mail sedgefield@knysna-info.co.za, web www.tourismsedgefield.co.za.
  Knysna Tourism, Main Street, tel 044-382-5510, e-mail info@knysna-info.co.za, web www.tourismknysna.co.za. For directions to the tourism offices, see pages 98 and 132.

If you really, really wanted to impress someone special, you would be hard pressed to find anywhere as seductive as the tree-top aspect of Phantom Forest Eco Lodge. Really.

Lake Pleasant Living. It was previously the family-oriented Lake Pleasant Hotel, but it has undergone a drastic facelift since becoming part of the Mantis (Shamwari) Collection. It is situated on the edge of Groenvlei Lake and offers suites and villas with all the mod cons one would expect from a modern, luxurious hotel. A touch of history remains; walls are adorned with glorious old black-and-white photos depicting the area's early settlement and woodcutting days, and some of the magnificent yellowwood floors and ceilings have been retained. All units face the lake, are self-contained for self-catering, and serviced daily. There's an on-site bistro, spa & gym, and rim-flow pool. Children are welcome. This is a destination for those seeking the highest level of relaxation and pampering to be had in the area, while the town and beaches aren't far away. B&B rates are from R1 700 for a

1-bedroom suite to R3 500 for a 2-bedroom villa. Tel 044-349-2400, e-mail reservations@lakepleasantliving.com or web www.lakepleasantliving.com.

The **Bistro on the Lake** is part of Lake Pleasant Living and is open daily from 08h00 until late for meals or just a drink. Members of the public are welcome. Seating is indoors or on the balcony overlooking the water, and dishes are a blend of local and European flavours. They offer a reasonably priced 'specials' board; the fish and chips is good value and popular with the locals.

LINEN, CALICO & CANVAS
The 3-star **Lake Pleasant Chalets and Lodges** has been owned and run by the Lidstone family for the best part of half a century, and has a reputation for clean and comfortable accommodation in expansive, verdant garden surrounds. Although close to the N2, the

traffic noise only vaguely penetrates the surrounding bush. At the top of the list are 5 atmospheric self-catering timber cottages, each sleeping 6, tucked beneath indigenous vegetation. They each have 2 bathrooms, indoor fireplace, TV, a large deck, from where good birding is enjoyed, a full kitchen and an outdoor braai.

A boardwalk leads up to a secluded swimming pool for the exclusive use of the 5 cottages. On the opposite side of the property are 8 fully equipped self-catering lodges each sleeping 4, with TV, patio and braai. The centre of the establishment is taken up by 55 electrified caravan and camping sites slumbering in park-like surrounds beneath the bows of ancient, spreading milkwood trees and a host of other arbour species. There are canoes, rowing boats and fishing rods for hire if you want to try for some of the lake's bass (average size 1,1 kg–1,2 kg) and trout. Health and fitness fans have the use of a gym, steam room, spa-bath and sauna, available at reasonable rates. There's a kids play area with another swimming pool, tennis courts, table tennis and a squash court. Rates for the timber cottages are from R265/ps, garden lodges from R240/ps, and caravan and campsites from R60–R100/p. Give Stuart a call on tel 044-343-1985, e-mail lake@mweb. co.za or web www.lake-pleasant.co.za.

Bungalô Bush Restaurant is 800 m past the Lake Pleasant turn-off when heading towards Knysna. Turn left and follow a short track through the bush. It's tucked under the trees and offers rustic seating in or outdoors. They're open Tue–Sun from 09h00–17h00 and serve breakfast and light meals including pancakes, rissoles and tramezzinis. It's fully licensed, so you can also just pop in for a frosty on the deck facing Groenvlei.

This is not a quiet spot as the N2 lies just below, but the atmosphere is invitingly laid back and in winter they light a fire inside to keep diners happy and warm. Owners Neels and Adri also have the kite surf shop on the premises, so speak to them if this exciting sport pulls your poop strings, tel 044-343-3118.

Ruigtevlei & Karatara Areas
Overnight in Ruigtevlei & Karatara
LINEN

One of the best ways to seek out the garden of the Garden Route is to find accommodation tucked into the foresty areas. **Teniqua Treetops** offers just this. Turn off the N2 onto the Ruigtevlei road, cross the train lines, and you're heading up through pine plantations. You'll pass a wee white church, and might spot a Knysna turaco flitting across the road as you venture deeper into the bundu. After 5 km there's a turn-off left to Karatara. Don't turn to Karatara, but continue for another 10 km and follow the signboards to Teniqua Treetops. The total distance from the N2 to the turn off is 15,5 km. It's a unique self-catering establishment situated on the edge of primeval indigenous forest.

Each of the 8 wooden units was designed and built by owner-managers Viv and Robyn Patz, with great respect for the environment. They are tucked into individual and private pockets of the forest, with views into or over the treetops. Each 'tree house' is unique and comes with special touches. Bathrooms are a treat, with glassed in, or open-air baths. There's a braai, double bed with electric blanket, and fully equipped kitchen; and facilities on the property include a communal pool area and lovely walks. This spot is very popular with honeymoon couples and families. If you have children, they're most welcome and the forest walk has a surprise waiting for littlies. Take a picnic and enjoy it under an ancient milkwood tree. Evidently there are those who claim to have sighted one of the rare Knysna elephants down at the Karatara River – whether that was after several pink gins one can only ponder.

Prices are R655–R1 870 per tree house per night. Tel 044-356-2868, e-mail queries@teniquatreetops.co.za or web www.teniquatreetops.co.za.

If you take the Karatara road, 800 m along there is a steep gravel road leading up to the right and a host of signboards at the base, one of which indicates **Hot Art**. About 2 km along this rough road is where renowned potter Lesley-Ann Hoets has her studio. She creates original, freestanding ceramic wood-burning fireplaces. Don't expect a polished tourist attraction or shop from which to buy; this is very much a working studio that welcomes visitors. Hot Art is open 09h00–16h00 Mon–Fri.

Follow the Karatara road: take the Ruigtevlei turn off from the N2 east of Sedgefield; after 5 km turn left to Karatara and follow the signboards for a further 13 km. Karatara lies on the historic Seven Passes Road, where you'll notice that plantations give way to pastures against a backdrop of the

Outeniqua mountains. The settlement of **Karatara** is hardly even a nod to a hiccup on the radar, but it has the ubiquitous liquor store, and small general dealers. The 'town' is a few streets long by a few wide and consists of institutional-looking houses, most in disrepair: this was where feral wood-cutting families were resettled in the 1940s, when all private cutting in the natural forests was outlawed. A little further up the road is Farleigh, a tiny settlement of wooden houses. There are a number of **mountain bike trails** (called the **Bigfoot Trails**) that start and finish at the Highland Café at Karatara. Trails range from 19–39 km and are suitable for novices and intermediate riders, depending on which you choose. They're open only on weekends due to the volume of timber truck traffic during the week. For info on these trails, visit: www.cycleworx.co.za.

Old mining machinery at the entrance to Bendigo Mine at Millwood goldfields.

Buffalo Bay & Goukamma

Buffalo Bay, or Buffels as the locals call it, is 9 km off the N2. The turning off the N2 is 13 km from Knysna and 12 km from Sedgefield. This is a large bay that stretches from the Buffels holiday settlement near Walker Point and curves east for 7 km to end in the hazy distance at Brenton on Sea (see under Brenton for details of this beach walk). **Goukamma** is, broadly speaking, the region between the N2 and Buffalo Bay.

Rates for accommodation are for weekdays and weekends respectively; rondavels R240–R320 for 2; Musselcracker R480–R640 for 4; Mvubu Bushcamp R560–R700 for 4; Groenvlei Bushcamp R480–R600 for 4. Prices are higher during peak season. To contact the reserve directly tel 044-383-0042 or for bookings contact Cape Nature (see page 20).

The first point of interest en route to Buffels is within 1 km of the N2, just after you've passed under the metal-girder bridge of the old railway line. There's a farmstall on your left, and shortly after this pull into the parking area also on the left. Walk through the wee tunnel under the railway line to reach **Niqua Choo-Choo Garden Café**. Although it's relatively new, it has great potential and is a vibrant, colourful restaurant owned by the talented Erica Louw who has some of her own paintings on display. They're open 09h00–16h00 Tues-Sat, and 09h00–15h00 on Sundays. Closed on Mondays.

Buffalo Bay is a collection of – mostly – unpretentious houses and, what's even more unusual, is that there are no large commercial or housing developments here such as have besmirched so many other once-charming places on the Garden Route. Some of the houses are the original fishers' cottages, built of clapboard, and many have intentionally kitsch names that'll definitely amuse you. Most homes are occupied only over holidays, making Buffels a quiet place for much of the year.

The best place to find a spot on the golden sand to work on your tan is at the main **swimming** area, which is below the only shop and restaurant. You can't miss it, there's a large parking area here. The other beach is called the **Wild Side**, on the right en route to the main beach; it's at the big parking area where the backpackers' lodging is located. The Wild Side is popular with **anglers** who cast their lines from the rocky outcrops or straight from the shore, but if you want to swim it's best at the main beach. Buffels rewards dedicated beach bums with uninterrupted views of the sun rising, and sightings of dolphins just about every day. The latter are sometimes seen surfing the waves. If you want a quiet beach holiday, autumn and winter months are a great time to visit and days can even be warm enough to catch a tan. A lot of the holiday houses offer self-catering accommodation, and there are some purpose-built guesthouses and B&Bs. Get info from Knysna tourism on 044-382-5510.

There are several surfing spots at Buffels, the favourite being inside Walker Point. Overlapping reefs create pretty much consistent although slow-breaking conditions, but in the right winds it can be a top spot. You can also catch waves along the Goukamma Nature Reserve, west of the road and river mouth; and at the mouth (said to be awesome when the sand is in the right place); and at Buffel's Wild Side. This is also the best place in the area for surf-skiing and kayaking.

Overnight in Buffalo Bay & Goukamma
CALICO

For us, the best place to stay to get the benefit of beaches and bush is at **Buffalo Valley Bush Lodges**, which are on a private 150-ha reserve 5 km from the N2 along the road to Buffalo Bay, and 4 km from the beach at Buffels. There are 3 self-catering timber cottages, 1 in the forest next to the Goukamma River, 1 on a small vlei, and 1 overlooking the river, and all are far out of sight and sound of one another. What you will hear is the roar of the sea 2 km downriver, birds, notably fish eagles, and the subdued chirruping of frogs; and no other sounds. Each unit is well equipped and there are solar-powered lights, paraffin lanterns, gas geyser, stove and fridge, and a selection of books that includes reference works. Thankfully there's no electricity so you can't charge your cellphone or laptop, and – bliss of all blissfulness – this means there's no white noise to devalue the bucolic charm.

There are braais at each cottage, and a recreation area with braais and tables on the riverbank. Plan to spend several days so you can explore the area by paddling 9 km upriver, or to the

YELLOWWOOD, STINKWOOD, AND MILKWOOD TREES

The Outeniqua yellowwood (*Podocarpus falcatus*) – the giant among several yellowwood species – is known as a *kalander*, it is the stately lord of these forests and is often draped in pale green lichen known as 'old man's beard'. It can reach a height of more than 50 m, and 100s of years in age; hence the few remaining large specimens are commonly referred to as 'big trees'. Before the forests were cut, these trees, as well 'real' yellowwoods (*P latifolious*) and stinkwoods (*Ocotea bullata*) would have formed a high canopy much more impressive than that visible today.

Many years ago, *kalander* timber was used for ships' masts, whereas today it's used for furniture. However, it is the more fine-grained real yellowwood that has been the preferred wood for furniture, and also flooring and beams. If you visit the glorious old colonial buildings of the Cape, you'll see where and how pale yellow yellowwood has been used, often together with much darker stinkwood. Today stinkwood fetches amongst the highest prices for timber in the world, its colour ranging from gold to black. Milkwood (*Sideroxylon inerme*) was once used in boat building, and occurs in coastal dune thickets, and forests, creating its own foreshore micro-environment. It often has a twisted, gnarled trunk with long-spreading branches.

Buffalo Bay caravan park is one cool spot – but you do have to play sardines sometimes.

sea. Canoes and life jackets are supplied free. The owners, Guy and Jo-Ann Thesen, also arrange for their lodge guests to have free access to Goukamma Nature Reserve hikes, which are worthwhile. Rates are R700–R1200 a unit a night depending on number of people and season. To book, tel 044-387-1111, e-mail bushlodges@mweb.co.za or visit www.bushlodges.co.za.

CANVAS

Buffalo Bay Caravan Park is a 4-star graded establishment on a grassy expanse near the point of the bay, right up close to the sea and just a short walk from the main beach. It has 85 caravan and 5 campsites, and is idyllically situated – in fact, if you rolled out of your sleeping bag too quickly, you'd end up on the rocky shore. This is an exposed park that can be hammered by wind in summer during a southeaster blow,

and in winter when a cold front moves through. The other thing to be aware of is the sardine run, and we're not talking of the fishy kind but rather of the packed-like-sardines kind, which happens over December holidays. Site rates are from R170–R350 for the first 2 people, thereafter R50/p extra. Pensioners pay R95 a night for 2. Tel 044-383-0045, e-mail info@buffalobay.co.za or visit www.buffalobay.co.za.

Buffalo Bay Backpackers is on a sand dune on the beach. Not near the beach edge, on the beach. The front of it opens onto the sand dune, so you don't get much closer to the sea than this. It's about 2 km from the main beach but in this gorgeous coastal environment, it's no hardship to walk there. It's fairly rustic and offers dorms at R100/p, doubles for R250 a unit, all opening onto a central courtyard. You can also camp, either in your own tent for R60/p or in one of theirs at R250 for the tent. They're a Baz Bus stop and offer an informal shuttle service to and from Knysna. Tel 044-383-0608 or 083-228-7851, e-mail info@buffalobaybackpackers.co.za or visit www.buffalobaybackpackers.co.za.

Rheenendal

The N2 and Rheenendal road junction is 8 km west of Knysna.

Rheenendal is a farming area between the N2 and the edge of the Knysna forests, encompassing fields with rickety gates and warped lichen-covered fence poles. Tangles of wild berries and bougainvillea grow alongside arum lilies on the road verge, and if you take a slow drive you'll see alluring signs to smallholdings, some of which are small commercial operations, like nurseries, that are open to the public. Just be aware that this road is also plied by impatient taxis and snail-paced timber trucks.

About 9 km along from the N2, the Rheenendal road reaches Portland Mini Mart and the turn-off left to Highway West. Just 1 km along the Highway West road brings you to **Forest Horse Rides**. They do supervised trails through pine plantations, indigenous forest, and across rivers; they also offer lessons. Booking is essential, call Liz Hattersley on 044-388-4764.

Overnight in Rheenendal
SILK
Staying on the Rheenendal road, and just past Portland Mini Mark is the entrance to the historical citrus and game estate of **Portland Manor**. The beautifully restored buildings include the Manor House and Hotel that offers 4-star accommodation overlooking a dam and fields. There's an 1860s English pub across the lawn, and a

Not too long ago Knysna and surrounds were well known for their hippy communities.

separate restaurant serving breakfast, lunch and dinner either in or outdoors. Day visitors are welcome. B&B rates start from R425/ps, to book tel 044-388-4604, e-mail portlandmnr@mweb.co.za or web www.portlandmanor.co.za.

Continuing with the Rheenendal road, a few kilometres further is **Totties General Store**. It's an old-fashioned general dealer, opened in 1922, that still has the original wooden shelves and much of its old character. Tottie van Reenen, so nicknamed by her granddaughters in return for calling them tiny tots, opened the shop to service the needs of the workers at the sawmill alongside and the woodcutters that lived in the nearby forest. Alongside it is the popular **Totties Eatery** that's open Mon–Sat 08h00–16h00 for meals and take-aways. Book for their Friday supper buffet, or Sunday lunch buffet – it's said to be excellent value for money, tel 044-389-0200 extension 3. You can order a Sunday lunch box from the take-away for your picnic in the forest and collect it en route, but it's best to order in advance – tel same as above. The general dealer's and pole processing plant alongside is also part of the historic family business; the sawmill has since closed but when it opened in 1921, it manufactured ox-wagon parts from stinkwood. For further info see their interesting and comprehensive website www.pjvanreenen.co.za.

LINEN
A few hundred metres past Totties, turn right to Bibby's Hoek, along a gravel road leading into the Knysna forest. A further 2,2 km along this road is a

Every region has its special secret place. We are only letting on about Drupkelders because the place is hard to get to, and it's tightly controlled by SANParks so you're unlikely to stuff it up.

junction, turn left and 1,5 km later you'll be at the multi award-winning **Forest Edge** accommodation where 5 replica **woodcutter's cottages** offer a peaceful respite from the busy coastal towns. The dedicated owners call it a nature lover's retreat, and indeed it is. The cosy cottages are just metres from the edge of the ancient forest and have 2 bedrooms each, a bathroom, plus outdoor shower, and a small open-plan kitchen and lounge area with TV, a selection of DVDs, and books. Our favourite place to relax is in the **hammock** on the covered veranda, where you can also dine al fresco.

A few hours lolling, listening to birds and reading will remind you of the finer things in life. You may see visiting bushbuck, baboons or monkeys (and porcupine, bush pig and honey badger by night); and if not, you'll still be entertained by the resident donkeys. While here, spoil yourself with a massage – the therapist will come to your cottage. Facilities include a braai, indoor fireplace and fans for summer, and the owner Ronél Pieterse can arrange permits if you want to visit Drupkelders gorge. Prices range from R500–R1 050 a cottage a night, depending on the season and number of people in the cottage. Tel 082-456-1338 or e-mail bookings@forestedge.co.za and visit their very comprehensive and informative website www.forestedge.co.za.

Drupkelders is a closely guarded secret, but we can tell you about it because SANParks controls it and allows only 12 people to walk down a day. Firstly, you have to pre-book and pay for a permit. If you don't have one,

their vigilant rangers will catch you and fine you very heavily. Secondly, the walk both down and up is not for the unfit, weak-kneed, or weak-minded. Initially the trail meanders up and down a few small hills, then you start going down a steep pathway, which in turn becomes a very steep rocky pathway. Have both hands free to hold onto trees and rocks. The reward is a deep and narrow gorge in pristine surrounding forest.

The unadulterated rock pools are filled with 'black' water (natually tannin-coloured); and there are small waterfalls at the top end of the gorge. The cliffs comprise layered rock formations, the trees reflect on the liquid surface, and it's a perfect place to take a picnic and make a day of it. Just don't think you can have a bottle of wine and climb back out! The name, Drupkelders means dripping cellar, and refers to a shallow cave on the left, where you can see a stalagmite forming.

To drive into the **Knysna forest**, follow the Bibby's Hoek gravel road up the hill, and a short distance after entering the woods there's an entrance boom that's manned during holiday periods. Distances to places where you can get out and walk or picnic are 2 km to Krisjan se Nek, 6 km to Jubilee Creek and 9 km to Millwood Mines. Please be aware that timber trucks and forestry bakkies use these narrow forest roads, and they tend to hurtle along, so take it easy and stick to your side of the road. There are some lovely **walks in the forest**, only some of which are mentioned here.

First stop should be at **Krisjan se Nek** picnic place, which has a magnificent 800-year-old **giant Outeniqua yellow-**

wood, locally known as a 'big tree'. The 9km **Circles in the Forest trail** starts and ends here, and takes about 3 hours, although there are some lovely swimming holes so take a picnic and make a day of it. There's also a 3km option here. The trails are fairly well signposted.

This is also the site of the **Dalene Matthee Memorial**. In recent times there's perhaps nobody whose name is so indelibly linked to the forests of Knysna than that of the late author Matthee. For many South Africans and foreigners, the mystery and magic of the Knysna forests and the people that once lived here were brought to life in a number of descriptive novels by this writer. Her book *Kringe in die Bos* was translated into *Circles in the Forest*, and became an international success in 1984. She wrote several other books based in

Dalene Matthee memorial at the big tree near Krisjan se Nek picnic site, Goudveld Forest.

and around the Knysna forests, and her works have been translated into 14 languages, winning both local and international acclaim. The inscription on her memorial reads: *'Dalene often came to Krisjan-se-Nek where she replenished her soul to write her stories about the forest. This is where she now rests.'*

The 19km circular **Homtini Cycle Route** is not ideally suited to novice mountain bikers; it starts and finishes at Krisjan se Nek, which offers shady parking and water. It's essential to get the detailed SANParks brochure from the tourism office before doing it. Homtini is a Khoi word meaning 'the passage' or 'difficult passage' and is thought to refer to the narrow gorges of the Homtini River. It's a relatively easy route that takes in the indigenous forest and plantation, with some rapid descents, but there is a 3km climb that is very steep; it's a good challenge for the fit, and is crucifying to the rest of us mortals. There are spectacular panoramic views at the top, but before doing this 310m ascent, take advantage of the swimming hole. The route takes a minimum of 2 hours, but double that if you want to enjoy yourself, or dawdle along the route. For further info tel SANParks 044-302-5606.

Deeper into the forest there's a fork in the road that's clearly signposted: left leads to **Jubilee Creek** picnic site, and to Millwood. Jubilee Creek is 31km from Knysna and has long been a favourite beauty spot with locals. A trickling, amber stream runs through 2 grassed areas that have tables and braai places. There's a delightful and easy 3,6km return walk to a swimming hole. En route look out for coloured fungi

Most visitors to Jubilee Creek are the park-and-sit kind. But a walk even a short distance up any one of the forest paths will lead you into a magical wonderland.

and chameleons, and you might even notice signs of the gold mining that once took place here (in fact a whole mining boom town has been swallowed up by the forest nearby). This is also the setting for the book *Circles in the Forest*. If it's a peaceful forest experience you want then it's best to visit during the week because on weekends and holidays the picnic site can be overrun with families with small children. Please ensure you follow the forest code. You may think your child is taking only one little flower, frog or fish home, but think of the impact hundreds of families who visit here each year could have.

Back at the fork in the road, turn right to **Millwood Tea Garden** and the **Materolli Museum**, which is owner-run by Kate and Don Severein. The museum has a pictorial display of the mining era. Make a point of stopping for Kate's muffins and scones, or light lunches. The Savereins do mine tours and are an excellent source of info on the area. Open Tue–Sun 09h00–16h30. For further info, tel 082-734-4552 or 072-129-3503, e-mail severein@tel-komsa.net. 1 km past the tea garden lies the long inactive **Bendigo Gold Mine** (a total of 33 km from Knysna centre) where you can explore the adits (accesses) with their moss-covered rock faces and croaking frogs.

To really appreciate this area you need a smattering of its history.... In 1876, **alluvial gold** was found in the Karatara River. In 1885, after favour-able reports, the fortune-seekers started arriving in hordes to prospect the Millwood tributary of the Homtini river where the gold was found to be accumulated. Between 1886 and 1888 Millwood village came to life and at the height of the gold rush the popula-tion stood at 400 permanent residents

FOREST ELEPHANTS

Elephants are an integral part of the area's history and even to this day they remain a most elusive and mysterious – and vital – aspect of local identity. Before European explorers 'discovered' these indigenous forests, elephants roamed here in their thousands. They did not live there permanently, but rather passed through on their seasonal migrations between grasslands over the mountains and the coast.

Numbers dwindled once the area was settled, through hunting them for their ivory. As the arable areas of the Cape colony were settled, the elephants were increasingly driven to take refuge in the forests. Many would have been chased off by tree felling activities as people's avarice consumed whatever could be gained.

By the 1870s, it was thought the 'Knysna elephants' numbered only 400–500 individuals along the entire 200 km coastal belt between the Outeniqua and Tsitsikamma mountains, and the ocean. By 1908 it was estimated only 20 elephants remained. In 1920, the Eastern Cape farming community lobbied for the remaining elephants here and at Addo to be annihilated. A Major Pretorius was delegated the task and, although he was diligent, the terrain and vegetation thankfully allowed a few to escape, which is why today a handful of Knysna forest elephants – the most southerly elephant population in the world – remain.

and 600 diggers living mostly in tents. Some 1400 claims were worked; 40 syndicates minded 27 reefs; the village grew to 75 buildings including 6 hotels, a bank, post office and government office. There were even 3 newspapers. However, by early 1890 the last die-hards had left, and the town became deserted – some say this was because no great riches were found, and others believed it was purely because discoveries on the Witwatersrand called them away. Some of the abandoned mining machinery is on exhibit at the mines. Of the original village, only one building remains, that of the aforementioned museum, and some street signs, graves, and mining shafts. The circular 5,6 km **Millwood Mine Walk** and **mountain bike track** takes you around Noltzy Kop and offers fynbos, pockets of indigenous forest, quartz reefs and wide views of mountains and valleys. Look out for fresh elephant dung and spoor of various small animals.

The Western Head & Phantom Pass Areas

Instead of taking the tar all the way from Rheenendal back to the N2, look out for the turning left onto gravel and take the eerily named **Phantom Pass** road down to Knysna lagoon. It is said you should never ruin a good story with the truth, so we must warn you that there are tourist-gobbling phantoms waiting in ambush. OK, this is a guidebook, so now we'll try to stick to the facts. Or rather, we'll share what's common knowledge – the 'phantom' is actually a moth, *Letho venus*, to be precise. Boring, maybe, and personally

There aren't many fully mature forest hardwoods left, but try to imagine what it was like when an entire canopy was made up of giants just like this centuries-old yellowwood.

we prefer the drooling ghosts version. However, there's a great legend behind how this moth came into being:

In 1881, the British Government brought around 40 Italian silk farming families to the area to create a silk industry. Unfortunately, the fellow who said there were mulberry trees aplenty did not research further or he would've discovered that the ones growing in the Knysna forest were not the ones upon which silkworms preferred to feed. So, the government abandoned the Italians. One of the silk spinners, Victoria Esposito, who was exquisitely beautiful, was infuriated by their mistreatment and, on a dark and stormy night she jumped on a horse to ride into Knysna in the hope of finding a ship on which she could take her family home. Lightning zigzagged across the sky, thunder shook the earth, and the wind tore at her clothes as rider and horse galloped feverishly along narrow paths. As they emerged at the top of Phantom Pass, they were struck by lightning and killed instantly. However, the girl's magnificent form did not turn to cinder but instead was transformed into a moth. Today, if you see one of these moths in spring, you'll see Victoria's striking eyes staring at you from its wings.

Overnight in Western Head & Phantom Pass
SILK

Our first choice of places to stay in or near Knysna is at the exquisite **Phantom Forest Eco Reserve**. A slew of sought-after awards recognises it as one of the top eco destinations, and the leading green resort in ... maybe the world. I'd say these accolades are a whole handful of turaco feathers in their caps! There is no space to write the poetic reams we'd like to, so we can only urge you to make a point of spending time here if you can afford to. Tree suites have been created on a private 147 ha nature reserve that includes 3 distinct ecosystems of Afromontane or yellowwood for est, coastal fynbos and estuarine wetland. Meandering boardwalks offer the opportunity to spot any of the 155 bird species, or perhaps even a bushbuck, and connect suites with the lounge, restaurants, bubble-barrel jacuzzi and spa. Each suite comprises a sitting room, bedroom and private deck with entrancing view; and some decks have an open-air spa-bath.

The evocative 'forest bathroom' invites nature to join you while you soak in bubbles and gaze through a glass wall and roof at the trees above; and the shower has a floor-to-ceiling glass partition allowing views straight into forest. Suites are completely private, so only the monkeys might spy on you. Care for the environment and thought for sustainability has gone into every aspect of both the interiors and exteriors and it feels as if the units melt into the forest. Wood-shingled roofs, coir carpets, silky linen, recycled water, biodegradable products and alien vegetation used in construction.

The **Body Boma** will pamper you from head to toe with an intriguing range of treatments utilising products from worldwide natural sources. In every way Phantom Forest's policy of 'touch the earth lightly' is literal and the result is soothing to both the eye and soul. Activities include forest walks, private jetty with canoes down on the river, 2-person sauna, bird watching, and 2 salt-water swimming pools. Their 2 on-site **restaurants**, **Forest Boma** and **Chutzpah**, offer inspired fine dining for the most discerning palate (see page 163). B&B rates depend on season and suite, and run from R1 400–R2 000/ps. Tel 044-386-0046, e-mail phantomforest@ mweb.co.za or web www.phantomforest.com.

White Bridge

The **White Bridge** straddles the upper reaches of the Knysna estuary about 6 km west of Knysna along the N2. It's a well-known Knysna landmark and also the junction with the roads to Brenton on Sea, Lake Brenton, Belvidere and Phantom Pass. (At the time of writing the road from here into town was undergoing major reconstruction, with attendant delays at busy times.)

You can't miss the huddle of **houseboats** at the **Lightleys** jetty as you turn off the bridge; and you don't want to miss them. In fact, ideally you want to be heading there to pick up your pre-booked craft on which you'll be spending a few glorious days on the lagoon. This is a highlight of any trip to Knysna.

An old Outeniqua yellowwood at the entrance to the bird sanctuary at Lake Brenton.

Granted, if you have children you'll not have a relaxing time because you'll be too busy getting them to shore to find things to do, unless you've taught your kids to do more than watch TV, in which case you should be OK.

There's nothing to beat puttering along the water, anchoring somewhere and having a drink or lunch, puttering some more, fishing, and just watching life on the water. It also allows you access to places you won't otherwise see, like the southern banks of the lagoon, and the sunsets and sunrises from the water can't be beaten. Even in the middle of the day, looking into the sun creates silhouettes on liquid mercury. OK, so we're wannabe old sea dogs, but you get the picture. You may be visited by habituated feathered beggars, like the vociferous Egyptian geese, and see pied kingfishers in action, so don't forget the binoculars.

You don't need a skipper's licence to drive one of these boats, but you do have to watch a short educational documentary beforehand and will be given instructions and a very com-prehensive folder of maps and info on rules and etiquette to be followed while on the water. Boats sleep 2–6 and are fully equipped for self-catering. You can also return to the Lightleys jetty to get the boat serviced while you pop out for a meal or to stock up on more bubbly and bait. Rates vary consider-ably depending on season, number of nights, and number of people. As a guideline, 2 people pay R510–R995/p, 4 people R350–R500/p and 6 people R250–R475/p. To book, tel 044-386-0007, e-mail info@houseboats.co.za or web www.houseboats.co.za.

Although we confess that we have not eaten at either of the following res-taurants recently, they're both well rec-ommended by locals. **Pembreys'** own-ers, Peter & Viv Vada, are very hands-on owner-chefs who offer no-nonsense seasonal dishes and great homemade pastas, and create unusual combinations for their salad buffet. The fact that this is quite popular with other local chefs on their days off speaks for itself. Peter's desserts are legendary. Their wine list is well thought out, and it's only the décor that patrons feel needs a lift. Enjoy your meal outdoors in summer or alongside a crackling fire on chilly nights. Open Wed–Sun from 18h30, and Sunday for lunch from 12h30. To book, tel 044-386-0005. **O'Pescador** is next door to Pembreys and has been around for a decade. It's a hit with local residents and offers genuine Portuguese cuisine and seafood in an intimate atmosphere. What a pleasure to have a restaurant that's not confusioning the issue with fusion food like everyone else! To book, tel 044-386-0036.

Crabs Creek must have among the best locations in Knysna, right on the edge of the lagoon. In fact, if you wanted to have a barney with the guy at the next table, one smack and he'd be face down in the mud, *pushing kappers*. That's how close it is to the water. It's an idyllic setting for sundowners, and if your timing is right, you might even see the moon rise and cast its shadow over the lagoon. Cat Stevens could have written his song 'Moonshadow' while quaffing beers here. It's been known for years for its 'pint of prawns' and ale on tap; the local Mitchell's brews, ale or bitter, are a house speciality.

Belvidere

Just 6 km from Knysna on the west bank of the lagoon lies the charming enclave of **Belvidere**. It's the kind of place you drive around and, even if you're far from retirement age, you can almost feel yourself settling down here for your dotage. It's an area that, according to the history books, has been continuously occupied for more than 200 years, and obviously far more so in recent times.

This land was acquired by George Rex (see Knysna history) in 1830, and in 1833, after his daughter married a Scotsman called Duthie, they bought the farm from old Georgie. Initially the young family lived in a cottage, which is now The Bell Tavern, but by 1848 they had 12 children (thank goodness for TV) and needed larger digs. Work started on what was later to become Belvidere Manor; by the 1870s, one of their sons had extended the house, creating a 2nd storey and adding verandas. Brent recalls: 'One hundred years

later, in the 1970s, we used to cycle hell for leather down the long avenue of oak trees leading to Belvidere Manor. It was a favourite playground for us kids.' Today, you can't even see the old house unless you're virtually on top of it, thanks to greedy developers. At least their architectural style reflects Georgian and Victorian tones.

Wherever you walk in Belvidere, lanes are tree-lined, you can still hear the hoot of an owl at night, and in spring the area is full of yellow blossoms frequented by families of guineafowl on a slow food hunt. The **Holy Trinity Church**, better known as the Belvidere Church, was built of stone and timber with lovely stained-glass windows, as a miniature of an 11th century Norman church. It was consecrated in 1855, and has long been a favourite for tourists. It's touching to read the book at the

Holy Trinity Church at Belvidere was built as a miniature of a C11 Norman church.

front of the church where one may request prayers; so many are written by people and for people far, far away.

The Bell Tavern, Knysna's smallest pub, is situated on the site of the original Belvidere farmhouse and the window in the floor looks into what is now a wine cellar. In its day, this is where freshly caught game would have been hung. Adding to the historic feeling, the small corrugated-iron building's floor is cobbled with ironwood and it has yellowwood ceilings. Pub meals are served outdoors in summer, or alongside a wood-burning stove in winter. It's open for breakfast, lunch and supper from 08h30–22h00 7 days a week.

Overnight in Belvidere
LINEN
Turnhill Cottage is a self-catering 2-bedroom cottage with panoramic views over the lagoon and mountains. Both rooms are en-suite and have extra-length beds, percale linen and down duvets. The lounge opens onto a patio and under-floor heating will keep you snug in winter. The kitchen is fully equipped for self-catering, although The Bell Tavern is just 150 m away and other restaurants are nearby. Brenton on Sea beach is 15 minutes' drive away (10 but for the speed bumps). Rates are R230–260/ps and the minimum stay is 2 nights. To book, call Gail on 083-535-0254, e-mail info@turnhill.co.za or visit www.turnhill.co.za.

Lake Brenton
The Brentons, as we shall refer to the both of them, are located on the western headland. Brenton on Sea is on the southern, sea side of this headland and runs down to the Indian Ocean; Lake Brenton is on the northern side that meets the lagoon. The history books claim they were named in honour of a Vice-Admiral Sir Jahleel Brenton, a British naval commander during the Napoleonic Wars, who visited in 1815.

Lake Brenton is also known as Brenton on Lake and lies 16 km from Knysna (the railway line is no longer used by the Outeniqua steam train, so you can ignore the crossing going up the hill). It's a tranquil residential settlement under a canopy of yellowwood, stinkwood and milkwood trees, where shy but semi-tame bushbuck live happily alongside the human inhabitants. The neighbourhood watch comprises several families of guineafowl, and it's not uncommon to see mongooses and tortoises on patrol too. Unfortunately, the wild ostriches and peacocks that once frequented the area are no more. When driving around, please do so slowly and keep a respectful distance from any animals. Although residents' houses are not on the water's edge, they're a short distance from it where there's a jetty and boat launch site. Try your hand at fishing or canoeing from here; or explore **Yellowwood Park bird sanctuary**, which has a 500+-year-old yellowwood tree.

Renette's Candles is at 371 Tuna Avenue and visitors are welcome to pop in. There's a small display of handmade, perfumed candles in sand holders, each individually boxed with refill instructions. Tel 044-381-0019, e-mail info@renettescandles.co.za or visit www.renettescandles.co.za.

The jetty and small-boat harbour at Lake Brenton, really just a small satellite settlement of the great Knysna lagoon area, but a particularly lovely and placid one.

Overnight in Lake Brenton
CALICO and CANVAS

Lake Brenton Holiday Resort is a large establishment that has 120 camping and caravan sites, mostly under indigenous trees; plus luxury brick, timber and log chalets; and rondavels. The big attraction here is not only its canopy of glorious trees, and grassed sites, but also that it lies right on the edge of the lagoon. Note that only mesh-type ground sheets are allowed. Facilities include a well-stocked mini mart, swimming pool, kids play area, trampolines, TV lounge, tennis courts, recreation hall with snooker and table tennis, and a full gym circuit and sauna. They also offer canoes, laundromat, and a limited number of moorings for boats. Rates start at R100/p a night to camp in low season, and units from R500–R1500 depending on number of people. To book, tel 044-381-0060, e-mail lakebren@mweb.co.za or visit www.lakebrenton.co.za.

CALICO

Glen House at 375 Tuna Avenue is situated under indigenous trees opposite the Yellowwood Park bird sanctuary and offers 4 self-catering units that each sleeps 4 people. They're fully equipped and have DStv; and the 2 downstairs flatlets each have a private and secluded garden and braai under a gazebo. The top flatlets have balconies overlooking the garden and gas braais. Facilities include safe under-cover parking. Brenton on Sea beach is just a few kilometres away over the hill, or it's a short walk to the lagoon where you can paddle and fish. Rates are from R150–R300/p, call Patrick Booysen on 044-381-0048, e-mail pbooysen@mweb.co.za or visit www. glen-house.co.za.

Brenton on Sea

This residential area, also 16 km from Knysna, is known for its lovely beach, cliff-top paths, whale and dolphin watching (the latter, especially, are a common sight) and fishing opportunities. It's totally different to Lake Brenton, in that it's not tucked beneath trees but rather it's an area of fynbos sprawling down the hill towards the sea. There's also a good chance you will spot some wildlife here, as indicated by the road sign warning of kudu. The beach is accessed by way of a long, gently sloping set of wooden steps and boardwalk.

Castle Rock is a Brenton on Sea icon, and although you need a bit of imagination to see the castle, it's a fishing hot spot – just watch out for those big waves. For a salt-air-infused walk you can't beat the 5,1 km **beach walk to Buffalo Bay**. What better than to work up an appetite for a breakfast at Buffels; or better still, take your own picnic and make a day of it. Be warned, there are strong currents along the coast so be careful where you swim and don't go far out. (There are various figures published in various media about the distance of this walk. We have confirmation that it's been GPS tracked and is definitely 5,1 km from the bottom of the stairs at Brenton on Sea, to the bottom of the stairs at Buffalo Bay.)

The **Brenton blue butterfly** is one of the rarest butterflies in the world, and it can be seen – only – on the south facing slopes of the coastal fynbos here, usually from late October until December, and again in February and March. The 2 ha reserve is marked by knee-high boundary poles adjacent to residential properties. A major effort resulted in the proclamation of the Brenton Blue Butterfly Reserve, the country's only 'special nature reserve', and while this has helped stabilise the small and only population known (there used to be another at Nature's Valley but none has been seen there for about 20 years), its tiny range means it is still classified as a highly endangered species. The site was saved from development by a strenuous public campaign. Access is strictly not allowed, unless you're with Dave Edge doing a tour, which costs R100/p. Call him on 084-312-4927 or 044-381-0014, or e-mail daveedge@xnets.co.za.

If taking to the air blows your hair up, you'll be pleased to learn that **Coastal Paragliding** has a launch site here, tel Hannes on 082-413-3007 or Elize on 082-499-0855, e-mail info@coastalparagliding.co.za or visit www.coastalparagliding.co.za. Soaring high above the Western Head is about as dramatic a flight as you'll ever enjoy.

Overnight in Brenton on Sea
LINEN
There are many accommodation options in Brenton on Sea: our favourite is **Dolphins Hill B&B** set high on the hill – turn right and follow the signs off the top road coming into the residential area – with panoramic views of the sea. We just love the elegant seaside décor, white and ocean blue colour scheme, and most of the rooms have sliding doors that lead onto a large covered patio that in turn leads onto a deck and pool. Spend the day catching some sun while you look out for dolphins and whales. It's owner-run by Mike and Penny Coetzee, a creative couple who make their own furniture and are responsible for the paintings you'll see in your room and

around the establishment. Rooms are all en-suite with bath and shower; and have good quality beds. There's a communal living area where you can while away the hours in comfort and choose from their selection of books.

Your hosts will recommend restaurants if you'd like to eat out, but if you pre-arrange an eat-in dinner with them, Mike dons his chef's hat and you're in for a treat. They also offer braais on the patio; and breakfast is served al fresco in warmer months. Children are welcome. Rates are from R350/ps in low season to R650/ps in high season; dinners are R120–R240/p depending on the menu. Tel 044-381-0527 or 083-290-2199, e-mail dolphins@mweb.co.za or visit www.dolphinshill.co.za.

LINEN & CALICO

There are 2 establishments alongside each other, offering similar lodgings in the form of timber self-catering chalets and cabins, so we'll mention both here.

Nature at Lake Brenton has not been pushed from the door, so bushbuck are still resident.

They're located on the slope on your right-hand side when heading to the beach parking, and are a short walk from the steps leading down to the beach. All units have sea views. **Brenton on Sea Cottages** has chalets and luxury chalets that sleep up to 6, cabins that sleep 2, and a honeymoon suite. Services include daily housekeeping, a few DStv channels, swimming pool, outside braais and shaded parking. Rates depend on number of people and season, roughly from R520–R650 for 2, and R750–R1 850 for 6 in high season. Ask about their pensioners' special. Tel 044-381-0082/3, e-mail info@brentononsea.net or visit www.brentononsea.net.

The other is **Brenton on Sea Chalets**, which has log cabins with spa baths that sleep 2, a honeymoon suite and a VIP house with kitchen, lounge with fireplace, 3 bedrooms and 2 bathrooms that can sleep a family of 6. Rates depend on number of people and season. The double log cabins cost R550–R820; the honeymoon suite is R710–R990 and the VIP house R1 200–R2 850 a night. Tel 044-382-2934, e-mail info@abalonelodges.co.za or visit www. brentononseachalets.co.za.

Nauticus Place is the only restaurant at Brenton on Sea and you'll spot it on the left going down the hill to the beach parking. While it lacks in sea views it should please you with its daily specials; the menu includes fish, grills, light eats and more. Their Sunday lunch is great and pizza is their speciality. Open from 09h00 daily, the kitchen closes at 22h00. Seating is inside, on the wide stoep, or up on the deck. To book in season, tel 044-381-0106.

Knysna 10

Starting town life as a thriving, if small, port that saw trade in timber, ivory and gold, today this sprawling mid-size town, built around a large lagoon fed by the Knysna River, lies between evergreen forests and the Indian Ocean.

Looking out through the Knysna Heads to the wild ocean: while the eastern Head has been allowed to become heavily developed, the western Head is the Featherbed private nature reserve.

Knysna is an intriguing place – starting with its name, the meaning of which has never been certain. Some people have thought it to be the Khoisan word for 'place of wood'; others say 'fern leaves'; and the most common belief is that it means 'straight down'. This is assumed to be in reference to the cliffs of the Knysna Heads – massive sandstone promontories that stand guard either side of the river mouth.

Whatever, Knysna is a place of many facets and mysteries; the main one being the enigmatic forests for which it is renowned. With their magnificent giant yellowwoods (*Podocarpus* sp) and other forest giants, unfathomable gorges and areas of impenetrable trees, ferns and undergrowth, the forests have long been a passion to those with a love of nature. While they were mercilessly cut for timber, much of their depths remain untrammeled and thankfully unexploited; and perhaps their greatest treasure is that they are still home to a handful of elusive Knysna elephants.

The estuary, or lagoon as it is more commonly known, enters the Indian Ocean through the striking geological feature called the Heads. On a clear summer's day, the water around the Heads is turquoise, the waves out at sea snowy white, and the sky above azure. Beneath the water, bright fish, seaweed and soft corals thrive, and this is also home to 1 of the rarest creatures on the planet, the endangered Knysna seahorse (see box, page 142).

The natural beauty surrounding Knysna has led to it becoming a sought-after holiday destination; today it offers visitors attractions from art

The Knysna Quays is the main tourist precinct of this waterside town. There are a few small eateries and curio places, and you can catch a ferry ride to the Featherbed reserve.

to zoology, watersports to shopping, adrenaline activities to world-class restaurants (and some not so), and an overwhelming range of accommodation. There's a host of craft stalls, flea markets and galleries, many of which are supplied by resident artists; waterside cafés ooze tourists; and although there's no sea frontage, beaches are within easy reach. It even retains some of the charm of Georgian and Victorian architecture, juxtaposed with modern buildings. All this attracts hordes of visitors, not to mention upcountry and out-of-country people in search of the perfect retirement spot. Year-round you will hear foreign accents, and in peak holidays such as December and Easter (as well as the week-long July festival time) the town becomes inundated with local tourists. Some people argue that is starting to suffer the fate of so

many beauty spots – the over-crowded victim of its own attractions.

Much of Knysna's appeal lies in the areas outside of the central business district. On the PE (east) side of town George Rex Drive leads off the main road (N2) to the right and takes you to the **Eastern Head**. A causeway off this road links to **Leisure Isle**, a small, affluent residential suburb of winding lanes and a small beach surrounded by the lagoon. Heading out of town the other way, west towards Sedgefield, the road winds along the lagoon to the 'white bridge' (a Knysna landmark) crossing the **Knysna River** before leaving the basin that the town lies in. Turning off at the white bridge and passing beneath the N2 will take you past the historic lagoonside suburb of **Belvidere** with its charming church. This road also leads to both **Brenton on Sea**, a residential area on the sea side of the **Western Head**; and to Lake Brenton, an idyllic and thickly wooded suburb with easy access to the lagoon.

Brent was privileged to grow up in Knysna and Plett when they were little more than specks on the road atlas. She recalls: 'My hometown may be a favourite playground now, but it was a totally different kind of playground between the late 1960s and 1980s. Back then, main street had no traffic lights and it was lined with magnificent old oak trees. It cost 12 cents to see a Saturday matinee at the local bughouse; and it was safe for us kids to play on the then-undeveloped hills around town. Our weekends were spent exploring every road, track, trail and beach in the area, leaving almost no rock pool undiscovered. There was hardly a pass we didn't know, a mountain not crossed, or a corner of the lagoon we'd not fished or snorkelled. We alternated between beach and forest; and in the

It's hard not to like Knysna, but a houseboat sojourn will help you to beat the crowds.

latter we spent hours looking for signs of the Knysna elephants, and found plenty. There were times when we got so close that their dung lay steaming on the road and we'd hear the almost imperceptible sounds of a large body moving away into the forest.'

History of Knysna
Little is known of Knysna's history prior to the arrival of white settlers, other than from the diaries of early explorers such as Francois le Vaillant. It's known that the earliest inhabitants of the area were Khoisan hunter-gatherers, evidence of whom has been found in caves and shell middens along the coast. The more detailed reports of settlers seem to focus on George Rex (1765–1839), who's described as the founder and first proprietor of Knysna; an enigmatic personality and a forceful one. Rumoured to be an illegitimate son of George III of England and a Quaker named Sarah Lightfoot, he was banished from England in 1797; it was said the king gave him land 'as far as his eyes could see' along the southern coast of Africa.

In 1804 he arrived in Knysna where he became the foremost timber merchant in the district, a leading landowner (acquiring the land on both sides of the lagoon and heads) and agriculturist. In those days, access to Knysna from the Cape was extremely arduous and it took weeks for ox wagons to negotiate the dense forests and deep ravines, and to cross many rivers. There was also the danger of large elephant and buffalo herds. This almost impossible access resulted in passage being sought via the sea and, in spite of the treacherous channel through the Heads, Knysna opened as a harbour in 1817.

It is written that the first ship to enter the Heads was the HMS *Emu* in February 1817, but that she never actually made it right through. After striking a submerged rock, she beached.

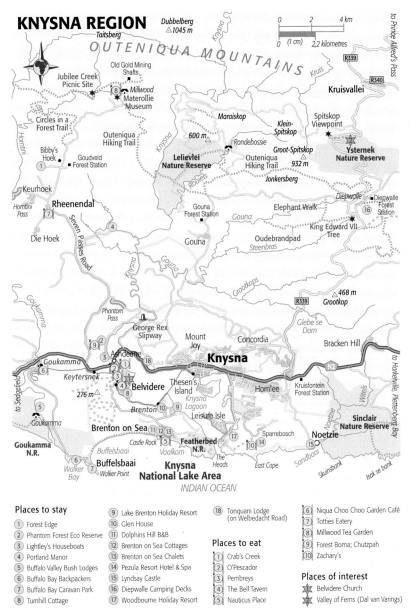

KNYSNA REGION

Dubbelberg
△1045 m
Taitsberg

OUTENIQUA MOUNTAINS

Knysna

Kruis

0   2   4 km

0 (1 cm) 2,2 kilometres

R339

R340

to Prince Alfred's Pass

Old Gold Mining Shafts

Jubilee Creek Picnic Site

8 ★ Millwood
★ Materollie Museum

Kruisvallei

Circles in a Forest Trail

Maraiskop

Klein-Spitskop

Spitskop Viewpoint

Outeniqua Hiking Trail

Knysna

600 m △

Rondebossie

Groot-Spitskop
△
932 m

Ysternek Nature Reserve

Bibby's Hoek
1

Goudveld
■ Forest Station

Lelievlei Nature Reserve

Outeniqua Hiking Trail

Keurhoek

Poolels

Jonkersberg

Hornttini Pass
7

Rheenendal

Gouna Forest Station

Gouna

Elephant Walk

King Edward VII Tree

Diepwalle

Diepwalle Forest Station
16

Seven Passes Road

4

Die Hoek

Gouna

Oudebrandpad
Steenbras

Gouna

Goukamma

Grootkops

R339

△468 m
Grootkop

Phantom Pass

George Rex Slipway

Mount Joy

Concordia

Glebe se Dam

Bracken Hill

9 2

Ashdeane

18

Knysna

N2

to Harkenville, Plettenberg Bay

Goukamma
6

Keytersnek

3
1

3

276 m △

4
8

Belvidere

Thesen's Island

Hornlee

Kruisfontein Forest Station

Witels

to Sedgefield

5

Goukamma

Brenton
10

9

Knysna Lagoon

Leisure Isle

Noetzie

Sinclair Nature Reserve

Brenton on Sea
11 12 13

Sparrebosch

10 14

15

Goukamma N.R.

Castle Rock
5

Featherbed N.R.

Vaalkom

17

Buffelsbaai

6
Walker Bay

7
Walker Point

Buffelsbaai

Knysna National Lake Area

The Heads

East Cape

Sandbaal

Skuinsbank

Isak se bank

INDIAN OCEAN

Places to stay
1. Forest Edge
2. Phantom Forest Eco Reserve
3. Lightley's Houseboats
4. Portland Manor
5. Buffalo Valley Bush Lodges
6. Buffalo Bay Backpackers
7. Buffalo Bay Caravan Park
8. Turnhill Cottage
9. Lake Brenton Holiday Resort
10. Glen House
11. Dolphins Hill B&B
12. Brenton on Sea Cottages
13. Brenton on Sea Chalets
14. Pezula Resort Hotel & Spa
15. Lyndsay Castle
16. Diepwalle Camping Decks
17. Woodbourne Holiday Resort
18. Tonquani Lodge (on Welbedacht Road)

Places to eat
1. Crab's Creek
2. O'Pescador
3. Pembreys
4. The Bell Tavern
5. Nauticus Place
6. Niqua Choo Choo Garden Café
7. Totties Eatery
8. Millwood Tea Garden
9. Forest Boma; Chutzpah
10. Zachary's

Places of interest
✸ Belvidere Church
✸ Valley of Ferns (Dal van Varings)

Knysna | **135**

The carronades (small ship's cannons) from the wreck were placed at Knysna Fort during the Anglo Boer War but never fired a shot. The second attempt to enter Knysna lagoon was made in 1818, and succeeded, resulting in a signal post and pilot being assigned. Can you imagine what these rock sentinels guarding our lagoon must have seen over the centuries? Those were the days of sail, and ships needed waves, wind and tide to be suitable before attempting to enter the Heads – still today considered an extremely treacherous undertaking. The lagoon offered calm waters for those who did make it, and it was an ideal place for repairs (given the forest on the doorstep). Vessels would be careened (put on one side), hard wood from the forests was used for repairs, and during their stay the sailors had plenty of game, fish and fresh water to sustain them. By the late 1800s, up to 12 ships would dock at Knysna harbour each month, bringing in mining machinery for the Millwood gold mines, and taking out timber.

Before George Rex arrived on the scene a chap by the name of Stephanus Terblans was reported to be the first white settler, and was granted a large tract of land on the eastern shore of the Knysna lagoon in 1770. This was the farm Melkhoutkraal (milkwood corral), later bought by George Rex. In time, the area was visited and settled by sailors, gold miners, hoi polloi in the form of colonial gentry, and woodcutters who came from various European countries. From the late 1700s it was the latter who were responsible first for the clearing of the forests through their uncontrolled harvesting of timber, with no thought for conservation, and later the first foresters, most notably Count de Vasselot, appointed as the Cape Colony's first superintendent of forests in 1889. Such was the devastation that from 1939–1967 the forests were closed to all harvesting to allow for their regeneration.

Knysna's history and economy has been interwoven with timber, shipbuilding and furniture making for decades, and there are still furniture factories to this day. However, the forests now fall under SANParks protection and limited harvesting is allowed under strictly controlled guidelines. Thesen's Island, now a swanky new part of town on the water, was originally owned by and named after 1 of the early baron-settler families. Until not so long ago it was still a timber- and shipyard; a Thesen-built yacht was a prize envied the world over.

The people of Knysna that you'll meet today are a hodge podge of settler descendents, and many who've fled from cities to grab a slice of what's deemed an idyllic lifestyle. There are

Cultivated oysters like these shlurpies helped to put the town on the culinary map.

those who flit between their homes in Europe and Knysna; and others work hard to supply services and retail outlets. Add to this a lot of earthy crafts people and some great artists, and you have a cosmopolitan mixture of friendly souls. Around the outskirts of town you cannot help but notice the 'twilight people' – descendents of Khoi, black and mixed-race slaves and servants, greatly added to by a more recent influx from the rural areas of Transkei. You might also notice their shanties occupy some of the finest potential real estate in the country.

ANNUAL EVENTS

The **Knysna Oyster Festival** is 10 days of fun and activities for the whole family. It's held each July, and although oysters are the highlight, there are also weekend sporting events, like the famous **Knysna Forest Marathon** (half and full), and the Argus Rotary Knysna Cycle Tour (road and off-road), and dozens of leisure and mid-week events as well. For further info visit www.oysterfestival.co.za.

The very colourful Pink Loerie Carnival is held over the first weekend of May each year and is the country's own gay Mardi Gras. For more info web www.pinkloerie.com or www.pinkloeriemardigras.co.za.

Gastronomica is held annually over the last week of September and celebrates food, health and lifestyle. Food is presented in all forms, from organic to local culinary artisans making breads and cheeses, as well as a long list of other enticing products. The festival encourages locals and visitors to become aware of how good food is produced and to be aware of what they eat; there are plenty of restaurant special offers. It includes exhibits, cooking workshops, and demonstrations. For further info tel 044-302-5749 or visit www.gastronomicakny.co.za.

Out and About in Knysna

Distances given are all from the tourist office in town.

Knysna comprises the main town, plus various outlying residential or peri-urban areas. Those west of town – **Belvidere, Brenton on Sea, Lake Brenton, Phantom Pass area, Rheenendal, Goukamma** and **Buffalo Bay** – have been covered in the previous chapter, Between Sedgefield and Knysna, on page 109.

As this book is about the *Garden Route*, we have elected to focus on the forests first, and then the Knysna lagoon and town.

FORESTS

Around Knysna, there are 3 main natural forest areas. **Goudveld** lies north-northeast and is accessed via the rural area and Rheenendal road; **Gouna** lies north of town and links up with **Diepwalle**, which lies more to the east. The map from Knysna tourism clearly indicates the different forests and access roads.

If you have a penchant for mystery and fantasy, you'll love exploring these forests, which resonate with unique life forms, ancient, giant old trees, bird song, and Mother Nature's brush strokes in the form of fungi, ferns, frogs and feathered friends. Look out for the flamboyant and famous Knysna turaco, and elusive and equally decorative Narina trogon. Read details of the ecosystem in the forest floor; be inspired by the intricate patterns made by moss and lichen as they wind around tree trunks; and search the shadows for the tiny blooms of the spur flower and Cape primrose. You can safely explore the forest as long as you stick to the demarcated trails. Just don't wonder off the paths because you'll get lost. Seriously lost. As in: you will never be found and, unless your surname is Khoisan X, you'll probably die.

The elephants of the Knysna forests are the only elephants in South Africa that are not fenced in and, contrary to popular belief, they are not a separate species. They are the straightforward *Loxodonta africana* (as are our savanna elephants found elsewhere in Africa) that were forced into the forest and have adapted to living here. In theory, they occupy what's left of the forest, an area of 43 500 ha; but in fact this is a fragmented area, dissected by the national N2 roadway and many other roads, thereby partitioning their territory even more.

> ## For information on
> Goudveld forest, which includes Krisjan se Nek, Millwood Gold Mine, Jubilee Creek, see under Rheenendal from page 116.

To reach **Gouna Forest**, take the N2 from town westwards, and from the traffic lights at the Main Road and Waterfront Drive junction, travel a fur-

ther 0,7 km along the lagoon, then turn right onto **Old Cape Road** (the 4th road right after the traffic lights). This road follows Salt River, passing a few rustic buildings, then climbs the hill to the Simola Golf & Country Estate. Past the entrance it becomes a gravel road and a little further you enter the forest. There is a small church, the **San Ambroso Catholic Church**, built in 1891 for Italian silk spinning immigrants, that – after being neglected for some years – was restored. However, at the time of writing there were no signs indicating where one could find it; nor could the Knysna tourist office direct us to it; furthermore the contact persons and numbers for the church seemed to be no longer in service.

From Gouna, it is possible to do the 11 km **Kom se Pad** loop road to the R339 near **Diepwalle forest** station. Alternatively, if you want to reach Diepwalle from Knysna, it's a total of 24 km. Take the N2 towards Plett and 5 km from the tourist office turn left off the N2 onto the R339. It's along this road you'll find the **King Edward VII Big Tree** and picnic spot. This tree is estimated to be 600 years old, with a height of 39 m and trunk circumference of 6 m. A little further on lies **Diepwalle Forest Station**, and it's near here you'll find the only place in the forest where you're allowed to **camp** – see Overnight in Knysna. From this station there are 3 different loops, 7, 8 and 9 km, through the forest that make up the **Elephant Walk**. Continue with the R339, 10 km north of the forest station towards Avontuur, and the road brings you to the turn off to **Spitskop viewpoint** (a total of

KNYSNA

Places to stay
1. Knysna River Club
2. Knysna Log-Inn
3. The Rex
4. Inyathi Guest Lodge
5. Hillview S-C Apartments
6. Paradise House
7. Greenside
8. Knysna Backpackers
9. Highfields Backpackers

Places to eat
1. Firefly Eating House
2. Fishermen's Cabin
3. 34 South
4. Robberg Seafood Safari
5. Boogies Restaurant
6. Ile de Pain

Places of interest
Knysna Charters
Ocean Odyssey
Knysna Quays and Waterfront

33 km from town). The track up to the viewpoint is rough so if your vehicle is low slung or has low profile tyres, forget it. You need reasonable ground clearance, and the rewards are panoramic views over the forest in every direction stretching to the horizon. On a clear day, you can see the coastal plateau to the south, and east lies Robberg Peninsula at Plettenberg Bay. Northwards are the Outeniqua and Tsitsikamma mountains. Just past the entrance to Spitskop lies a picnic site and the **Dal van Varings**, meaning valley of ferns. There's a short walk here through incredible tree ferns

(*Cyathea capensis*), a protected species that grows in groups and can reach up to 6 m.

Petrus se Brand mountain bike route starts at Diepwalle forest station and that's also where you get your permit. It's a 24 km one-way north-to-south trail that finishes at the Garden of Eden; it is challenging but can be done by average fitness riders. The track follows the contoured bed of the disused forest railway before joining the Petrus se Brand track and then descending and ascending a couple of times through forest and pockets of fynbos. The last climb

If you turn your back to the town – and the highway – it's hard to imagine you're smack in the middle of the busiest spot of South Africa's most popular holiday town.

is more than 4 km, and if you don't fancy the fast single-track at the end, there's an alternative to the N2. It's best to get up-to-date info and a map from Knysna Cycle Works bike shop (see page 150 for their listing), and remember you're not allowed to leave the marked trail.

The best-known piece of forest, and the most easily accessed, is the **Garden of Eden**, 16 km east of Knysna along the N2. There's not much parking on busy days, but plenty in quiet times; and the trails going into the forest are wheelchair friendly. This is where you can get a taste for the magic of the forest without having to mount a small expedition. The Garden of Eden is a superb example of 'wet high forest' and has tall stinkwood, yellowwood, witels and many other tree species that grow in moister forest areas.

Look beyond the pathway at the tightly curled frond of a fern, the intricate patterns of the lichen, and the variety of fungi that sprout just days after rain. Lilac moss grows alongside orange bracket fungi, and smelly stinkhorns can be spotted because of their bright red colour. NB: never touch wild fungi – some types are so poisonous even tiny amounts have been known to kill. Listen out for rustling leaves on the forest floor, there's a good chance you'll see a chorister robin-chat – or it could be elephant eggs hatching.

LAGOON
Please note:
♦ This glorious body of water is a protected marine reserve – respect it!
♦ It's permanently open to the sea and tides rise and fall an average 1,7 m.
♦ A remarkable diversity of species is recorded here – the highest in any

South African estuary.

◆ It comprises swamp, salt marshes, and eelgrass areas.

Life on and around a glorious body of water like Knysna's lagoon is in itself sufficient to entice you to visit, never mind all the other attractions. If you don't have your own boat and want to explore the lagoon a little, there are several companies offering **boat**, **yacht** and **catamaran trips** and if conditions are right you may be taken right into the Heads.

Synonymous with Knysna are **oysters** and they're best enjoyed with some bubbly on a boat, so join **Knysna Charters**, which operates from Thesen's Island. They offer trips to the Heads, a sunset cruise and one up the **Knysna River**, and a fascinating **Oyster Farm Tour** that visits the oyster beds and will teach you all you want to know about these tasty molluscs and their wild coastal counterparts. Take in the tranquil lagoon waters, pass by the bustling waterfront, and soak up some sun. Trips include drinks and snacks, and are of varying lengths and prices, from R200–R400/p. Call 082-892-0469, e-mail info@knysnacharters.com or visit www.knysnacharters.com.

One of the Knysna icons is a pair of headlands called **The Heads**, and no, there are no presidents heads carved into the rock.

These are vegetation-covered Table Mountain sandstone cliffs that guard the waterway from the sea into the lagoon. They're probably the most arresting geological feature along the entire Garden Route coastline. The **Eastern Head** is 6 km from town and you can drive right to the top, where there's a small parking area and short walk to the cliff-edge lookouts that offer fabulous views down onto the rocks below, and across the lagoon to Leisure Isle and town. You can also walk around to the sea side on a boardwalk that offers stunning coastal views. There are railings, but they're not necessarily childproof so keep a lead on the kids.

Around the base of the Eastern Head you can reach **Coney Glen**, a sheltered cove that has interesting rock pools, a small beach, and braai facilities. Be aware of wave action here when swimming or snorkelling.

UTILISING THE KNYSNA ESTUARY

The Knysna estuary (lagoon) might look like it's in good condition, however, it is under a lot of strain as it tries to balance its delicate ecological state. It's a sensitive salt marsh environment, which is the foundation upon which so much of the estuarine food chain is built. As with just about every esturay in this country, its tidal bore (the energy source that maintains the ecosystem) has been negatively influenced by human activity: in this case by road and rail bridges, filling in of marsh areas and the building of marinas and housing developments along the water's edge.

The estuary is a protected National Lake Area and controlled by SANParks. There are restrictions in place with regards to fishing, bait collecting and access to certain parts of the lagoon, so be sure that you get the necessary permits and follow the information signs.

THE KNYSNA SEAHORSE

Another elusive and endangered local creature is the Knysna seahorse (*Hippocampus capensis*), the only known purely estuarine seahorse in the world; it is found only in the Knysna, Keurbooms and Swartvlei estuaries. These diminutive creatures have horse-like heads, chameleon-like eyes that move independently of each other, insect-like body armour and a prehensile monkey-like tail – but this is a fish. It has gills and fins, measures an average length of 7 cm; and blends into its surroundings of dense eelgrass vegetation by skilfully changing colour. It feeds on tiny crustaceans (zooplankton). Pregnancy occurs in the male, who gives birth to between 5 and 190 well-developed young. Once born, these babies receive no further care from their parents. Take note that it's an offence to disturb them, and you'll be hung, drawn and quartered if you even think of trying to catch one.

Hippocampuss capensis is the most beloved of all Knysna's many natural treasures.

At the bottom of the Eastern Head there are 2 restaurants (see Eating Out in Knysna). There's also a walkway to the beacon, and on the lagoon side there's a wooden cabin (at time of writing it was in need of repair) with steps going into the water that's been a favourite swimming spot for years. 'When we were kids, this was a safe snorkelling area, and today you can still see little fish there,' recalls Brent.

There are several **scuba diving** sites in the Knysna Heads and surrounds. Explore a few old wrecks, *Paquita* (1903) is a shore entry dive, *Phantom* and *The Fairholme* (1888) are wrecks; or the reefs and banks. Depending on where you dive, you might see beautiful corals, game fish, bright invertebrate life, sharks and even seahorses. Visibility is from 0–20 m, with an average of 5–6 m; summer water temperatures average 21°C, and in winter 15°C. However, the incoming and outgoing tidal currents are extremely strong, so dive with the guys in the know – namely **Hippo Dive Campus** (named after the Knysna seahorse, *Hippocampus capensis*). They operate from The Heads and charge R100 a dive plus R250 for a full set of diving gear. There are no other hidden costs. This is the company that hosts the Navigation Drift Dive Challenge during the Oyster Festival; and they also offer snorkelling. Tel Stefen on 044-384-0831, drop them an e-mail at hippodivecampus@gmail.com or web www.hippodivecampus.co.za.

The **Western Head** is home to **Featherbed Nature Reserve**, a privately owned and registered reserve, and a South African Heritage Site. It can be reached only by ferry, for which there are several options. One includes a 4-hour eco-experience that offers some spectacular viewpoints; and another offers a 4-star dining experience on their Paddle Cruiser, the country's only paddle-driven vessel. Bookings are essential, tel 044-382-1693, e-mail bookings@featherbed.co.za or web www.featherbed.co.za.

Another fabulous way to enjoy the Knysna estuary is to spend time on a **houseboat** – see **Lightleys cruises** on page 124.

The closest beach to town is **Bollard Bay** on Leisure Isle, which has a glorious view over the water to The Heads and is also perfect for kidlets to paddle around. **Buffalo Bay** is 22 km from Knysna and is generally the only beach around this area suitable for unsupervised swimming. It runs 7 km in a gentle curve around to **Brenton on Sea**, which is much closer at about 12 km from town. For further info see page 109 (section: Between Sedgefield and Knysna). Although **Noetzie** has a beach, it is definitely not a swimming beach because of its very dangerous **rip currents**, and there are no lifesavers or rescue personnel anywhere nearby. Also, the private castle owners might try to evict you on the grounds that it is a 'private' beach – it isn't, so tell them to have a nice day.

Ocean Odyssey holds the official boat-based whale-watching permit for Knysna and does daily trips out to sea in search of dolphins, whales and other sea life. They can legally approach whales within 50 m; different species are seen at different times of year with the southern

Coney Glen is a maze of rocky ridges and tiny beaches at the base of the western Head.

rights around from July to November. The coastal scenery is spectacular from the ocean, and looking back gives you a different perspective of the Heads. Imagine the guts needed in the old days to even contemplate navigating a cumbersome wooden ship through that treacherous gap. Luckily, you don't need to worry about that today. You're in safe hands with skipper Dave Huisman, who'll ensure you have a great trip. Call him on 083-543-3773 or 082-852-9402, e-mail info@oceanodyssey.co.za or web www.oceanodyssey.co.za.

Most visitors won't have their own boats, but you can **hire canoes** and **small boats** from Lightleys. The 2-person canoes cost R165 a half day or R275 for full day, or R60 an hour, R90

The lagoon is navigable for several kilometres upstream, but if you want to explore the more secretive upper reaches of the Knysna River you'll need to go by canoe.

for 2 hours. The 8 hp 'Poppet' is suitable for 4 adults and costs R295 a half day, and R550 for a full day. Picnic hampers can be ordered 24 hours in advance. To book tel 044-386-0007, e-mail info@houseboats.co.za or web www.houseboats.co.za.

Fishing is very popular on the lagoon, along the coastline as well as from the beaches. Or, as the pro's call it, estuary, surf, rock and river fishing. We call it water therapy – you sit with fishing rod in hand and watch the gentle lapping motion of the water. Make sure to get relevant fishing and bait collecting permits from the post office at the eastern end of the main town's street.

Leisure Isle

Leisure Isle has a circumference of roughly 4km, is 1,6km in length, and half a kilometre across at its widest point. When Knysna was first settled, this was a grassy sandbank where birds, small mammals and a population of steenbok once roamed, hence its name back then, Steenbok Island. It belonged to the colonial government until 1821, when it was given to George Rex, and remained in his family until 1929, when George Cearn, an American who'd farmed coffee in Kenya, purchased it. Cearn was only 53 when he retired here, and his vision was to turn the island into a place where people could live in idyllic surroundings. He renamed it Leisure Isle.

Today, some of the original milkwood trees remain on the island, and the main attraction is the small beach and wide sand flats that are exposed at low tide. Bollard Bay is particularly good for toddlers who can paddle in the calm lagoon water. In cooler months, take a picnic, let your body melt into the soft sand, and enjoy the scenery. The southern side has an uninterrupted view across the usually tranquil water of the lagoon to The Heads, while the rest overlooks Knysna and the Outeniqua mountains. On a perfect day, you could hardly find a more attractive setting. It's ideal for stretching your legs, or working off that crème brûlée on a bicycle.

The island is tranquil out of holiday periods, and residents enjoy their own tennis and bowls facilities. Apart from wall-to-wall houses, there is an art gallery and coffee shop. There are several places you can park: the sea wall along the stretch between Greenhole and Bollard Bay has been collapsing for some time so it's best to park at the Steenbok Nature Reserve under the gum trees. Just don't park on private lawns or you'll pique off the locals.

The **Steenbok Nature Reserve** runs along the northern shore of the island, in an area that was once a 9-hole golf course, and has been set aside to protect the indigenous vegetation (around 300 species) found here. The main entrance is near the Leisure Isle Gallery and it's a pleasant place for a stroll along the water's edge or plonk yourself on a bench and upload the scenery into your memory banks. At low tide there are plenty of **birds** to be seen on the mud flats just off shore, and in summer you may spot waders such as grey plover, greenshank, curlew sandpiper, and whimbrel. The Woodbourne Marsh at the turn-off to Leisure Isle is especially bird rich.

TOWN

If you don't have wheels, or prefer a guided tour, get **Amatuktuk Safaris** to show you the town in one of their genuine 3-wheeler tuk-tuks, imported from Thailand. They conform to safety regulations and are covered to keep off the sun and rain. Although they operate from the **Knysna Quays**, you can negotiate for pick-ups from your guesthouse. Rates are for a person and, depending on which tour you take, cost from R30–R150 and may include trips to The Heads or Brenton on Sea. They do custom tours and evening charters. Tel 084-863-2808 for details.

There's a lovely historical side to Knysna, although you have to look hard between the more modern glitz and glamour to spot it. Pick up a street map from the tourist office.

Knysna has a quaint wood and iron museum, **Millwood House**, in Queen Street near the municipal offices. It's a typical example of the dwellings built at Millwood village during the gold mining days in the 1880s, and was dismantled there, and re-erected here. It's open Mon–Fri 09h30–16h30, and on Saturdays until 12h30. Tel 044-302-6320. See also page 121 on the **Materolli Museum** at Millwood.

There's also the **Old Gaol Museum** in Queen Street, which has a fascinating room telling the story of the Knysna elephants; plus an art gallery, restored jail cell, and angling display. The building was erected in 1859 to house convicts en route to the Prince Alfred's Pass construction camp.

The stone **St George's Anglican Church** in the main street was completed in 1855, and is also worth a look. It has wide yellowwood floorboards, exposed trusses and a timber ceiling. When it became too small for the community, a larger church was built on the same property.

George Rex's grave, which is fenced off, has been well maintained. You'll find it at a place called Old Place just off the N2. Pass the turn-off to the Heads, continue for 1,2 km, and before you start going uphill east out of town, you'll see the national monument signpost indicating his grave to the right. Then turn immediately left onto a short road that runs parallel to the N2 and ends under big old oak trees that shade his grave. He died in 1839, and his gravestone reads 'Founder and Proprietor of Knysna'.

Remnants of the old stone **Knysna Fort** can still be visited today. It sits on the hill above the Knysna provincial hospital, and was built during the Anglo Boer War (1899–1902). It's said that it 'never experienced a shot fired in anger', however, it was the most southerly fort dating to the Anglo Boer War. The best way to reach the fort is by entering the hospital grounds and parking at the back where concrete steps and then a pathway lead straight up a steep hill to it. Get further info from the Millwood House Museum.

There is a ribbon of shops selling **crafts, shells, wooden items** made from Knysna wood, and kitsch knick-knacks masquerading as tourist mementos; all of which are fun to browse, especially when the weather's miz. Pick of the bunch is **Birds of Africa**, a small factory-cum-shop in the main street that creates indigenous birds that are collector's items. Each is individually made by the hands of skilled artists, with the wood being sourced from forests in the region. Tel 044-382-5660.

Pledge Square has a few interesting shops and corners to explore and the highlight is the excellent 2nd-hand bookshop called **Knysna Book Exchange**, which you'll find upstairs on the left when you enter the square. It's also where you'll find an information kiosk, which you'll need to visit to gain admission into **Pledge Nature Reserve**. This 10 ha reserve is a mere 200 m above the main road and offers trails through wetland, forest and fynbos. There's an info hut and toilets at the Bond Street entrance and the pond area has benches in the shade. Stop for a picnic lunch at the table at Fern Grove, or the viewsite that overlooks Knysna and the Heads. You should spot some of the 60+ bird species, butterflies, dragonflies and other small animals. For further info about tours and forest breakfasts, call the curator Jill Dempere on tel 072-784-7357.

Art Galleries are scattered around the town and on Leisure Isle, showcasing local painters, potters, sculptors and various other artists. Several local artists exhibit countrywide and also sell their work overseas, or are com-

Pledge Square on Knysna's Main Street, complete with renovated water mill.

So here we are at the Knysna Quays: it should be everything you wished for and more, but if it's just not your cuppa you can get your bearings here to … just about anywhere else.

missioned. If you're into art, you're bound to recognise some famous South African names around town. **Die Ou Fabriek** was once a thriving warren of creative shops. Today it's probably best known as the long-standing location of Stephenson and Son **Bookbinding**, an oft-overlooked craft.

Thanks to Lex Mitchell, Knysna has brewed its own handmade traditional beers since 1983. **Mitchell's Brewery** offers tours and tastings Mon–Fri at 10h30 or 15h00; or just go and taste Mon–Fri 08h30–16h30, or Saturdays 09h00–12h30. For further info and to book a tour tel 044-382-4685. It just might be the finest pint you enjoy in South Africa.

To stretch your legs and view Knysna from a different angle, tackle the paved path, called the **Costa Sarda Walkway**, along the edge of the lagoon that stretches from Knysna Yacht Club, passes the Knysna River Club in Costa Sarda suburb and ends at George Rex Drive. It's popular with runners and cyclists too. You can detour off the walkway to **Thesen Harbour Town** where a collection of mostly overpriced 'label' shops cater for bulging wallets. This is also where you'll find the **Knysna Oyster Company** and the **SANParks offices**. At the time of writing, the **Knysna Oyster Company**, which was established in 1949 and has been cultivating oysters in the estuary ever since, was undergoing some tender times …. The outcome of the current business tender was going to be announced only after submission of this text, so for the latest news, tel 044-382-6941/2, e-mail knysnaoysterco@mweb.co.za or visit www.

knysnaoysters.co.za. If you want to see the famous **Knysna seahorse**, there are a few in a tank at the SANParks offices; and 34° South deli-restaurant on the Knysna Waterfront also has seahorses in a tank upstairs in their wine shop.

Thesen Harbour Sunday Market happens on the first Sunday of the month from 11h00–16h00. Stalls include handmade pottery and soaps, lovely Indian clothing, artworks, and those selling edibles such as roti, spring rolls, and liqueurs. If it's raining, the market is held under cover.

The largest organised Rastatarian community of its kind in the country is based just outside Knysna: **Judah's Square Rastafarian Community**. Here, around 30 families have created an eco-tourism experience. You can visit and join them on a forest walk that's been created with SANParks, or spend a night. For further info contact the tourism bureau.

It's par for the course, ahem, that there are those of you who'll prefer to do your walking across manicured greens. Knysna has **3 golf courses**, the longest established being **Knysna Golf Club**, which lies on the eastern shore of the lagoon, on the left of George Rex drive. It's thought to be the only golf course in the country to have holes below sea level, call 044-384-1150 or www.knysnagolf.co.za. **Simola Golf & Country Estate** is just a few kilometres up the Salt River Road and has a spectacular view over the lagoon and down onto the Knysna River, tel 044-382-4116 or www.simolaestate.co.za. **Pezula Championship Course** is on the Eastern Head and has spectacular panoramic views over the ocean and coastline, and is rated amongst the best and most scenic golf courses in the world. For further info tel 044-302-5300 or visit www.pezula.com.

Whether you're a foodie, an eatie, or

Pezula is certainly one of the most dramatically sited golf course estates in the world, but it is not without its detractors who think the Eastern Head would be much nicer au naturel.

THE KNYSNA OYSTER

Synonymous with Knysna (and known to make most readers' mouths water), the Knysna oyster has its own interesting history. First experiments to cultivate oysters in the Knysna lagoon began in 1946, but it was only in the 1970s (how's that for being tenacious!) that a commercially successful species, the Pacific oyster (*Crassostrea gigas*), proved to be ideal for conditions here.

Today, the Knysna Oyster Company farms 16 ha of the lagoon. They're grown in fine plastic mesh bags, which allow water flow, and tied to specially created racks secured in the intertidal zone. At low tide they dry out, preventing them becoming covered in marine growth but, no, you can't go and help yourself to oysters when the tide goes out! To be sure, don't go near the oyster beds: not only are you likely to puncture the bottom of your boat on an unseen pole, you're also likely to get shot at by the oyster-sniper who sits in the bush on the Western Head.

just looking for an alternative but constructive way to spend some free time in Knysna, one way is to head to **Kilzer's Kitchen Basics** for a range of cookery courses. Their custom-designed facility is on the hill above town, overlooking the lagoon, and courses emphasise correct preparation methods resulting in simple, tasty, wholesome food. Tel Albin and Jenny Kilzer on 044-382-0135, e-mail kilzerkb@iafrica.com or visit www.kkbcooking.co.za.

A fun way to start Friday evening is to visit the **Friday Market** in Welbedacht, a residential area 3 km west of Knysna. It happens between 16h00 and 20h00 every Friday from beginning September to end June. It's located on the Montessori school fields and is signposted from the N2 turn-off to Welbedacht. For details tel 044-382-5316.

Out of Town

Birding is good all around Knysna, with habitats spanning the lagoon, rocky shores, forest, grassland and fynbos. You can bird watch wherever you are, on the beach, in a garden, or nature reserve, and it's said that species number somewhere in the 260s. Special sightings include the Knysna warbler, Knysna woodpecker, Narina trogon, and a couple of the flufftails, to mention a few. There is always the chance of spotting a brilliant green and red flash of the **Knysna turaco** (lourie) in the leafy town suburbs and in the forests. It's unmistakable as it flies, flashing scarlet wing windows through the treetops. Their distinct Egyptian-like eye makeup of red and white, along with a maroon beak, stands out beneath their green crown. They have an inelegant song for such an exquisite bird and if you hear a *korr, korr, korr* type call, keep your eyes peeled.

There is a **'Timber route'** that Knysna Tourism promotes, but it's not one on which you'll be able to savour the timber heritage. It's more of a list of shops, studios and factories where you can buy wooden items, including furniture, and watch them being made at various outlets that use indigenous yellowwood and stinkwood. Also on the Timber Route is the southern hemisphere's largest timber structure (Knysna Log Inn); and a 'big tree'.

The Knysna forests offer fabulous **mountain biking** trails (detailed under their relevant sections, e.g. Rheenendal). You can also pootle down George Rex Drive from the N2 to the Heads and/or Leisure Isle. It's a steep climb to top of the Heads, but well worth it, and a ride around Leisure Isle is all on the level and pure pleasure out of season when there's little traffic. A great place to get cycling info, and whatever you need for your bikes, including superior servicing and repairs, is at **Knysna Cycle Works**. You'll find them at 13 Nelson Street, just 1 street below Main Road behind the Knysna Mall. This company is owner-run by Jacques and Altha Brink who've been in the cycling game for many years, and know the area really well. The shop is open 08h30–17h00 weekdays, and 09h00–13h00 Saturdays. They also hire out bikes with front or full suspension, tel 044-382-5153, e-mail freejacq@mweb.co.za or visit www.knysnacycles.co.za.

If you need to work off those dozens of oysters you've been *slukking*, lace your boots and hit one of the many **hiking trails**. Whether you prefer forest, beach, coast or fynbos, there are varying degrees of difficulty and each offers different scenery. Get info from the 'Calls to the Wild' chapter, or Knysna tourism.

The **Knysna Elephant Park** which does not have Knysna forest elephants but African savanna elephants rescued from elsewhere. Also, it's not in Knysna but in Harkerville, about 9 km from Plett. See **Harkerville** section under Plettenberg Bay, page 188.

Prince Alfred's Pass – see entry on page 165.

There are **4x4** trails in the area but it's best to visit the tourist office to get info on the various options.

Knysna Nightlife

Apart from the dozens of restaurants, there are plenty of pubs, a cinema, and clubs like **Tryst Dance Club & Cocktail Bar**, which caters for a range of ages and has a VIP lounge. The really cool youngsters hang out at **Zanzibar** in the Main Street; and **Harry B's**, also in the Main Street, is popular with various age groups.

Overnight in Knysna

There are more than 300 accommodation establishments in and around Knysna, scattered from the centre of the busy town, right out to the coast, and deep into the forests and mountains. The choice here is vast, from 5-star hotels that'll cost you up to and over R10 000 a person a night, to affordable hotels, lodges, guesthouses, B&Bs, self-catering units and houseboats, right through to backpackers and caravan and camping sites. You name it, Knysna's got it. If you look at the town's places to stay on a graph, there are probably more top-of-the-range places than budget, but whether you're one of a couple or a family, budget conscious, backpackers or enjoy outdoor living, you're sure to find somewhere memorable for your holiday. Just be sure to

If it's colour you're looking for, the Knysna Quays and lagoon around sunset dazzle with a combination of natural and artificial light: you should see it at full moon.

book well in advance, as it seems these days there are few months when it's not busy with both local and overseas holidaymakers.

Please note:
Listings below are split into the following areas:
◆ Central
◆ Welbedacht 3 km west of town centre
◆ Hunter's Home en route to Leisure Isle
◆ Leisure Isle
◆ Between Leisure Isle and the Heads
◆ The Heads
◆ Noetzie
◆ The forest (Diepwalle)

NB: For areas outside of town, such as **The Western Head** and **Phantom Pass area** (includes Belvidere, Lake Brenton,

Brenton on Sea), Rheenendal, Buffalo Bay and Goukamma, see Between Sedgefield and Knysna on pages 109 to 130.

GOLD-THREADED SILK

Let's start at the very top of the range, which is definitely only for those whose wallets suffer from obesity. **Pezula Private Castle**, situated at Noetzie beach, is part of the 5-star Pezula Resort Hotel & Spa and, depending on whether you want to rent the main castle, which sleeps 3 couples, or the castle complex, costs are from R55 000 to R100 000 a night. Yes, a night. However, the price is inclusive of meals, drinks, refreshments, spa treatments, golf and other activities, plus an executive butler, chef and luxury vehicle with a driver waiting to pop you over the hill to

Pezula Castle is 1 of several similar follies built at Noetzie, a small bay just to the east of town. You can stay there, but you'd better have a good relationship with your bank manager.

the main hotel. Naturally, it's rumoured to have seriously famous guests but they're too discreet to admit this, never mind give any names.

Pezula Resort Hotel & Spa is perched (rather rudely) atop Knysna's Eastern Head and is popular with golfers, but not exclusive to them. It incorporates 78 luxury suites, an incredible 18-hole golf course (see activities), a spa, and a gourmet restaurant (see **Zachary's** under Where to Eat). Rates depend on season and suite type, and run from R4 500–R13 500 a unit. To book, call 044-302-3333, e-mail reservations@pezula.com or peruse www.pezularesorthotel.com.

Central
SILK

Knysna River Club, which is a multi AA Awards winner, is nowhere near the Knysna River, but is in fact on the eastern edge of the Knysna lagoon on the inland side of the N2, offering spacious, well-appointed wooden self-catering chalets with large windows so you can enjoy the view over the water. Each unit has an open-plan fully equipped kitchen and living room, the latter opening onto a veranda deck where you can braai and enjoy your meals al fresco.

The Costa Sarda Walkway (see page 147) runs between the River Club and the water's edge, so if you're a walker, you'll enjoy the convenience of popping along to the Knysna Quays by heading west along here. Chalets have 1, 2 or 3 bedrooms, each of which can accommodate 2 extra guests on a double sleeper couch in the lounge; and they are serviced daily. Rates depend on whether the chalet has a garden or lagoon view, and run from R800–R2 500 a unit a night. To book, tel 044-382-6483, e-mail info@knysnariverclub.co.za or visit www.knysnariverclub.co.za.

Knysna Log-Inn is a **4-star luxury hotel** conveniently situated at 16 Grey Street between the town centre and the waterfront. It's reputedly the largest timber structure in the southern hemisphere and is certainly impressive if you're into wood. The light and airy lobby has huge carved trunks for pillars and a solid staircase, both of yellowwood, and the large stained-glass windows on either side depict scenes from Knysna's wood cutting days. The 57 double, twin and family rooms are spread over 2 floors with those on the 1st floor opening onto private balconies. If you enjoy a lie-in ask for a room away from the road, with traffic starting around 6 am. All rooms have air-conditioning, TV, fans and tea/coffee facilities, and there's an all season pool and sun deck, spa-bath, and sauna downstairs. Breakfast is served in the **Tribes Restaurant** downstairs, which has tables inside, or outside through the French windows on the *stoep* – they also do suppers from an à la carte menu. They have a 24-hour reception. B&B rates are from R560–R875/ps. They offer a shuttle service to and from George airport. Tel 044-382-5835, e-mail info@log-inn.co.za or visit www.kli.co.za.

One of the newer upmarket establishments in town, managed by the Three Cities hospitality group, is **The Rex Hotel** at 8 Grey Street, a block past Knysna Log-Inn towards the lagoon. It has a 4-star grading and offers apartment-style hotel rooms. It's modern, light, and has all the luxuries of a hotel with the added bonus that all units are equipped for self-catering. Of their 30 rooms, 4 have 2 bedrooms. Their restaurant, **Dish**, at street level, is reasonably priced and the bar is the place to be seen sipping cocktails on Friday evenings when they're on special and there's some kind of live music playing. Rates are R900/ps, less 25% during winter. Tel 044-302-5900, e-mail reservations@rexhotel.co.za or visit www.rexhotel.co.za.

LINEN

The 3-star **Inyathi Guest Lodge** at 52 Main Street is just past the BP garage when entering from the Sedgefield side and offers some of the quirkiest lodging you'll find in these parts. Set slightly back from the main street and built on a gentle slope, this one-time craft village comprises 10 small en-suite timber cabins and a family unit, decorated with ethnic African arts and crafts, so you almost get the feeling of being in an African village. Units nestle in a lush garden alongside a central path and unusual features make each one unique. The proprietors, Riaan Louw and Helen Watkins, are laid back and if they're not fully booked they'll show you around and you can choose the unit you like best. It's a great place for folks who enjoy places with a difference. There's secure off-street parking. Rates are R280–R350/ps including a full breakfast. Give them a call on tel 044-382-7768, e-mail info@inyathi-sa.com or web www.inyathi-sa.com.

Hillview Self-catering Apartments at 8 League Street, are on the hill behind the tourist office, so have lovely lagoon views out to The Heads. They offer 4 exclusive boutique-type self-catering apartments – 3 doubles and 1 family unit, all of which have full bathrooms and are tastefully equipped with luxurious linen, DStv, DVD and free internet access. Some have indoor fireplaces and private entrances, and there are braai facilities and an atmospheric central courtyard area with loungers and swimming pool. Self-catering rarely comes with such style at such good value for money. The town centre is a short amble away. Self-catering rates are R450 a night for 2 people, R350 a night if you stay longer than 5 nights. Breakfast baskets can be ordered. Contact Karen Gschwend on tel 044-382-3940 or 072-518-7509, e-mail hillview@cyberperk.co.za or web www.hillview.co.za.

Paradise House is in a quiet cul-de-sac at 6 Protea Street on the hill behind town about 1 km from the centre, and also has fab lagoon views. There is 1 spacious self-catering apartment with TV, braai, fridge, lounge and fully equipped kitchenette; plus 4 elegant en-suite rooms with TV, braai, fridge and coffee tray – there are shared microwave ovens, crockery and cutlery in 2 purpose-built nooks in the entrance hall for basic self-catering. Rates are R190–R350/ps plus R30 for breakfast. Contact Johan and Zita Petzer on tel 044-382-6705 or 083-412-7097, e-mail info@paradisehouse.co.za or visit www.paradisehouse.co.za.

CALICO

Greenside at 12 Rawson Street, is opposite the Knysna Bowling Club in between Knysna's Main Road and Waterfront drive. It has 2 budget options – they're small but clean and equipped for self catering. Both units – the Cottage and the Flatlet – are en-

Idyllic Knysna lagoon: the story goes that George Rex, an illegitimate son of George III, was given oodles of land surrounding the estuary to get rid of him. Poor unfortunate fellow!

The short walk into the Garden of Eden is like an intravenous shot of raw nature.

suite, have a fully equipped kitchenette, braai facility, patio and secure off-street parking. The flatlet is like a bedsitter and adequate for a couple, while the cottage, although open plan, has a double bed and a sleeper couch and is cosy for a small family. Rates are R350 for the cottage and R270 for the flatlet. Contact Sandra and Frank Norval on tel 044-382-3677 or e-mail sandran@sanparks.org.

Backpackers – there are several in town, all costing around R100 a dorm bed; all have pools, self-catering facilities in communal kitchens, and double rooms. The longest running and possibly the best of the bunch is **Knysna Backpackers**, located in a century-old house with yellowwood floors and bay windows on either side of the front steps. They're situated up the hill from the stone Anglican church, on the corner of Queen and Newton streets,

which is within easy walking distance of the town centre. Accommodation includes 3 doubles with TVs, a twin, a family room and an 8-bed dorm, all sharing 3 communal bathrooms and a kitchen. They accommodate budget-conscious travellers as well as international backpackers but **booking is essential**, as they don't take drop-ins. They will book all the main activities in the area for you and recommend places to eat and drink. Speak to Muriel Blumer or Hannes Visser on tel 044-382-2554, e-mail info@knysnabackpackers.co.za, or web www.knysnabackpackers.co.za.

Just a few blocks away at 2 Graham Street is **Highfields Backpackers**, which has a real chilled-out vibe. They offer 2-, 4- and 5-bed rooms upstairs as well as 2 dorms. There's a braai and swimming pool area out back and breakfasts can be ordered from ingredients on a blackboard. Rates are: dorms R90/p, doubles R250 and R125/p in the family room. For inside info call Dave Price on tel 044-382-6266, e-mail dave@highfieldsbackpackers.co.za or visit www.highfieldsbackpackers.co.za. It's also home to the **Adventure Centre** that's been around for 10 years and does canoe hire, tours, adrenaline sports and more. Tel Jay Thornton on 083-260-7198 or web www.theadventurecentre.co.za.

Welbedacht
Welbedacht Lane is 3km west of Knysna off the N2.

SILK
If views of sea, lagoon and mountains aren't a prerequisite for your visit to

Knysna, but tranquil surrounds are, 1km along Welbedacht Lane lies what we feel is one of Knysna's best accommodation establishments – and we're not saying that just because it has won more awards than are given out on an average night at the Oscars.

The 5-star **Tonquani Lodge** is everything you look for when planning to recharge and relax over a romantic weekend or extended short break. If you have the pleasure of meeting 1 of the owners and hosts, Sheldeen Robson-Parsons, you'll immediately see that her genuine and open personality has been woven into the fabric of the Tonquani experience.

Accommodation is set in tree-rich gardens in log chalets sleeping 2, or family suites sleeping 4. Most units have king-size beds, full bathrooms, bar fridge, air-conditioning, private patio with a kettle braai, and a host of personal touches. For those who enjoy a fireplace and spa-bath, or private splash pool, some have those too. If the interiors don't entice you to spend your time wrapped in their warmth then reclining next to the pool might.

Should total relaxation be your priority there are 2 things not to miss: order breakfast in bed, served on trays covered by silver domes; and in the evening have marshmallows, popcorn and a flask of hot chocolate delivered with your choice of DVD from their extensive library. Ah, then there's the spa offering many enticing ways in which to pamper yourself. B&B rates are R500–R1400/ps, less 30% in winter. To book tel 044-382-4355, e-mail tonquani@mweb.co.za or web www.tonquani.co.za.

Hunter's Home

Behind the Knysna golf course the neighbourhood of Hunter's Home spreads across the gently sloping hills and is ideally situated between the town centre and the landmarks of The Heads and Leisure Isle.

LINEN

There are a number of guesthouses tucked along the narrow streets but our pick of the bunch has to be the 3-star **Bamboo Guesthouse** at 9 Bolton Street. Here Jayne Court and Gordon Turrell have created a tranquil and lush haven through which boardwalks meander to various double and family units. Each has its own private entrance, and patio with braai, DStv, bar fridge, coffee tray, fans/heaters, a snack basket and complimentary bottle of wine.

We highly recommend the Palm unit built at the top of a slope and looking across the garden. In the morning wander through the vegetation, which includes a large stand of bamboo, admiring the many birds at the feeders hung in the trees, then settle down for breakfast in the open-fronted boma alongside the pool. Children are welcome. Garden rooms cost R300–R445/ps; Courtyard rooms R280–R400/ps; family suites R1000–R1350 a unit. They can also arrange sundowner trips on the lagoon. Tel 044-384-0937 or 082-812-8838, e-mail info@bambooguesthouse.co.za or web www.bambooguesthouse.co.za.

Leisure Island
LINEN

Having turned off George Rex Drive and crossed the causeway take the first

The navigational beacon on the side of the treacherous channel through the Heads has saved many a soul and ship from a watery death, but not all: you can visit some by scuba diving here.

turn left into Woodbourne Drive and follow the road until it curves around to the waterfront where it becomes Cearn Drive. At number 37 Cearn Drive, **The Tree House** hides among the spreading branches of an ancient milkwood tree. It's a very well-equipped 2-bedroom unit looking across a stretch of the lagoon to The Heads, a view best relished from the sun deck built around the tree's trunk. Both bedrooms – a double and a twin – are en-suite and have French windows opening onto the private back garden. The open plan lounge/dining room/kitchen is cool, light and airy, and furnished in a modern theme. It has everything guests would need for an extended holiday including TV, video and sound system, washing machine and outside braai. Guests have the use of a canoe, bicycles and a mooring for a small boat. Rates for 2 people in low season are R585 plus R130 for an additional adult; mid season costs R785 for 2 plus R190 an additional adult; and mid-Dec to mid-Jan the unit costs R2 000 a day. Call Sheena and Peter Maré on tel 044-384-0777 or 072-127-6648, e-mail saltdog@mweb.co.za or web www.tree-house.co.za.

If a view over the lagoon isn't a priority then **Belle Ile** around the corner at 10 George Avenue is a self-catering 1-bedroom flat with a fully equipped open-plan kitchen and lounge opening onto a spacious deck. It has its own entrance and parking, a TV and sound system, and can sleep an extra 2 people on a sleeper couch. A minimum stay of 2 nights is required and children are welcome. Rate for 2 people is R550–R1 050, and for 4 R780–R1 450 low/high season.

Call Veronique Leach on 044-384-1355, cell 083-753-7762, e-mail fungy@mweb.co.za or visit www.belle-ile.co.za.

Between Leisure Island and The Heads
CALICO & CANVAS

Between the turn off to Leisure Isle and The Heads **Woodbourne Holiday Resort** offers 3-star self-catering chalets and is also the closest campsite to Knysna town. The resort is a private estate and the grounds on which it stands was once part of George Rex's farm, Melkhoutkraal. The fully equipped chalets each have a *stoep*, braai and SABC TV; they range from quaint wooden cabins sleeping 2 to larger units for up to 8 people. The electrified campsites are grassed, and nestle in the shade of large milkwood, oak and syringa trees, which come alive with prolific birdsong during the day. There's a pool, trampoline and playground for the kids. For adult amusement the grassed bank overlooking the adjacent wetland is a good spot to park off and start a new bird list. A minimum stay of 7 nights is required during the December peak season. Rates for chalets range from R390–R760 in low/high season a night a unit for 2 people, and camping R120/R280 a site for 2 people. Discounted prices are applicable for each extra person. For full details tel 044-384-0316 or 072-466-1459, e-mail w48@mweb.co.za or web www.woodbourne.co.za.

The Heads
SILK

Under Milkwood is one of the best-known **self-catering** establishments around, probably due to its heavenly setting on the lagoon-side of the Eastern Head. It's a collection of timber chalets tucked beneath and between glorious milkwood trees. The units are split into waterfront, hillside and middle chalets, each with its own prices: each has 2 bedrooms (1 twin, 1 double), fully equipped kitchen with mod cons, and a sun deck and braai. They're serviced daily. There's a beach right in front of the chalets that's safe for swimming, depending on the tide. Rates, depending on the situation of the chalets, range from R860–R1300 a unit for 2 people in low season, and from R2500–R3500 a unit for up to 4 people in high season. They also have a few B&B rooms from R260 to R600/p sharing. Call 044 384-0745, e-mail admin@milkwood.co.za or web www.milkwood.co.za. Affiliated to Under Milkwood is the upmarket **Milkwood Bay Guest House** situated in a Mediterranean-style villa next door. For further info tel 044-384-0092, e-mail milkbay@milkwood.co.za or visit www.milkwood.co.za.

LINEN

If you enjoy quieter, more individual establishments contact **Owl's Roost**, a self-catering apartment enjoying an elevated location on the corner of Ou Pad and Paquita Drive at The Heads. It has a private entrance, equipped kitchen, lounge, DStv, bedroom, full bathroom with separate toilet and a private balcony with a beautiful view across the lagoon and Leisure Isle to Knysna and the Outeniqua mountains. If you like to watch your own meat sizzle on a grid there's a small boma down

South Africa's earliest inhabitants the Khoisan. The water is so-coloured by humic acids leached from the vegetative debris on the forest floor.

Although today the emphasis is on the environment rather than its castles, Noetzie became known for these stone buildings that look as if they belong somewhere in Scotland, rather than along the South African coast. Unfortunately, the castles are not historically significant, although there are those who will lead you to believe some incredibly romantic story of smugglers and pirates, which is far more enticing than the truth. The beach, which is reached 100+ steps down from the small car park, is pleasant for a stroll, a nosey at the castles, and time spent daydreaming on your beach towel. It is strongly advised that you do NOT swim here more than just a dip; the beach shelves deeply, there are strong currents and no lifesavers, so wet your toes but don't be tempted into the crashing breakers.

LINEN

For romantics, location alone is enough to send the heart a-flutter. When there is a castle thrown in, and it's inviting you to stay over, well, 'tis enough to make a girl swoon. **Lyndsay Castle** is a guesthouse. No, guesthouse sounds too ordinary for a castle, and it certainly can't be called a B&B, but you get the picture. It overlooks this glorious Noetzie beach, with its busy oyster-catchers and salty sea air that smacks of mystery and intrigue, and offers 4 double en-suite rooms upstairs and 1 twin with separate bathroom downstairs for those who can't face the climb. Dinner costs R150–R200 and is served in a candlelit dining room in a stone-walled tower. B&B rates are R600–R1 200/ps. Ask about winter specials. Tel Julia and Wayne Hullet on 044-384-1849, e-mail reservations@knysnacastles.co.za or visit www.knysnacastles.com.

Prince Alfred's Pass

The R339 to Uniondale turns off the N2 at the top of the long hill that climbs from Knysna towards Plettenberg Bay – opposite the Noetzie turning. This mostly gravel road traverses huge tracts of indigenous forests around Diepwalle and has numerous beautiful picnic sites with associated walks and big trees, and some stunning viewpoints (see Diepwalle forest on page 138). About 45 km out, the road starts to wind up and over the Prince Alfred's Pass and eventually joins up with the R63 that runs east to west along the Langkloof. Just before reaching the pass the road goes through the isolated farming settlement of De Vlugt, which is where Thomas Bain set up his construction camp in 1863 and later settled with his family. The pass can also be accessed from Plettenberg Bay via the R340, which turns off the N2 just across the Bitou River.

The history of Prince Alfred's Pass goes back to the mid 19th century when, because of Knysna's increasing importance as a port and trade center, it became necessary to establish a route over the Outeniqua mountains to the interior. Andrew Geddes Bain was summoned to survey the possibility in 1856, but it wasn't until 1863 that his son Thomas (see page 70) started on the arduous task of constructing the road. It took 4 years to complete the pass, which happened to coincide with a visit to Knysna by Prince Alfred, the Duke of Edinburgh (Victoria's beloved husband), who took part in an elephant hunt here, hence the origin of the name. If you have not yet driven the Seven Passes route, this one will fill you with the spirit of the Garden Route.

LINEN & CANVAS

If you've had enough of the sea head for **Outeniqua Trout Lodge**, an establishment that comprises 4 timber self-catering chalets sleeping 4 to 6 people with fireplaces and deck with braai. Also ideal for, but not exclusive to, small groups is their tented camp, made up of 4 tepees sleeping 4 each with separate private bathroom and cooking boma. It's something different and good fun – in winter there's even a small ceramic fireplace inside each tent. The property forms part of the Keurbooms Conservancy so the 'garden' here is well looked after. The main activity is fly-fishing for rainbow and brown trout on 2 rivers and 3 dams on a catch-and-release basis.

If you're not a fisher don't fret as there're plenty of other activities including hiking, mountain biking, bird watching, swimming and horse riding. You can't get much further into the mountain's embrace than here so if you're a country bumpkin at heart and love peaks and valleys, put this on your must-stay list. Rates are from R600 a chalet for 2 people. The tepee camp costs R400 a tent for the first 2 people and R50 for the 3rd and 4th person – 3 night minimum stay over December. There's also a conservation fee of R20 a person a night. Fishing rods can be hired and day visitors are welcome. For inside info call Ingo and Naomi on tel 044-752-3140 or e-mail troutlodge@iafrica.com or web www.outeniquatrout.co.za.

On a clear day from Spitskop, a viewsite near Diepwalle forest reserve you can see all the way across the Outeniqua mountains, to heaven – a personal kind of heaven.

Plettenberg Bay

11

including Harkerville, Kranshoek, Bitou, Keurbooms & Wittedrift

Plettenberg Bay, or rather, Plett as it's known locally, is an area of outstanding natural beauty, with sweeping golden beaches, a dramatic rugged peninsula, rivers that flow into a picture-perfect lagoon, a temperate climate, and panoramic views that stretch to the horizon. It has long been a favourite for tourists and socialite mavens.

Another gorgeous day dawns over the Keurbooms lagoon, part of the watery attractions of Plettenberg: not hard to see why the Portuguese first named it 'the beautiful bay'.

As with just about all natural beauty spots, the place Portuguese sailors named the 'beautiful bay' has grown from a small fishing settlement – where early morning walkers could spot pansy shells on the beach – into a sprawling modern holiday town.

The main beaches and town lie on a north–south axis, easily seen from the lookout point on Signal Hill that offers views to the horizon. The exquisite brush strokes of Mother Nature lie surrounded by great slashes of houses, such as those above Robberg Beach where, until not at all long ago, the landscape was pristine and untouched. Fortunately, the long rugged finger of Robberg Peninsula in the south remains an unscathed nature reserve; the seductive curve of Robberg Beach is still one of the finest along the coast.

The town's main street and associated central business district is relatively compact and sits perched high on a hill above the beaches. From here it slopes seawards, flattening out around the Keurbooms River lagoon to the north and, in the south, the Piesang River valley. At the mouth of the Piesang River is a tiny island, atop which stands the iconic Beacon Isle Hotel that looks somewhat like a giant wedding cake.

The main 'downtown' street is short and flanked with shops and restaurants aimed mostly at the holiday trade; there are 2 other retail areas: 1 being a largish shopping centre at the eastern entrance; the other being a small collection of shops just across the Piesang River, which lies at the bottom of the hill that Plett's main street arcs across.

North of town lie the estuaries of the Bitou and Keurbooms rivers, which run into the Keurbooms River lagoon, a long-time favourite with campers and water sports enthusiasts. In fact, both of us grew up holidaying regularly in Plett back in the 60s and 70s when there was still a bamboo bridge across the lagoon and the town was framed by endless vegetation.

With mostly mild winter (May–September) weather, and glorious summer days, Plett's beaches are the

WHY VISIT PLETT
For the beaches; and to have a really good belly laugh at the property prices.

WHAT'S WACKY
The fact that what was once Lookout Beach is now the Keurbooms Lagoon mouth. Huge winter storms during the mid 2000s washed away the main beach and re-bored the river's course. The beach will probably come back … some time.

TOURIST INFORMATION
The only reason to visit this office is to pick up brochures – you'll find them upstairs in the Melville Shopping Centre, which is on the corner of Main Street and Marine Way (near the dolphin circle). Tel 044-533-4065, for accommodation queries email info@plettenbergbay.co.za or for general info e-mail frontdesk@plettenbergbay.co.za, web www.plettenbergbay.co.za. In truth we never got a reply from our e-mails.

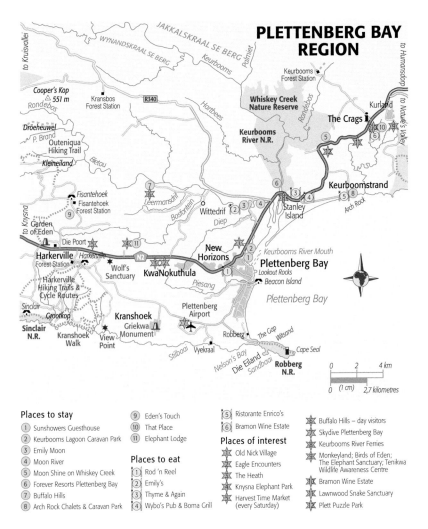

PLETTENBERG BAY REGION

Places to stay

1. Sunshowers Guesthouse
2. Keurbooms Lagoon Caravan Park
3. Emily Moon
4. Moon River
5. Moon Shine on Whiskey Creek
6. Forever Resorts Plettenberg Bay
7. Buffalo Hills
8. Arch Rock Chalets & Caravan Park
9. Eden's Touch
10. That Place
11. Elephant Lodge

Places to eat

1. Rod 'n Reel
2. Emily's
3. Thyme & Again
4. Wybo's Pub & Boma Grill

5. Ristorante Enrico's
6. Bramon Wine Estate

Places of interest

- Old Nick Village
- Eagle Encounters
- The Heath
- Knysna Elephant Park
- Harvest Time Market (every Saturday)
- Buffalo Hills – day visitors
- Skydive Plettenberg Bay
- Keurbooms River Ferries
- Monkeyland; Birds of Eden; The Elephant Sanctuary; Tenikwa Wildlife Awareness Centre
- Bramon Wine Estate
- Lawnwood Snake Sanctuary
- Plett Puzzle Park

main attraction; and also a haven for schools of dolphins and visiting whales. The quieter months are our favourite, when there are only a few souls enjoying the beaches. However, if you are keen to see and be seen, then head here in December when it crawls with tens of thousands of holidaymakers – some of whom arrive in their helicopters and private jets. The locals are a delight in general, and probably remain even-tempered in December because they've doubled their prices.

History of Plett

Plettenberg Bay has a rich heritage relating to the history of the Griqua people, and the 'strandlopers' or beachcombing Khoisan people. The latter found the location ideal in terms of the climate, plentiful fish, game and fresh water; natural shelters in cliffs near the ocean, and large marine animals that provided skins. Rich evidence of this existence has been found in middens and caves dating back some 12000 years. Archaeological findings in Nelson's Bay Cave on Robberg Peninsula, and Matjes River Rock Cave at Keurboomstrand indicate that a Middle Stone Age culture inhabited them more than 100000 years ago. A burial site was discovered, with the remains of around 100 people; and archaeologists discovered an 11-year-old child's remains that was radio-carbon dated to around 70000 BP. In later years, the Khoisan lived in these caves and, although excavations are still taking place, deposits of their ornaments, tools and food debris have been found.

The Portuguese explorer Bartholomeu Dias arrived in the bay in 1487; and 90 years later, another Portuguese explorer Manuel da Perestrello named it Bahia Formosa, or 'bay beautiful'. The first semi-permanent inhabitants were the 100 survivors of the wrecked *San Gonzales*, which sank here in the mid 1630s. The ship was on its way back to Portugal from India when it anchored in the bay to repair leaks; it was overloaded so 100 sailors swam to shore and 400 remained on board. During a fierce storm, the ship sank and those on board all drowned. The castaways were stranded for 9 months, living off the land, planting seeds and trading with the Khoisan. In time, they managed to build 2 boats and set off, being picked up eventually by other Portuguese vessels.

The 15th–17th centuries were colourful ones, full of European explorers; and in 1763, white stock farmers, frontiersmen, hunters and tradesmen from the Cape began to settle in the area permanently. Today some descendants of these pioneers still live or own property in Plett. The Cape governor, Baron Joachim van Plettenberg, renamed the settlement Plettenberg Bay in 1779; in 1787 a woodcutters' post was established, a timber storehouse built, and a year later the first wood was exported. The Cape was chronically short of tim-

PANSY SHELLS

These fragile and unusual 'shells' are actually the internal structure of sea urchins (*Echinodiscus bisperforatus*). Although once commonly seen along coastal beaches of the Garden Route, they were so avidly collected you'll be very lucky to see one in the wild today. When the urchin has died, a flat, white disc-like calcium plate remains, with an intricate 5-petalled flower pattern on its upper surface, and 2 slits for 'eyes'. The pansy shell reveals that radial, 5-armed structure that associates these marine organisms with sea stars.

The back of the so-called shell is equally pretty; and being the unofficial logo of Knysna and Plett has undoubtedly contributed to its seriously depleted populations. NB: It is illegal to collect anything, including shells, in a national park; and most definitely illegal to collect pansy shells anywhere.

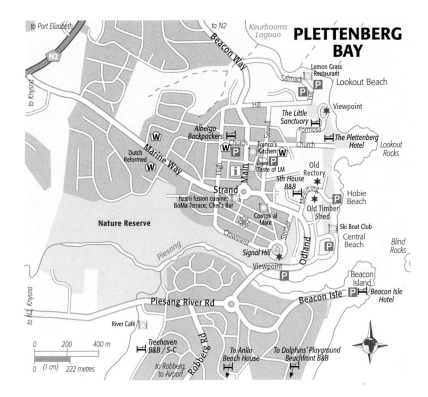

PLETTENBERG BAY

to Port Elizabeth
to N2
Keurbooms Lagoon
Beacon Way
N2
to Knysna
Lemon Grass Restaurant
Salmack
Lookout Beach
Viewpoint
The Little Sanctuary
Formosa
Albergo Backpackers
Church
Franco's Kitchen
Church
The Plettenberg Hotel
Lookout Rocks
Dutch Reformed
Marine Way
Taste of LM
Old Rectory
5th House B&B
Strand
fu.shi fusion cuisine; BoMa Terrace; Chef's Bar
Hobie Beach
Old Timber Shed
Nature Reserve
Cornuti al Mare
Crowsnest
Ski Boat Club
Central Beach
Blind Rocks
Piesang
Signal Hill
Viewpoint
Odland
Sinclair
Main
Sewell
Beacon Island
Piesang River Rd
Beacon Isle
Beacon Isle Hotel
to N2, Knysna
River Café
0   200   400 m
0   (1 cm)   222 metres
Treehaven B&B / S-C
Robberg Rd
To Anlin Beach House
To Dolphins' Playground Beachfront B&B
to Robberg, to Airport

ber and the indigenous forests around here were a welcome source.

By the mid 1800s, the timber trade had developed sufficiently to necessitate a pass into the interior, and Thomas Bain completed the Prince Alfred's Pass in 1868. He also built the 90 km of forest road through Tsitsikamma to Humansdorp that encompassed 3 major passes and took 16 years to complete (the Tsitsikamma Road, as it was then called).

The current site of the Beacon Isle Hotel was once a whaling station; with placid southern right whales – so named because they were the 'right' whales to harpoon as they floated once killed, and were rich in oil and baleen – being relentlessly harvested. Whaling operations ceased in 1916. Today, you can still view the original slipway and blubber cauldron, as well as a harpoon mounted in the hotel grounds. The first hotel was erected here in 1940, and replaced in 1972 with the current and well-known landmark.

Out and About in Plettenberg Bay

NB: See also the following areas:

West of Plettenberg: Harkerville and Kranshoek – see page 188.

North of Plettenberg: Wittedrift – see page 192.

East of Plettenberg: Keurbooms River and Keurboomstrand – see page 193.

The 'whale tail' lookout point off Formosa Street above the Baia Formosa: a near perfect bay with a most appealing aspect of the Tsitsikamma mountains. Paradise for a chosen few.

Plett **beaches** are world famous to those who travel in search of the most glorious spots to tuck their toes into the sand. What they lack in tropical-beach assets such as palm trees, they more than make up for in length (around 15 km altogether), cleanliness, visits by dolphins and views. The most frequented beach is **Central Beach**, also commonly referred to as **Main Beach**. This is the one at the centre of the bay, north of the Beacon Isle Hotel, and it's reached by travelling down the hill from town (on Odland Drive) and turning left into a large car park. It's here you'd go over the Christmas holidays if you're keen to squeeze through the oiled bodies and flash your designer bikini and sunglasses. Out of season it's a delight, with only a few colourful brollies, no queues at the nearby kiosks and restaurants, and it's the place to spend time watching the comings and goings of the fishing boats that launch from here. Between here and the Lookout Rocks (a small outcrop) to the north, lies **Hobie Beach**. These 2 beaches are often thought to be 1, as they're both short stretches of sand that adjoin. Hobie Beach is reached either by crossing the invisible line from Central Beach, or by turning into Meeding Street, which leads you past the Old Timber Store and down to a small parking area. Its name is derived from the line of hobie cats that are usually parked here, and in the right conditions, it sees much sail action. The bay is excellent for sailing, and sailboats may launch off Hobie Beach.

Further north of Central Beach, things get a bit tricky. This is where **Lookout**

Beach once was, but major flooding in 2006 drastically changed the beach, which was then swallowed up during a big storm in March. Today, there's virtually no Lookout Beach because the mouth of the Keurbooms River lagoon is in its place. This used to be the main surfing beach.

Robberg Beach stretches from the Beacon Isle Hotel roughly 4,5 km southwards to the Robberg Peninsula, and offers sun lizards ample space to bake. There are sections where lifeguards are on duty, so it's best to stick to those if you're planning to get into deep water; if you're more of a paddler-in-the-shallows type, then you can dip your toes in anywhere. There are several accesses to the beach but only a few small parking areas along Beachy Head Drive, which is the residential road running parallel with the beach and also known as Millionaire's Row because of the elaborate holiday houses. In summer parking could be a problem, so get there early. This beach is working towards full Blue Flag accreditation, and hopefully will have achieved it by the time you read this. South Africa was the first country outside Europe to win Blue Flag accreditation for some of its beaches. This status assures the public that the beach is clean, safe and environmentally friendly, and aims at educating the community about the need to care for the coastline.

Keurbooms River lagoon is right on the edge of town, and not to be confused with Keurboomstrand, which is about 12 km east of Plett. It's formed by the combined Bitou and Keurbooms rivers, which culminate in an estuarine lagoon. It's a magical, mostly protected body of water ideal for swimming, wind watersports, and boating. There's a beach here, and the shallow water is ideal for kids. Take the main street, heading east down the hill, near the bottom of the hill turn right into Cupid and follow this road to the end where there's limited parking, and easy access to this beach. From this beach, it's just a few short kays up to the bridge where the N2 crosses the Keurbooms River itself. The lagoon opens into the sea and is tidal, whereas upriver the water is dark brown river-fed. See page 193 for further info on Keurbooms River.

Dolphin- and whale-watching can be enjoyed from the shore, but there are a number of operators you can go out to sea with, and boat trips leave at scheduled times on a daily basis. As there are no harbour facilities in Plett, the operators have a unique way of launching their boats – go and see for yourself. Getting the boat out of the sea is equally exciting as they power it through the surf to beach it (locally it's taken for granted, but visitors often

With old favourite Lookout strand washed away, Robberg has become Plett's beach of choice.

stare agape when first they see it: unlike some other places, South Africa generally does not over-pamper people).

With regards to whale-watching, some Bryde's (pronounced 'broodies') whales are resident off the coast all year round, while others migrate; southern right whale season is June–November; and humpback whales are migratory but mostly seen in the area in June–July, and again in Nov–Dec. Orcas are sometimes seen, any time of the year. When you really start to get into the nitty gritty of the incredible marine life around here, you'll discover, for instance, that this is the only place in the world where scientists have seen and filmed the rare tropical beaked whale. Licensed boats will approach whales but must stop within their specified distance (they may not approach closer than 300 m unless they have a special licence). Then they will sit and wait for the whales to approach them, which (more than often) happens so there's a good chance you'll have a close encounter.

Ocean Blue offers 2 types of boat trips, both lasting 1,5–2 hours (children younger than 3 go free). Their Standard Encounter runs year round, departing at set times and costing R400 an adult, and R200 a child under 12. The other is their Close Encounter trip that runs from July–Dec, in which you get within 50 m of whales; this costs R650 an adult and R350 a child under 12. If you're conservation minded you'll be pleased to know they're actively engaged in a large conservation programme, and they also have a programme that involves the local black community from informal settlements. For further

info, tel 044-533-5083 or 083-701-3583, e-mail info@oceanadventures.co.za or web www.oceanadventures.co.za.

Ocean Safaris conducts trips lasting 1,5–2 hours with 1 boat legally permitted to approach whales within 50 m, as opposed to the regulation 300 m. Trips cost R400 (discovery), and R650 (close-encounter) an adult, with children under 3 for free on the discovery trip, and roughly half price on the close-encounter trip. To check daily departure times tel 044-533-4963 or 082-784-5729, e-mail info@oceansafaris.co.za or visit www.oceansafaris.co.za.

Dolphin Adventures is a specialist company offering sea kayak trips on boats that are adapted for ocean paddling. Even if you're not experienced, these are extra-stable kayaks. Although we've never done one of these trips,

Old hippies never die, they reincarnate at the Global Village market in the Piesang Valley.

we've been told that dolphins will approach you, and you may see small fish jumping nearby, and be entertained by playful seals. Trips are 2 hours and cost R250/p (R150 for children under 16), and leave at 09h00, 12h00 and 15h00 in summer. For further info, tel 083-590-3405, e-mail kayak@dolphin-adventures.co.za or web www.dolphin-adventures.co.za.

There's great **fishing** around Plett, starting with the beaches as described above, plus the Robberg Peninsula and, heading east, rock angling at Keurboomstrand. Rock anglers can catch elf (shad), roman, galjoen and steenbras. Permits are essential, also for bait collecting, and obtainable from the post office. No bait collecting is allowed around Robberg Peninsula, as it is a protected nature reserve (see Calls to the Wild section); most food stores also stock bait, and ice. If you'd like to take a **deep sea fishing charter**, there are also several companies that offer this; try **Plett Fishing Charters**, owned by Graeme Pollard. Trips last 5 hours and are fully equipped. The boat launches off Central Beach between 06h00–07h30, depending on season and takes about 25 minutes to reach the fishing grounds. You may catch Cape salmon or cob in summer, and hake or red roman in winter, and you can keep the fish you catch. NB: Bag limitations apply. For further info tel 083-324-6331, or look at their website www.deep-seafishing.co.za.

Scuba diving can be good in and around Plett, and there is a good selection of sites like Redbait Reef, Deep Blinders, Shallow Blinders, Groot Bank and Jacob's Poort. Depending on where you dive, you should see soft corals, nudibranchs, game fish, sponges, a range of butterfly fish (chaetodons) and sharks (mostly ragged-tooth). It's best to join a guided dive with a local dive company like **Pro Dive**. They're based in the Beacon Isle Hotel and offer both shore and boat dives, and dive courses – in fact, 1 of the shore dives is straight off the private beach in front of the hotel. Shore dives cost from R100/p, and boat dives from R200/p. Give them a call on 044-533-1158, e-mail plett@pro-dive.co.za or visit www.prodive.co.za.

Surfing spots are many. Lookout Beach and its surfing conditions changed drastically in 2006/7, but there are still some surfing opportunities closer to the river mouth. The Wedge is a spot within sight of the Beacon Isle Hotel but near the rocky outcrop to the north. Under the right conditions it offers a short barrel. Keurbooms is a firm favourite, altho' the brus tune you gotta be patient, man. When it's good, it has glassy tubes and crystal water. A highlight here is the school of bottle-nose dolphins that are often around. A lowlight is it can be sharky.

Another way to enjoy the water, without necessarily getting into it, is to walk along some of the 4 km-long peninsula of **Robberg Nature Reserve**. Refer to Calls to the Wild on page 22. Eden Adventures has been awarded the tender for **abseiling on Robberg** – see the Wilderness section for their details.

To get an overall feeling for this spectacular section of coastline from the air, **Skydive Plettenberg Bay** offers tandem skydiving that requires no experi-

Wooden boardwalks take walkers through sensitive floral sections of the Robberg Peninsula, a nature reserve run by Cape Nature with a particularly high conservation status.

ence and only 10 minutes of instruction. Once in the air, you can enjoy a 20-minute scenic flight up to 10 000 feet and then the adrenaline starts to pump as you exit the plane with your tandem master and experience the rush of a 35-second freefall at 220 kph before the chute jerks opens and you glide gently down to earth. They operate from Plett airport, and if conditions are right they'll jump all day, every day, as this is 1 of the busiest drop zones in the country. What we really love about them is that they plant trees to offset their carbon emissions, thereby reducing their carbon footprint created by their need to burn fossil fuel. Jumps cost from R1 600/p, and if you want a DVD of your jump it's R400 for the cameraman. To book, tel Tim on 082-905-7440, e-mail info@skydiveplett.com or web www.skydiveplett.com.

When all the water- and beach-based activities pale, head to **Old Nick Village**, a famous Plett landmark on the left on the N2 just beyond the bottom (east) entrance to the town. The building that the Old Nick Shop is situated in today was a farm trading store built in 1880, which closed only in the 1960s when the local population moved away to a newly built area. The Old Nick Shop sells ceramics and textiles made on the premises, and other shops and galleries showcase South African crafts that include weaving, pottery, clothing, soaps, jewellery and mosaics. At one point, an Englishman ran an antique shop in the old gaol on this farm, and called it Old Nick in the slang of his home country – a name that's stuck ever since. There's a **weaving museum** that houses 19th-century power looms on the property, and the buildings are set in lovely gardens that are great for children to stretch their legs in.

While they burn off some energy, parents can top up theirs at **São Gonçalo's Kitchen**, which is open for breakfast, tea and lunch and offers Portuguese flavours and a great bakery. To book a table in busy times, tel 044-533-6016. For further info on the village, web www.oldnickvillage.co.za.

If you're keen to see what's inside that giant wedding cake, the **Beacon Isle Hotel** is open to the public if you'd like to go and have a drink, a meal in one of their restaurants or tea in the lounge. It also has a lovely little shop called **Gecko** that stocks Plett gifts and really magical hand-painted T-shirts by a local artist, Kelly Naudé.

If you enjoy history you'll be interested in the ruins of **The Timber Store** at the bottom of Meeding Street. After governor Van Plettenberg's visit here in 1778, he recommended that timber from the local forests be exported from this 'port', but the trees had a 9 year reprieve before cutting began in earnest. The Dutch East India Company commissioned a man called Jerling in 1787 to build a timber store, and the following year the first load of timber was floated out to sea and loaded onto a ship. Much of the timber store's walls, windows and lintels remain today and, evidently, a renowned Dutch historian stated that it is '1 of the most exciting historical remnants in the whole of South Africa'.

Whatever you do, don't miss the **Knysna Elephant Park** – see under Harkerville on page 188.

Golf addicts will enjoy Plett's own course at the **Plettenberg Bay Country Club** in Piesang Valley. For details tel 044-533-2132. Alternatively, there's the Gary Player-designed **Goose Valley Golf Club**, a short drive east of Plett just off the N2. They offer luxury accommodation near to and on the course, tel 044-533-5082.

The other way to pursue a white ball is from the back of a horse, and in recent years Plett has become known for its private polo estates. **Kurland Estate** is said to offer state-of-the-art facilities, and hosts international test matches. Members of the public are welcome to attend polo matches at any of the venues in Plett; entry is free so just grab your picnic, straw sun hat and head out there. Practice chukkas start mid-August and matches take place between December and April. It's a great day out, even if you don't know the game well, and you'll be called onto the field to replace the divots, which is jolly good sport, what. For summer fixtures, have a look at the Plett Polo website www.plettpolo.com.

Antique shop, farm stall and now craft shop, but never a goal – that's Old Nick on the N2.

The Robberg is deceptively big, so this signpost at The Gap is not just for decoration.

While in Plett, if you've had a bit too much to drink, or don't feel like driving, try **Vogue Cabs** tel 078-906-6677.

Overnight in Plettenberg Bay Central
SILK

If you're very picky about where you stay and like to treat yourself to the very best, make a beeline for **The Plettenberg Hotel**, perched on a headland overlooking the coastline. This 5-star establishment is a member of the exclusive Relais and Chateaux accommodation collection and they will pamper you and cater to your every whim with dedicated professionalism. They have air-conditioned rooms and suites aplenty, a terrace from which to spot whales and dolphins while sipping your pink gin, and if the surf is a bit rough for you there are 2 swimming pools, 1 of which is heated. B&B rates for doubles range from R2 250–R3 500 a unit, and suites are R4 000–R8 000 a unit. Go on, spoil yourself and call 044-533-2030,

e-mail plettenberg@relaischateaux.com or web www.collectionmcgrath.com.

LINEN

Treehaven is a 3-star **self-catering** or **B&B** establishment at nos 45 & 47 Hanois Crescent that overlooks the Piesang valley and is just a few minutes from town and the beaches. They offer 3 fully equipped units. Beneath the main house the studio apartment has a private entrance and big windows with sliding doors opening onto a deck fronted by indigenous trees. It sleeps 2 and has a full kitchen, SABC TV and DVD player. On the adjacent property are 2 units each sleeping 4, with SABC TV and private patio. These 2 units can be combined to accommodate groups of up to 8. The establishment is perched on a steep slope of thickly wooded indigenous garden that instils an atmosphere of tranquillity and hosts numerous birds, including a nesting pair of Knysna turacos. This will appeal to folks who enjoy quiet moments with the binos and bird book. The owners, Feo and Carol Sachs, live next door and will arrange birding tours. Children are welcome. Unit rates are R550–R800 for the studio, and R800–R1 700 for the larger units next door. Tel 044-533-1989 or 082-798-7907, e-mail info@treehavenholidays.co.za or visit www.treehavenholidays.co.za.

The Little Sanctuary at 14 Formosa Street, near what's known as the 'Whale Tail lookout', has gorgeous views across what's left of Lookout Beach, the Keurbooms lagoon and the Tsitsikamma mountains. The house is hired on a self-catering basis and can accommodate 10 in 3 purpose-designed en-suite rooms in the main house and 2 in a separate cottage. Facilities include a swimming pool; and it's within walking distance of the busy main street up the hill. It's suitable for a large family or group of friends. Rates are R1 500–R3 100 for the unit depending on season and there's a minimum stay rule ranging from 3 to 7 nights. Call Sonja van Rensburg on 044-533-1344, 082-775-8157, e-mail tlsatplett@telkomsa.net or web www.littlesanctuary.co.za.

5th House B&B at 4 Meeding Street carries a 3-star grading and is located in the 5th house ever built in Plett. The walls are half a metre thick and there's lots of the original sandstone still to be seen. It's situated on the hill above the main beaches, just a 3-min walk from Hobie Beach and they offer 3 en-suite rooms, 1 of which can be combined with a 4th to make a family unit. If you're after value for money,

this establishment is pleasant, clean, crisp and close to the beach. There's also a large deck to recline on out front and the views across the bay from the elevated position are mesmerising. B&B rates are R300–R600/ps depending on season. Contact the friendly owners, Daphne and Charl, on tel 044-533-3180, e-mail info@5thhouse.co.za or web www.5thhouse.co.za.

The 4-star **Sunshowers Guesthouse** is situated at 15 Susan Street in the Poortjies area near the shore of the Keurbooms lagoon. This modern establishment offers B&B in 2 en-suite doubles, and an upstairs luxury suite with great lagoon views; and there's a self-catering family unit downstairs. The luxury unit is worthy of a honeymoon stay-over and includes a spa-bath and large private balcony. All rooms have patios and are equipped with tea/coffee making facilities, TV and fridge. The communal lounge and dining room are

It's been called a giant wedding cake and a mutant barnacle, but the Beacon Isle Hotel has a spectacular setting on a small island that was once a whaling station.

on the 1st floor surrounded by large glass windows; and there's an indoor braai for the use of the guests. The beach and calm waters of the lagoon are a frisbee throw away making it great for families, or those who like a quick dip before breakfast. Rates for the B&B rooms are R220–R420/ps in low season and R300–R650 in high season. The self-catering unit costs R225–R360/ps. For further info, call Lindy on tel 082-575-0663, e-mail info@plettafrica.co.za or web www.plettafrica.co.za.

CALICO

Albergo for Backpackers is as close to the centre of town as you can get, at nos 6 & 8 Church Street, which is just off Plett's main street. Accommodation ranges from dorms to en-suite doubles and, even if you're not a backpacker, it's a good place to choose if your budget is limited and you don't mind sharing a communal kitchen. Facilities include hammocks in the garden, an honesty bar and pool that's set away from rooms, and they have bonfires at night. At their internet café there's ADSL and they'll put photos onto disc for you. They offer the usual backpacker services, are a Baz Bus agent, and have a One Stop Action Shop where you can book activities and shuttles. Dorms cost R120/p, doubles from R300, camping R75/p. Look out for their winter discount specials. Give Leslie and Mirjam a call on tel 044-533-4434, e-mail info@albergo.co.za or web www.albergo.co.za.

CALICO & CANVAS

Keurbooms Lagoon Caravan Park, 2 km east of town along the N2 – oppo-

site the landmark, Old Nick – is set in a stand of blue gums on the shore of Keurbooms lagoon. It has 270 sites, 32 of which are located on the edge of the lagoon, and the others are just a stone's throw away. This location is ideal for watersports enthusiasts, and families with young children who can frolic on the soft beach sand and splash around in the calm waters that are just a stroll from your campsite. All sites are grassed and have electrical points, there are ample ablution blocks and the park has all the facilities you'd expect, plus stuff for the kids, and canoe and boat hire. Rates are from R80/p in low season to R220 a site for 2 people in mid-season, and R500 a site for up to 4 people in high season. Tel 044-533-2567, e-mail info@keurboomslagoon.co.za or web www.keurboomslagoon.co.za.

Robberg Beach Area
LINEN

Dolphins' Playground Beachfront B&B is at 3 Tillamook Ave off the far end of Beachhead Road. With little passing traffic and the beach just 50 m away, it's the place for a quiet getaway with romantic strolls and cooling dips. It's owner-run by Pam Meara, whose warmth and friendliness immediately put you at ease. The rooms and large deck face Robberg Beach and once you've wiped the sleep from your eyes, the bay and distant mountains are there to usher in each new day. The 3 B&B rooms offer twin/king-size beds, full bathrooms, DStv and tea/coffee making facilities. If you like holidaying with the extended family or group of friends, the whole house can be hired on a self-

Time and tide do seem to stand still when you've got all the time in the world to enjoy the Keurbooms lagoon, part of the Plett holiday mecca for many generations.

catering basis taking the total number of bedrooms to 5. While munching your muesli on the breakfast deck, there's a good chance of spotting dolphins and whales, and the view may entice you to linger until lunchtime. It's not officially graded but is easily 4-star quality and good value with B&B rates R295–R345/ps in low season and R445–R595 high season. Rates for the whole house on request. Have a chat with Pam on tel 044-533-3654 or 083-613-0428, e-mail info@dolphinsplayground.co.za or web www.dolphinsplayground.co.za.

Also in the Robberg Beach area the 4-star **Anlin Beach House** at 33 Roche Bonne Ave offers self-catering options from garden suites to a family unit with 3 bedrooms on the 1st floor. The interiors are all decorated in modern contemporary style with quality fittings and attention to detail. Each has its own patio/balcony with sun-loungers and

they are neat, compact and comfortable and comprise a lounge/kitchenette, bathroom with shower, bedroom with king-size bed and a sleeper couch for a 3rd person. There's DStv and all the luxuries of a 4-star establishment. Continental breakfasts are delivered to your unit. It's just a 2-minute walk to the beach, and the hosts Dermot and Fran Molloy will supply beach towels, brollies, chairs or toys for the kids. Rates depend on season and are R395–R710/ps for the suites, and R1 800–R3 120 for 4–6 people in the family unit. For more details tel 044-533-3694, e-mail stay@anlinbeachhouse.co.za or web www.anlinplace.co.za.

Bitou River Area
SILK
Emily Moon is different enough to elevate it into the extra special category. The rooms and restaurant overlook

the meandering Bitou River below, and distant Tsitsikamma mountains. The Valentine family has created a time warp back to the era when explorers ventured into the unknown lands of the east and the depths of the 'dark continent' to barter for exotic treasures. Accommodation consists of 8 en-suite units – 7 doubles and 1 family unit – most with king-size beds. All have a fireplace, DStv, tea/coffee station, mini bar, fans/heaters, full bathroom with underfloor heating, private entrances and a laundry service. Some have outdoor showers on the deck while others have baths inside large picture windows.

Listen for the *craaacking* wake-up call of the resident blue cranes in the

Just a short drift inland of the bustle of Plett is the bucolic Bitou River valley.

valley, spend soporific afternoons gazing at the great views from your private deck and then stay put for the decadent sunsets across the valley filled with liquid light. They offer mountain bikes and canoes for the energetic. Although you're not obliged to eat in their restaurant, make a point of doing so at least 1 night – it's part of the experience. Even the view of the valley comes second to the ambience of **Emily's** (see Eating Out in Plett), especially at night when lanterns, fires, candles and fairy lights lift it to an enchanting level. To get there, turn off at Pennypinchers on the N2 a few km east of Plett, and follow the road to their driveway, which leads up the hill to the parking. B&B rates are R1 100 a lodge in low season, and R1 100 a person in high season. Tel 044-533-2982, e-mail info@emilymoon. co.za or web www.emilymoon.co.za.

LINEN

Across the Bitou River, 5 km east of Plett along the N2, the R340 leads off left to Wittedrift and Uniondale. A little over 1 km along this road, amongst the wetlands and abundant birdlife, stands **Moon River** self-catering apartments on the banks of the Bitou River estuary. The Garden Deck is an open-plan en-suite room sleeping 2 with a deck looking onto the garden, while the Top Deck is a first-floor unit sleeping 4 in 2 bedrooms with a deck overlooking the river. Both are fully equipped and have SABC TV. Moon River is owner-run by Mick and Wendy Jones who'll happily set you adrift on the lazy river in a canoe or point you in the direction of walks in the surrounding fields. Apparently fishing in the Bitou River is tremendous and the property's lawns make a comfortable spot to wait for that piscean strike, while for keen bird watchers the waders push species numbers up. The units are reasonably priced at R240–R330/ps. Tel 044-535-9595, e-mail moonriver@telkomsa.net or web www.moonriver.co.za.

Eating Out in Plettenberg Bay

There are around 50 eateries in and around town, and the cuisine ranges from top class where you'll pay top euro, to take-aways. If you enjoy fish, we recommended you have at least 1 meal of locally caught fresh fish, preferably eaten overlooking the sea. If you don't enjoy fish, what are you doing so close to the water?

For a fine-dining experience, enhanced by a glorious bay view, head to the Upper Deck Lifestyle centre at the dolphin circle. This is where you'll find the award-wining **fu.shi fusion cuisine**, a restaurant that lives up to the meaning of its name, 'house of happiness'. The pan-Asian fare is the greatest source of happiness, however, its location adds greatly to this, without increasing prices too much. The serene interior is enhanced by a small fish tank that forms part of an interior wall, huge picture windows, and a stainless-steel-and-glass wine rack that displays a carefully structured wine list. When we ate there the chef dazzled us with a cornucopia of fine cuisine that included favourites such as tempura prawns, soft-shell crab, dragon rolls, dim sum and outstanding Thai green curry. Dishes are evocatively described using adjectives

such as 'bejewelled' and 'enchanted'; a highlight of the menu is the sushi, which comes in numerous combinations. Leave room for the wasabi crème brûlée, or 'concubine whisper' of chilli chocolate fondant with pistachio nut brittle. Open daily from 11h00–22h30. Tel 044-533-6497, e-mail info@fushi.co.za or web www.fushi.co.za.

Adjoining fu.shi is **BoMa Terrace** champagne and cocktail bar, which is a particular favourite for Sunday brunch al fresco. It's a spacious terrace overlooking the busy main street and bay. The Chef's Bar downstairs from fu.shi is an intimate late-night bistro that opens from 16h00 til late.

I hope we won't get into trouble with the locals for sharing the secret of **The River Café** with readers. This down-to-earth café is situated in a wooden cabin in Piesang Valley and is a favourite for breakfast and lunches. The location is very special, and if you enjoy bird watching, bring your binos because when the café is quiet you can see several species on the wee section of lily-covered Klein Piesang River that the deck overlooks. There's plenty of lawn for the kids to charge about on, just be aware of the swimming pools nearby and keep them away from the mulberry tree.

Owner-chef Kirsty Sinclair is known for her home-made mulberry jam that's made fresh from the tree each year. The café is fully licensed and in winter there's a crackling fire to snuggle around. It's tricky to find, so here are directions: from the traffic circle between the Piesang River Road and Longships/Odland, head into Piesang

Valley, pass the first road left (Robberg Road) and take next left to the water park, Wild Waters.

Turn right across the large car park and head into the corner, cross the model train lines, follow the sand road that curves up and right, squeeze through the gate and park under huge old pine trees. Open Tues–Sun 09h00–17h00. Tel 044-533-3815 or 083-459-4550.

DOLPHINS AND WHALES

Dolphins – common and bottlenose – can be seen all year round along the Garden Route coastline. They're particularly fond of surfing in the waves, and when the water visibility is good, this is an awesome sight to watch from the beach. Bryde's whales are rarely seen because they lie low in the water, are relatively sluggish and seldom come close to shore, but are not at all rare and occur along the coast year round. Humpback whales visit from April–January, on their annual migration cycle up the east African coast. Southern right whales are the real stars of the Cape's cetacean show, arriving from Antarctic waters in June to birth and breed, and returning south from November, with their numbers peaking around September. Since receiving international protection status in 1935, southern right whale numbers have vastly increased (from the brink of extinction) but it's still estimated only around 3000 (of the world's 7000-odd) visit our waters annually.

If it's value for money you're after, and al fresco dining in warmer months, head to **Rod 'n Reel**. Our most recent Saturday lunch we had there must be the best value-for-money meal we've ever had on the Garden Route. It's a straightforward family restaurant with tables in various rooms or outdoors on a deck that has views over the bay and lagoon. Directly below the deck is a large expanse of lawn for kids to play on. The extensive menu covers everything from breakfast to grills, and their fish and chips is excellent. To find it, coming from Knysna on the N2 – before you reach the main traffic circle into Plett – turn right onto the Piesang Valley Road. Almost immediately you'll see large gates on your left, and a sign for the restaurant, which is alongside the concrete fortification of Castleton Estate. Open daily from 08h00 until last supper orders, depending on the time of year. To book, tel 044-533-0165.

The elegant **Lemon Grass Restaurant** has one of the most idyllic locations in Plett, thanks to the phenomenal weather in 2006/7 that shifted the lagoon mouth. The result is that the Lemon Grass Restaurant is now perched on the edge of the channel and diners can sit on the terrace and spit their olive pips into the estuary mouth. The other joy of this location is that you can watch sea birds diving for food or tanning themselves on a sandbank across the waterway, and the frenetic activity of the fishers, while enjoying international cuisine. They're fully licensed and have a small cocktail bar. To book, tel 044-533-5520, e-mail info@milkwoodmanor.co.za or web milkwoodmanor.co.za.

Situated near the dolphin statue circle you'll find the Upper Deck Lifestyle Centre and fu.shi fusion cuisine restaurant– ground zero for fine dining in Plett … and more bay views.

The **Plett Ski Boat Club** is pretty basic but offers a square meal at a reasonable price in an awesome setting right on Central Beach. Their fish and chips is usually good, their beer's always cold, and if you're lucky you'll get to spot some watery entertainment in the form of boats launching and beaching, the moon rising over the sea, or even some gorgeous bodies gliding through the ocean (dolphins, that is). Be warned, this is a Plett locals' hangout; don't attempt to get through the door on Friday nights or when big games are televised. It's open from around 08h30–20h30 Mon–Sat and 08h30–15h00 Sun. You can't book, but if you want to check how busy they are you could call 044-533-4147.

There are usually several pizzerias in Plett, and one that's been around for years is **Cornuti al Mare**. It's perched on the hill just off Odland Road (the main road down to the sea) and offers sweeping vistas over the bay that are best enjoyed from their deck. The food is usually good, and the pizza often great, but it's a bit pricey. As with most good pizza places these days, their selection of toppings is inspired, and their bases are very thin. The pasta is authentic Italian fare and if they still have the vongole (clam) sauce, give it a try as you don't find this dish on too many menus. They also have a cocktail bar if you want to rub shoulders with the polo set. Be warned, this place gets seriously packed in season. To book tel 044-533-1277.

Franko's Kitchen is our other pizza place of choice, based on price, which is very reasonable. It's in the main street next to the Caltex garage – but don't let its proximity to a garage put you off.

Dining is in a modern, uncluttered setting with large picture windows offering a view of the bay over the roofs of the residential area. They also do other light eats at lunchtime and a variety of fresh dishes, grills and seafood for dinners; tel 044-533-3693.

Taste of LM in Plett's main street has a loyal local following and an atmosphere that's both rustic and sophisticated. Walls are clad with rough wooden *latte* (rough staves) and adorned with photos depicting scenes from Mozambique. The food is Mozambican, which is a combination of Portuguese, Indian and African fare – some dishes come with lashings of fiery peri-peri and, according to the regulars, it's a great evening out; tel 044-533-1420.

If you're after a dining experience, rather than just a meal in a restaurant, **Emily's** should appeal to you as much as it does to us. It's a fabulously exotic restaurant at the **Emily Moon River Lodge** just 3,5 km east of Plett. It's not specifically a fine dining restaurant, although they have their finer points. Rather, it offers an escapist ambience, with décor that speaks reams about Africa, including collector's pieces, crisp table settings and an awesome view from their elevated position high above the Bitou River. Start with a drink on the deck as the sun sets or, if you're there for lunch, sit outside beneath big brollies in the adjoining courtyard. The latter offers live entertainment in the form of birds bathing in the water feature above the swimming pool, and you'll get good sightings of various species as they hang around the feeders in nearby trees. The eclectic menu utilises international flavours that inspire and elevate simple dishes. The menu changes regularly and, in quieter times during winter, there's a set menu and crackling fire around which to sip after-dinner liqueurs. They're popular so it's best

What, here! With its genteel atmosphere, it's sometimes hard to remember that the area is very much a part of Africa and that wild elephants once roamed here: the Knysna Elephant Park.

Plett represents the easy life for many wealthy holiday home-owners: little has changed in that respect for 100 000 years, since Stone Age beachcombers found an easy life hereabouts.

to book. Open Tue–Sun 12h00–15h00, Mon–Sun from 18h00. Tel 044-533-2982, e-mail info@emilymoon.co.za or visit www.emilymoon.co.za.

Drinking and Nightlife in Plett

When in Plett you don't want to sit in a poky pub or smoky joint when you can salute the sunset overlooking this incredible bay and its beaches. If cocktails and poncy chit chat appeal, head to **Cornuti's, BoMa Terrace** or the sophisticated **Sandbar** in the posh Plettenberg Hotel where the polo set preen. If you want to have salt air with your Sauvignon Blanc, sidle down to the **Lookout Deck** on the remains of Lookout Beach; or slink into **Beacon Island Hotel's** surrounds with its lounge that hangs over the sea. Movers and shakers should mosey along to **Moby Dick's**, where many meet mates amongst the seafaring paraphernalia. It has a fabulous location right on Central Beach. Nightlife venues

come and go: at the time of writing **Flashbacks**, in the main street, was the place to groove. They call themselves a 'pub, lounge and kitchen' and the latter serves pizza. This is the place to come for gigs, parties and regular sports events shown on 3 screens. For more info visit www.flashbacks.co.za.

West of Plett along the N2

The first noteworthy stop heading from Plett to Knysna along the N2 is **The Heath**. This collection of rustic buildings, tucked in the shade of big old pine trees, offers crafts, furniture, clothes, a play area for kids, a labyrinth and a restaurant. For us, the highlight is **Eagle Encounters** run by Dennis and Janet Robson. It's a rehabilitation centre that aims at community awareness, and the rescue-rehabilitate-release of birds of prey. As this is a non-profit organisation, they use the necessary exercising and training of birds as an opportunity to share with tourists in the form of an interactive flying display. Don't miss this. You'll be amazed by demonstrations, and the speeds raptors can achieve. A number of species are exercised during each display, our favourite being the handsome owls, and you can have a hands-on experience. A day pass costs R40 an adult, R20 a child. Fees charged help to support the centre, and the 45-min shows are held daily at 13h00 and 15h00, with an extra show at 11h00 over weekends and public holidays. For further info tel 044-532-7537, e-mail janet@eagle-encounters.co.za or web www.eagle-encounters.co.za.

West of Plett – Harkerville

Harkerville is a rural area of farms, smallholdings and a forest reserve that lies about 10 km west of Plett along the N2 towards Knysna.

NB: For info on the **Garden of Eden**, see under Knysna on page 140.

The surrounding indigenous forests are well known for their mysterious Knysna elephants, and it is these elusive mammals that inspired the **Knysna Elephant Park**. The park lies 9 km from Plett, and if you want to be 'touched by an elephant' as their logo states, you're going to love this experience. First, though, it's important to understand that this is not a circus-elephant type of set up. The park is also not simply a tourist attraction; quite the contrary: it's a project that provides welfare to a number of elephants that have special needs for various reasons, and the aim is to rehabilitate these animals to a sufficient degree that will allow them to be re-released. Those that cannot be

released are given a very comfortable home here. It's a controlled free-range environment and management system that allows the breeding herd to roam freely over the 60-hectares, and only interact with visitors on their – the elephants'– terms.

Lucky for us humans, the elies are keen to interact, and there are jumbos big and small to feed and stroke or just take a stroll with. The herd currently numbers 10 individuals and while it's not the Kruger National Park, they seem happy with their 60 ha of relative freedom. Tours to where the elephants are grazing leave the reception every half hour from 08h30–16h30 daily and a day pass costs from R160/p. For those with fatter wallets there are 2-hour elephant-back safaris during the day R620/p and sunrise and sunset safaris, costing from R980/p. Not only is the experience of being in such proximity to these incredible creatures food for the soul, but you'll also acquire information that will add value to your next visit to a national park, starting at the informative visitors' centre. It's easy to spend the whole day here; you can enjoy a leisurely breakfast or lunch at the restaurant, and visit the curio shop. Better still, spend several days in their unique accommodation – see Overnight in Harkerville starting on page 190. For further info tel 044-532-7732, e-mail info@knysnaelephantpark.co.za or web www.knysnaelephantpark.co.za.

A kilometre closer to Plett is **Adventure Land** where kids can frolic away the hours 7 days a week from 10h00–17h00. Fun includes a water slide, play park and quad bike trails.

The Heath is one of several of what can best be described as Garden Route 'eco-village-markets'; you can stop to browse and also here visit the Eagle Encounters raptor centre.

To get your farmer's market fix, head to **Harvest Time Market** alongside the N2, 12 km from Plett. It's open every Saturday from 08h00–12h00 and has around 40 stalls selling fresh produce, arts, crafts and curiosities. The highlight for many is the hearty breakfast bought from a stall that advertises the huge quantities of eggs, bacon and other ingredients they've cooked since opening this stand years ago. The atmosphere is jovial and friendly, as locals and visitors interact, eat and drink around the central tables and seating area.

The Harkerville area offers 4 circular **mountain bike trails** that are recommended by local cyclists. All start and finish at the Garden of Eden on the N2, where permits must be obtained; distances range from 12–24 km and from gentle to technical. Routes include some gravel road, forest slip-paths and

sections through forest. One passes by a glade of coastal redwood trees that were planted in 1927; another leads to a shaded swimming hole; the 24 km red route is one of the most scenically diverse in the country. It is tough if you're not a fit rider, and takes 3–5 hours. It encompasses long stretches of off-road riding and inlcudes a section of coastal fynbos near the sea-cliff tops. For further information about these trails, contact Knysna Cycle Works on 044-382-5153, e-mail freejacq@mweb.co.za or web www.knysnacycles.co.za.

The **Harkerville Hiking Trail** is a 24 km, 2-day circular trail that is aimed at fit hikers that don't have a fear of heights. It begins and starts and ends at the Harkerville forest station where the main trail hut is located. The first day covers 15 km and takes roughly 7 hours. It meanders through indigenous forest,

Looking down onto The Island and Nelson's Bay on Robberg is a time-travel experience, because this is where Strandlopers lived for millennia before the arrival of 'new' people.

along to the cliff top, and then a very steep climb down to the rugged coastline. The next 4 km along the shore is slow going due to loose, boulder beach, then it's up, up, up to the cliff top again to reach the overnight hut. This last part is a steep ascent that could give you vertigo. After following the cliff edge, you'll turn inland to Sinclair hut, which overlooks the coast. The hut sleeps 12, and is equipped with bunk beds and mattresses, a veld toilet and plenty of firewood.

The second day follows the cliff edge for about 2 km, then another steep descent using chains, and a chain ladder brings you to the sea. Some 5 km later it's up the cliff again, then inland through the forest and you're back at the forest station. To book the huts or get further info tel 044-302-5606, e-mail cathyv@sanparks.org or visit www.sanparks.org.

Overnight in Harkerville
LINEN

The Elephant Lodge offers a unique experience to lovers of wildlife, and specifically elephants. The 6 luxurious rooms have access to an elevated central lounge that opens onto the elephants' sleeping quarters. This means that a privileged few get to enjoy a drink in comfort while watching the elies settle down for the night. If there are bottle-fed babies, you'll have the opportunity to nip downstairs and help feed them; then, when you go to bed, you can almost hear them snore. Or, you could follow the example of guests who have spent the night on the lounge couches in order to maximise their time near the elephants. Depending on the room you choose, rates are from R600–R1 200/p for room only. The best option is the room with a spa-bath and window overlooking elephants' sleeping quarters. To book, tel 044-532-7732, e-mail info@knysnaelephantpark.co.za or visit www.knysnaelephantpark.co.za.

Eden's Touch is located halfway between Knysna and Plett, 4 km along the Fisanthoek road. It will appeal to those who want to spend time in a tranquil, natural setting without skimping on comfort. The 7 wooden self-catering chalets are on an 85 ha farm covered in fynbos and indigenous forest. Each chalet has a private splash pool, DStv, covered entertainment area and private braai, and some even have views from the bath. A nice touch is that all the furniture and fittings have been handmade by members of the local community. There are various hiking and mountain biking trails, good birdlife, and horse riding with the nearby Southern Comfort horse farm. Take a picnic and a slow stroll through the forest to a shady spot or babbling brook. Rates range from R520 a night in low season for a 1-bedroom cottage to R2 350 a night in peak season for a 3-bedroom chalet that sleeps 8. To book, tel Shirley on 083-253-6366, e-mail info@edenstouch.co.za or web www.edenstouch.co.za.

The 4-star **Tree Top Forest Chalet** is situated in the Harkerville forest along the road that leads to Kranshoek. It's well equipped and has DStv, although why you'd want to watch TV in this pristine environment is beyond us. The large viewing deck overlooks a wide valley, and facilities include 2 en-suite bedrooms, and spacious living quarters. It's ideally located to enjoy nearby mountain bike and hiking trails, or just enjoy the embrace of the forest. Rates are from R875 for 2, plus R200 an additional person self-catering. Winter rates are lower, while in December holidays you'll pay more. Tel 044-302-5606, e-mail cathyv@sanparks.org or web www.sanparks.org.

West of Plett – Kranshoek

Kranshoek is a forested area in the Harkerville region. The turn-off lies about 12 km from Plett when travelling west along the N2, and is at the Harkerville garage and shops. Follow the gravel road past smallholdings, then stop at the boom where you'll obtain a self-issue permit. You then enter the indigenous forest and travel through a tunnel of trees (where you might spot your cousins, Bob and Jaan) before arriving at the main picnic area. From here, there's a 100 m signposted walk along the top of the gorge, and a point where you can look back and see a small **waterfall**. The **Kranshoek Coastal Walk** also starts at this main picnic area; and if you follow the road towards the coast you'll reach the **Kranshoek viewsite** on the edge of a very steep forest-covered drop down to the sea far, far below. There must be excellent fishing down there, but you'd not want to carry a good catch back up this cliff. Keen birders should keep a lookout in the fynbos between the picnic area and viewsite. In winter, Cape sugarbirds are visible displaying over the proteas, and orange-breasted sunbirds occur here, as well as a veritable scattering of avian jewels that could include amethyst, southern double-collared, greater double-collared and malachite sunbirds.

The spectacular 9 km circular **Kranshoek Coastal Walk** covers a section of the Harkerville coastline, but should not be confused with the Harkerville 2-day coastal trail (see under Harkerville). The Kranshoek walk mirrors much of what's to be seen on the Harkerville Trail, but should not be underestimated, especially in hot weather. Descents and ascents are 200 m and extremely steep. The terrain varies from cliff-top scenery and fynbos, down lots of steps into a gorge, and includes rocky and boulder-strewn shoreline, forested valleys and waterfalls; and some of the trail is slippery in wet weather. Information boards along the route inform hikers about aspects of the environment. Keep a lookout for birds, and carry plenty of drinking water. If you want to stay overnight, SANParks has a tree-top forest chalet

nearby (but not on the trail). A shorter, 3 km, loop of the above walk can also be taken. Tel 044-302-5606, e-mail cathyv@sanparks.org or web www.sanparks.org. See aforementioned tree-top cabin listed under Harkerville.

North of Plett – Wittedrif

When those perfect days spent lolling on the soft sand and frolicking in the lapping surf get a little too much and you desire a change of routine, head for **Buffalo Hills** for an African adventure. Take the N2 east of Plett for 4 km, turn left onto the R340 to Wittedrif, 4 km later turn left again towards the settlement of Wittedrif, after 1 km turn right onto Stofpad. The reserve is well signposted on the R340. Buffalo Hills offers a range of activities for **day visitors**, plus fully catered accommodation.

Day visitors can expect **game drives**

If you go hiking on the Garden Route today, you might be in for the kind of surprise that you'll find when you park your toes over the edge of Kranshoek, on the Harkerville Trail.

and **game walks** with optional breakfast, lunch or dinner as part of the deal and priced accordingly from R250–R650, children under 12 half price. If you have a few extra buffalos (R100 notes) we recommend the **half-day safari** that starts in the freshness of early morning with coffee and rusks, then a fascinating guided walk, followed by a hearty breakfast. Next comes a 2-hour game drive, a visit to the mampoer distillery, and it culminates with lunch. Then you'll probably head back to the sea wishing you'd booked into one of their safari tents. They also have mountain biking and trail running products, plus birding and horse riding options.

If you're interested in the production of *witblits* (moonshine), this is where the **Nyati Mampoer** distillery is located and a quick tour and free tasting is offered between 09h00 and 15h00.

Overnight North of Plett
LINEN

Buffalo Hills accommodation is either in a **lodge** or **luxury tented camp**. The lodge offers 4 en-suite bedrooms and a communal dining room, pub and lounge beckon those who want to socialise. Alongside, the cottage has 2 double rooms, lounge and a separate bathroom. There's also a swimming pool, and a boma for drinks and meals. On the other side of the riverbed, the 9 en-suite tents offer a colonial-feel safari experience. Beds are twin or king-size, all have a private deck, and 6 have spa-baths with views of the forest through big picture windows. All meals are served at the lodge; and rates include a daily game walk and drive. The game

viewing here is guaranteed and you'll get close to impala, wildebeest, eland, zebra and giraffe, plus other antelope on the open pastures of what used to be a dairy farm; and there are 150 bird species. The owners, Tony and Maria Kinahan, are hands-on hosts who will ensure you have a wonderful stay. Ask them about their 'kids go free' and other specials. This is also a popular wedding venue. Dinner, B&B rates are from R950/ps. Tel 044-535-9739 or 082-771-9370, e-mail buffalohills@mweb.co.za or web www.buffalohills.co.za.

East of Plett –
Keurbooms River

The name 'keurboom' comes from the keurboom tree (*Virgilia oroboides*) that has pretty purple flowers in summer and is typically found around forest edges and river banks in the fynbos biome. The Keurbooms River flows for about 60 km, and 12 km of it is navigable by boat – although the top 2 km is reserved for canoes only.

Keurbooms River Ferries offer trips up the river through the gorge of the unspoilt Keurbooms Nature Reserve. It's a special way to spend a few hours. Take a picnic lunch and grab a seat for a gentle cruise 5 km up the river. Your guide will tell you all sorts of interesting facts about the river and environs, and if you go with Russell he might show you the white-backed night heron – which, if you know your birds, is a rare treat. Twitchers will also be thrilled that there's a good chance of spotting the half-collared kingfisher and, in winter, the African finfoot. Once you reach the turning point of the tour, you'll stop on a natural river beach and can enjoy your lunch and walk through the forest, or swim before returning to the boat an hour or so later. Drinks are available on board, and picnic baskets must be ordered 24 hours in advance. Trips run from April–Nov at 11h00 and 14h00, and from Nov–April they do an additional 'sundowner' trip. Trips cost from R130 an adult, and R55 a child under 12, tel 044-532-7876 or 083-254-3551, e-mail ferry@ferry.co.za to book, or web www.ferry.co.za for further info.

Keurbooms River Ferries also hires **self-drive boats** licensed to carry 4 adults. The 5 hp engines are easy to use, and once they've shown you how and given you the rules of the river and safety equipment, you can head off for a day's fishing along the 5 km towards the mouth, or head upriver and stop at any of 3 river beaches, which all have braais, toilets and shade, and are safe for swimming. Prices are from R95 an hour with a minimum of 2-hours booking required. Ask for day- and half-day rates. Call Mark on 082-487-3355. Alternatively, the Plett Angling Club on the opposite side of the river also offers boat hire on a half- or full-day basis.

Something really different is the 2-day **Whiskey Creek canoe trail** (maximum 10 people) to an overnight, stilted log cabin with dormitory-style sleeping 7 km up the Keurbooms River. This used to be a straight paddle but, following floods a few years back, there are now a few minor portage points before reaching the cabin. There are solar powered lights and hot water, a large deck with braai area you won't want to leave in a hurry, and all you need to take is food, drinks and sleeping bags. It can be reached only on the river so come late afternoon it's just you, those who came with you and the creatures of the forest. The self-catered, self-guided option is reasonably priced and is sure to be 1 of the main entries in your holiday diary. It's run by the long-standing Garden Route company **Eden Adventures** from their office at the **Keurbooms Nature Reserve**. They also hire out canoes at an hourly or daily rate and will set you on your way with various paddling options up and down the Keurbooms River, as well as on the Bitou River. A good one to try is a morning paddle up the Bitou, bird-watching as you go, to Emily's (see Eating Out) for lunch and then, when the food and drink have made you mellow, they'll fetch you and transport you back to their office. To find the option for you tel 044-877-0179 or 083-628-8547, e-mail info@eden.co.za or web www.eden.co.za.

Overnight at Keurbooms River
CALICO & CANVAS

Forever Resorts Plettenberg Bay is situated within a conservation area among indigenous forest on the banks of the Keurbooms River. The various accommodation options include 116 caravan sites with electricity points, 9 timber chalets sleeping 2–6 people, 12 brick chalets with indoor fireplaces sleeping 6, and 8 luxury log cabins that sleep 6 and have views of the river. The location of the resort is conducive to long bouts of quiet contemplation listening to the

The place where land meets sea in Plettenberg Bay can be a watery deception, with far more water than land, what with 3 lagoons – Keurbooms mouth here – trying to break out.

surrounding sounds resonating across the gorge. Tangled forest spills down the slopes of the adjacent hill where vervet monkeys bounce through the treetops. When you've had enough rest, take yourself off on a canoe or pedal boat trip up river, and lose yourself in an image of paradise.

Resort facilities include a swimming pool, trampolines and volleyball court, or try a touch of fishing on the wide stretch of river frontage. There is also plenty to keep the kids amused, and the bird watching is incredible. Rates for camping and caravanning depend on the position of the site and cost R65–R80/p out of season, and R470–R535 a site for 4 people plus R80–R90 each additional person in season. 'Season' is generally over Easter weekend and December school holidays. Chalets range from R590 for 1 bedroom to

R1 325 for a log cabin out of season, and R930–R1 770 for the same in season. Out of season pensioner discounts are available on all options (this is a very popular resort with caravanners who set up temporary homes and make new friends of their neighbours). Day visitors have the use of a separate area. To book, tel 044-535-9309, e-mail plettres@foreversa.co.za or web www. foreversa.co.za.

East of Plett – Keurboomstrand

A short distance past the Keurbooms River along the N2, there's a turn-off right to Keurboomstrand, a sleepy hamlet comprising mostly holiday hous-es, a restaurant and accommodation on a section of the coast that has good beaches, interesting rock formations and is a very popular venue for fishers. From the end parking outside Enrico's Restaurant, it's a

15-minute walk to the well-known **Arch Rock**, and a bit further to Cathedral Rock; this is the area where the Strandloper Cave was recently discovered.

Overnight at Keurboomstrand
CALICO & CANVAS
If you want to stay over, **Arch Rock Chalets & Caravan Park** has 17 self-catering options sleeping from 2 to 6 people. These range from forest lodges, and log cabins, to the original beach-front cottages and more modern units – all with equipped kitchens, TV, braai, bedding and towels. The beach is easily accessed from the resort via steps down the embankment. There's a whole string of rates depending on position, view, type and size of unit, and time of year. As a ballpark figure they range from R500 for 2 people to R1 100 for 6 people low/high season and prices skyrocket during December school holidays. The 20 campsites are shaded by milkwood trees and set a bit back from the beach. They're a little cramped and the facilities are showing wear and tear, but it's quite cosy if you're not fussy. Camping rates are R70–R140/p for low/high season, plus R15 for electricity. Tel 044-535-9409, e-mail info@archrock.co.za or web www.archrock.co.za.

Eating Out in Keurboomstrand
Thyme & Again is on the N2 about 8 km east of Plett, before you turn off to Keurboomstrand. It's a farm stall with shelves groaning with preserves, much of which they produce themselves, and a whole range of other items including those that come straight from the bakery oven. Their restaurant serves food from breakfast to lunch 7 days a week and the menu has interesting combinations. Grab a bottle from their wine room and head out onto the deck for a lazy meal in the shade of brollies; tel 044-535-9432.

Ristorante Enrico's is an Italian restaurant situated on Keurboomstrand overlooking the beach. The menu is somewhat rustic, with lots of seafood, pasta and pizza that's accompanied by a small selection of Italian wines and the usual South African suspects. It's a hit in warmer months when locals and visitors flock there to sit at wooden bench-tables on the large terrace that has good views of the coastline; and in winter the interior is cosy and filled with appetising smells and authentic Italian music that'll have you tackling the grappa. It's open daily from 12h00 until late. To book, call 044-535-9818, e-mail info@enricorestaurant.co.za or web www.enricorestaurant.co.za.

Wybo's Pub and Boma Grill is at the turn-off to Keurboomstrand. It's a typical South African steakhouse that is popular with locals who are fans of venison, but their large menu has much more on offer, from pasta to grills, and home-style comfort food. They're fully licensed (there's a separate bar too) and always have a special on offer. Opening hours are Tue–Sat from 12h00–22h00 (kitchen closes at 21h00), and 12h00–16h00 on Sundays for a roast. To book in busy times, tel 044-535-9942.

East of Plett – The Crags
The Crags is a rural area that lies 20 km east of Plett, below the Tsitsikamma mountains. Take the N2 from Plett, cross the Bitou and Keurbooms rivers,

Let's imagine: the man showing his children Cathedral Arch on Keurbooms beach once stood at that same spot many years before, while his dad held his hand under the landmark rock.

and wind up the hill – at the top lies The Crags. Over recent years this area has become home to some top attractions that have transformed the region from a purely beach destination into one that now offers wildlife encounters with monkeys, birds, elephants, and large cats; plus some wine tasting and polo to end off the day.

Out and About in The Crags

Many of the attractions in The Crags are animal related. One of the best-known wildlife attractions near Plett is **Monkeyland**, which is well sign-posted off the N2. Here primates that were previously confined in cages have been released into a free-roaming environment in 12 ha of forest that closely resembles their natural habitat (although they originate from all over the world). There are a host of different species of monkeys, lemurs and apes swinging in the trees in what is thought to have been the first and currently the only multi-species primate sanctuary in the world. Entrance is free if you just want to sit on the forest deck and sip a drink or have a bite to eat while watching the primates nearby. This is a great option if you're watching your budget.

However, we recommend you join a 1-hour guided walk with a ranger who'll track down the primates and fill you in on loads of interesting stuff while wandering through the forest and across the 128 m swing bridge through the treetops – don't forget comfortable walking shoes. A visit is fun and interesting, and some of our cousins are really cute. These walks depart every half hour and cost R120 for adults, R60 for children aged from 3 to 12 years.

Right next door to Monkeyland, and another brainchild of its owner, Tony Blignaut, is **Birds of Eden**. Spanning 2,3 ha of indigenous forest it's – again – reputedly the largest single free-flight aviary in the world, and is home to more than 3 000 previously caged birds of 220 African and exotic species. They've been freed from cages to once again feel the exhilaration of flying in the forest canopy. While wandering along 1,2 km of walkways, some elevated,

WHY VISIT THE CRAGS?
To take an elephant by the trunk and go for a walk.

WHAT'S WACKY?
Having a range of animals in captivity that roamed free in this region centuries ago.

TOURIST INFORMATION
The Crags is such a hip and happening place that the various stakeholders decided to create a more visible destination route. Their unmistakable pink fold-out map and brochure called Cruise the Crags is a travelling companion that details where to cruise (activities and attractions), snooze (accommodation) and chews (places to eat). They also have a website www.cruisethecrags.co.za and can be contacted on e-mail info@cruisethecrags.co.za or tel 044-534-8622.

the darting streaks of coloured feathers and cacophonic squawks will keep you enthralled. There's a mist system to add to the rainforest effect, and a small man-made waterfall you walk behind. It's not hardcore birding, but the collection of species is amazing and it makes for a great family outing. Set aside a minimum of 2 hours, preferably more, and take a breather or have a meal at the restaurant or snack bar. Entrance costs R120 for adults, R60 for children aged 3–12 years. We recommend you go for a full day's outing taking in both establishments and then the combo price is R192 for adults, R96 for kids. Both are open 08h00–17h00 daily. For more info, give them a squawk on 044-534-8906, e-mail info@birdsofeden. co.za or web www.monkeyland.co.za or www.birdsofeden.co.za.

The Elephant Sanctuary, 400 m before you reach Monkeyland, is home to a small herd of rescued African elephants that comprises 5 females and 1 male. It's a pachyderm halfway house and the management system is based on a foundation of trust, with bonds built through humans exercising and stimulating their 4-legged counterparts daily: the idea being that when the elies are old and experienced enough, they'll be released back into the wilderness. What the visitor can experience is close contact in the form of brushing and feeding them, a sunrise or sunset tour, and the highlight is the trunk-in-hand experience. This centre's aim is to focus on education through interaction, but you are likely to find – like we did – that after holding that trunk in your hand, your brain goes mushy with sentimentality and you don't remember many of the facts being shared. Being in the company of such magnificent beasts is humbling, and it is a privilege, albeit a man-made one, to hold their trunk and go for a stroll. The 1-hour tours are available throughout the day from 08h00, or try their popular 2-hour sunrise or sunset experience. Fees vary according to the option you choose. The Trunk-in-Hand programme lasts about 1 hour, of which you're actively with the elies for half that time, and the rest is pre- and post-education on their anatomy and habits. Entrance fees are R150 for children (3–14yrs) and R295 for adults. To find out more give them a trumpet on 044-534-8145, ele-mail crags@elephantsanctuary.co.za or web www.elephantsanctuary.co.za.

In the same area **Tenikwa Wildlife**

A rescued barn owl gets good care at Eagle Encounters before being set free again.

They're far from being pets, but you can pet them, at Knysna Elephant Park.

Awareness Centre is home to a host of wild felines from the African continent and beyond. It's well signposted from the turn-off on the N2 and offers 1-hour guided tours leaving every half hour from 09h00–16h30 every day of the week. There's a tearoom overlooking a dam that's home to waterfowl, blue cranes and other birds, so if you have to wait a while it won't be a hardship. Although the centre focuses on the 'lesser cats' such as genets and African wild cat, they offer a **sunrise experience** that lasts 2–3 hours when you join the cheetahs for a walk, and watch them clamber about in trees and play. This sunrise tour must be pre-booked. Give Len or Mandy a purr on 044-534-8170, 082-414-4416 or 082-486-1515, e-mail info@tenikwa.co.za or web www.tenikwa.co.za.

Another interesting wild experience to ssssqueeeeze into a visit to The Crags is **Lawnwood Snake Sanctuary**. They offer 1-hour guided tours starting at an indigenous snake pit, followed by other outdoor exhibits including meeting Billy, the cuddly monitor lizard. Yes, these underrated reptiles really are cute. Then the tour moves into the snake housing in a large dome where South African and exotic ssssspecimens live; and finally you get to see the huge pythons and other giant constrictors. The owners, Michael and Emily Caithness, rescue and offer sanctuary to snakes and put emphasis on education. Most of us are socially conditioned to believe all snakes are dangerous and should be killed; after a tour like this you'll have learned all sorts of interesting facts and leave with a less fearful approach to these creatures. They're open Tuesday–Sunday from 10h00–16h00, and every day during school holidays, but closed for the month of May. If you want further info give the owners a hiss on 044-534-8056 or 082-667-6588, or e-mail lawnwood@polka.co.za.

Feel like taking in a show one night? The original **Barnyard Theatre** is located in a rustic barn and hosts national and international artists. To check out what's on and book, contact Figo on tel 044-533-5432 or 082-973-1246.

Plett Puzzle Park is well signposted on the N2, 10km from Plett towards The Crags and offers a very different and, 'scuse the pun, a-maze-ing way to keep the family busy for half a day. The 3-D maze and Forest Puzzle Walk is a subtle workout for mind and body. After that the young ones can get stuck into the kid's rope maze, while mom and dad work their way through some light refreshments. It's important to wear comfy shoes for the hour or more that you'll be in the natural forest; and a hat for when you're doing the maze, which is a lot of fun and suitable for all ages. Open daily 09h00–17h00 and costs vary according to which puzzle you want to undertake: adults R50–R100, children under 12, R40–R80. For more info tel 044-534-8853, e-mail info@plettpuzzlepark. co.za or web www.plettpuzzlepark.co.za.

Those who think any chance of doing a little wine tasting lies several hundred kilometres towards Cape Town will be pleasantly surprised. Peter and Caroline Thorpe, who own **Bramon Wine Estate**, are producing a very palatable sauvignon blanc Cap Classique sparkling wine; new cultivars planted will increase their range. This, we believe, is the most-easterly wine farm in the Western Cape and the only winery in the region – the closest being in the Little Karoo around Calitzdorp. They're open for tasting and sales from 11h00–17h00. If this tipple tickles your tonsils, they also have an on-site restaurant – see Eating Out in The Crags. Tel 044-534-8007, e-mail peter@bramonwines.co.za or visit web www.bramonwines.co.za.

Overnight in The Crags
LINEN
Moon Shine on Whiskey Creek is our favourite place to stay hereabouts, 10 minutes from Plett and situated off the N2 without it being a long drive to the middle of nowhere. The welcoming owners, Albert and Sue Bröhm, have created 4 handcrafted wooden cottages – with great respect for the unspoiled indigenous forest – on a north-facing slope; each is isolated just enough to ensure privacy. The cabins are fully equipped for self-catering and come with fireplace, private elevated deck with a mountain or forest view, and braai area. Depending on where you stay, you might get a wraparound deck, or the 1 with the mosaic shower – it's awesome; and so is their Forest Jacuzzi, built on a deck overlooking the valley. Make the time to soak in 38°C bubbles preferably with a bottle of your own bubbly nearby; it's food for the soul, especially if you've just returned from the mountain pool walk. The latter is a hike down the kloof to Whiskey Creek (a tributary of the Keurbooms River) and is best done at a leisurely pace so you can look out for fungi, ferns and birds, and explore the pool when you get to the bottom.

For those not wanting the schlepp of making a meal, Sue sells homemade pre-cooked frozen lasagne, lamb curry and chicken pie; just take your own salad and wine. Moon Shine welcomes children, and there's a swimming pool and playground for them. There's also a restored farm cottage on offer, which has fabulous views enjoyed from the wide veranda. Self-catering rates are from R480 for 2 people in low season to R1 300 for 6 people in high season. To book, tel 072-200-6656, e-mail moonshine@mweb.co.za or web www.whiskeycreek.co.za.

Ever tried to remember the name of a super place you stayed, and couldn't? Well, the owners of this one have saved you the trouble by naming their quirky self-catering house **That Place**. It's a

Nearly 2,5 ha of covered forest and home to some 3 000 birds representing 220 species, all freed from cages – that's Birds of Eden, where you play the Big Explorer on the swing bridge.

cheerful 3-bedroom house, just 700 m off the N2 and overlooking a verdant valley. The main bedroom comes with en-suite bath and shower and sweeping forest views; and the kid's bedroom comes with toys. The second bathroom has shower only. A long wooden table and braai on the covered patio is great for relaxing around with friends; or, if you're the quiet type, there's a wooden deck with that same valley view, which can be enjoyed from the hanging seat or recliner. If the weather's miz, there are tons of books of various genres, games, DStv and a selection of DVDs, or you could hop into the on-site sauna; and in warm weather there's an inviting swimming pool to loll in. Rates for the house are from R750–R1 500 a night self-catering. To book, tel 044-534-8886 or 082-578-1939; e-mail info@thatplace.co.za and have a look at their fun, interactive website that allows you to explore That Place, www.thatplace.co.za.

Eating Out in The Crags

If you like a casual atmosphere, good food, and some alcohol-induced hilarity head to **Bramon Wine Estate's Restaurant**. Caroline Thorpe has created a stylish wine-farm eatery with garden seating alongside vineyards; or indoors beside a crackling fire, and serves classy home-cooked 'peasant food'. Take your time to enjoy mezze lunch platters that include dolmades, olive butter, smoky eggplant dip, garden salads and great homemade bread. The smoked duck goes particularly well with the sparkling wine made on the estate. If you spot some elephants next door, it won't necessarily be because you've had too much wine – unless they're pink. The neighbouring farm is an elephant sanctuary. Open daily, 11h00–17h00. To book, tel 044-534-8007, e-mail caroline@bramonwines.co.za or web www.bramonwines.co.za.

The small **Crags Superette** is open from Mon–Fri 06h45–19h00, Sat 07h30–19h00, and Sundays from 08h00–18h00. It sells fairly basic groceries, take-aways, ice, gas and fuel, and there's an Absa bank ATM.

Tsitsikamma Region 12

Here, at its furthest eastern end, beyond the holiday hullabaloo of Mossel Bay, Knysna and Plett, lies the true garden we have been looking for, but up to now have found intact only in patches. This is where wild forest meets craggy rocky shore; where the bootprint of mankind has not beaten roughshod over the wonders of nature. Here, at last, we find communion with nature and peace of body, soul and mind in a green world.

The rocky shoreline at Storms River Mouth is part of the most important marine reserve in southern Africa and a vital breeding area for many fish species that are elsewhere in peril.

Nature's Valley

Some 30 km east of Plett lies the small settlement of Nature's Valley at the mouth of the Groot River. This area forms part of the Tsitsikamma National Park, also known as the De Vasselot Nature Reserve, and it is our absolute favourite place on the Garden Route; it may well be South Africa's most pleasing 'natural' built place. It's 14 km off the N2; turn onto the R102 at The Crags and you'll travel along a fynbos plateau before zigzagging down the **Groot River Pass**, with its glorious indigenous forest and giant yellow-woods. If you stop to admire these trees, there's a chance you'll hear the Knysna turaco *craaaking* high up in the branches.

Thomas Bain completed this pass in 1880, and evidently all that's changed since then is that it has been tarred. As you near the bottom, there's a fleeting glimpse of the Indian Ocean, then you're back in the shade of the trees before turning right to the village. Except 'village' is not quite what Nature's Valley is. It's more of a collection of 400-odd (some odd indeed) holiday homes, around 100 residents who are fortunate enough to live here permanently, and over summer holidays it quivers with frenetic energy as it's inundated with city folk on their annual getaway.

Prior to becoming a village in 1953, the valley was one of the original pioneer farms in the area; and today – out of season at least – Nature's Valley retains a tranquil farm-like atmosphere. Spend a few days and you'll see bushbuck wandering into residents'

gardens; bush pigs are also said to visit occasionally at night. The quiet times are also when you're guaranteed a large stretch of sand all to yourself, and the beauty of this environment can be enjoyed at a leisurely pace.

This is a valley full of nature's bounty; long beaches overlooked by the Tsitsikamma mountains, the amber waters of the river and lagoon, all intertwined with emerald forest that's inhabited by small wildlife and innumerable species of birds. South lie the azure waters of the Indian Ocean, and on most days of the year the sun shines down on this scene from a deep blue sky. Certainly, humankind has made its mark in the form of houses, many of which don't blend into their surroundings, but the theory is that because the village is encircled by national park, it cannot be developed or extended.

NB: It should be noted that the

WHY VISIT NATURE'S VALLEY
To get in touch with nature.

WHAT'S WACKY
In December holidays, the population shoots up from 100 to 2500!

TOURIST INFORMATION
Info is best sought via your host if you're booking accommodation here, or from the shop on tel 044-531-6835, e-mail beefy@xnets.co.za or web www.natures-valley.co.za. The shop also arranges letting of holiday homes.

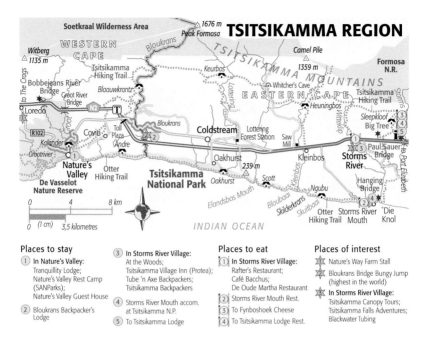

TSITSIKAMMA REGION

Places to stay

① **In Nature's Valley:**
Tranquillity Lodge;
Nature's Valley Rest Camp
(SANParks);
Nature's Valley Guest House

② Bloukrans Backpacker's
Lodge

③ **In Storms River Village:**
At the Woods;
Tsitsikamma Village Inn (Protea);
Tube 'n Axe Backpackers;
Tsitsikamma Backpackers

④ Storms River Mouth accom.
at Tsitsikamma N.P.

⑤ To Tsitsikamma Lodge

Places to eat

① **In Storms River Village:**
Rafter's Restaurant;
Café Bacchus;
De Oude Martha Restaurant

② Storms River Mouth Rest.

③ To Fynboshoek Cheese

④ To Tsitsikamma Lodge Rest.

Places of interest

🏹 Nature's Way Farm Stall

🏹 Bloukrans Bridge Bungy Jump
(highest in the world)

🏹 **In Storms River Village:**
Tsitsikamma Canopy Tours;
Tsitsikamma Falls Adventures;
Blackwater Tubing

residential area consists of 1 main loop road, with some side roads, that leads to the restaurant and shop at the 'end' of the village.

Out and About in Nature's Valley

Having turned onto the R102 from the N2 at The Crags, make a point of stopping at **Nature's Way Farm Stall & Country Deli** a few km along. This is the most authentic farmstall we've ever had the pleasure of visiting. It, and the farm, belongs to Pete and Judy Wilson and as you enter the short driveway, you'll smell the surrounding dairy paddocks. Man, there's nothing like this aroma to bring visions of creamy milk and rich cheese to mind. The farmstall is right near the entrance, so you can't miss it. It's the wooden build-

ing that's fenced (to keep children in, and chickens out, except these are no bird-brained chooks) and while you're enjoying coffee, a light lunch, or a cheese platter on the stoep, you'll be serenaded by the lowing of the lactating 4-legged lasses. The farmstall has a variety of deli items, preserves and great honey; if you take your own container you can fill up with fresh Jersey milk. It doesn't get fresher than this! They also sell olive oil on tap, locally produced home bakes, free-range eggs, as well as fruit and veg. However, for us, the highlight is Judy's selection of local and imported cheeses, including their own, Loredo Sweetmilk, which is made from Jersey milk in a natural process without the use of hormones or antibiotics. You can taste various cheeses, which are shaved off large rounds, and they'll cut to order. They're open from 09h00–17h00 daily, except out of school holidays they close on Sundays; but take note that over winter months from June–Sept the farm stall is closed. To contact Judy, tel 044-534-8849 or 082-875-7044, e-mail loredo@global.co.za or web www.cruisethecrags.co.za.

Once you get to Nature's Valley, activities are nature based. Summers are hot, and winters fairly mild interspersed with some gloriously warm days, allowing plenty of time to enjoy the outdoors. It could be argued that lying on the **beach** is essentially an activity; certainly it's nature based. Lazing languidly like a lizard lapping up the rays, you can tune into the sound of the surf and occasionally dip your bod in the sea – couldn't get more in touch with nature if you tried (unless you're one of those who has to have an iPod to ensure your fix of noise pollution). There are several kilometres of unadulterated beaches with various access points, the easiest being at the river mouth or near the shop where a tunnel through the trees takes you onto the beach.

If you're not staying over and just want to picnic, drive past the entrance to Nature's Valley and a little further east there are some **shady picnic sites**.

The **Groot River** lagoon – the mouth of which opens and closes according to the whims of tide and flood – is a large body of water that's suitable for water sports like windsurfing, and is especially good for small children to paddle and play in. It's also fun to take drinks and snacks, hop on a canoe and head upriver to explore; when you tire, pull out the grub to re-energise while you float on the dark waters.

The Groot (big) River is in fact not very big at all, rising just kilometres away in the mountains backing Nature's Valley, but it is part of the bigger picture in this special place.

Not all forest in the Tsitsikamma area is of the high, moist kind: the Otter Trail traverses mainly stunted, dry forest that grows on the sea-facing edge of a plateau that traces the coastline.

There is a network of scenic **hiking trails** in the area, and they take anything from 2–6 hours. Maps and general info on the trails and tides are available from the shop (part of the village restaurant) or SANParks office at the campsite. Our favourite walk is to **Salt River mouth**, a 3 km jaunt west from the beach area in front of the shop. It is an exquisite piece of paradise where emerald forest meets white sand, which meets, er … brown, or green water, depending on whether the river mouth is open or not. It's essential to have good walking shoes and cross the rocks only at low tide. Take note that the rocks can be very slippery in places. There's also an 8 km round trip that takes you inland to/from Salt River mouth. You'll need to put aside at least 4 hours for this if you want to stop and enjoy the views. In both cases, there are some steep climbs. If you want to enquire in advance about the weather, the shop owners, Beefy and Tish Mance and will assist if you call between 08h30–20h30, tel 044-531-6835.

The **Lagoon Walk** takes a couple of hours and leaves from the campsite, crosses the Groot River, follows the eastern shore of the lagoon and returns via the lagoon mouth and the western lagoon shore. If the mouth is open, check the tides for your crossing. It's a fairly easy walk along the flat, and follows a track that's also suitable for **mountain bikes**.

Nature's Valley is the ending point of the famous **Otter Trail** – see The Big 6 of Hiking Trails on page 31. If you're a wanna-be Otter trailer, hang around the beach east of the river mouth where hikers arrive – usually mid-morning, and you can chat to them as they walk across the beach and head for their first

The man who founded Nature's Valley was a road camp overseer on the Groot River Pass in the 1880s. Reynier Barnardo laid the basis for a nature-loving community that remains intact.

taste of luxury in 5 days (the offer of a cold drink would be a welcomed conversation opener).

On your various wonderings, keep an eye out for **wildlife**: 88 species occur in the vicinity. You're almost guaranteed to have great sightings of bushbuck if you're staying in the campsite; and if you're not too busy watching the inside of your eyelids while lying on the beach, there's also a good chance of seeing dolphins. Then, if you're incredibly lucky and the nature spirit that's said to bring good fortune is on your side, you'll glimpse a Cape clawless otter. However, you're more likely to spot its spoor; and locals have seen leopard spoor as well. We felt very privileged to have a brilliant sighting of a spotted genet in front of our forest hut in the rest camp; and the **birdlife** is

enough to send twitchers into raptors, er, raptures – see the SANParks website. Our primate cousins, Bob and Jan (baboons, from the Afrikaans *bobejaan*) also love this area and are often seen on the Groot River Pass; just one thing though, please do not feed them.

Fishing is popular all along the coast, and with necessary permits you may cast your line in from the rocks, lagoon or beach. **Swimmers** should be aware that the area has dangerous undertows when the swell is big, and the surfer dudes say it's 'very sharky' out at the best surf sites.

If you need beach buckets and spades to build that castle you've always dreamed of, the **shop**, which is the only retail outlet here, stocks the basics, including gas, ice, sunscreen and wood, plus essentials like wine. They're obviously more expensive than the large town supermarkets, due to transport costs alone, but they operate every day of the year from 08h30–17h00, except Christmas Day when they're closed.

Overnight in Nature's Valley

Nature's Valley/De Vasselot campsite (see also Calls to the Wild page 20).

SILK

If you prefer a luxurious accommodation, **Tranquility Lodge** is the place to head. It's next door to the restaurant;

THE MAN WHO MADE NATURE'S VALLEY

Perhaps the greatest hunter of the Tsitsikamma in the mid-19th century was one Reynier Barnardo. At the time the area 'frequented only by elephants, buffaloes, woodcutters, hunters and bandits'. His brother Hendrik was a foreman on Thomas Bain's Groot River construction camp.

When the Tsitsikamma Road was completed in 1885, Oom Hendrik bought a 69 ha plot of land where the Groot River meets the sea, built himself a house of yellowwood, married 3 times in all and fathered 19 children. There he farmed and his many friends were always welcome – but they had to abide by his strict rules: to burn and bury all waste, and not to harm even one branch of any indigenous tree. He called his paradise Nature's Valley, and there his spirit and dream remain intact.

---

it's an attractive, mostly wooden building tucked into a neat garden that is a-twitter with birdlife. Rooms are either standard or superior twins or double. Standard rooms are downstairs and have a shower only; superior rooms are upstairs, have shower and bath, selected DStv channels, mini bar and private deck area. The honeymoon 'penthouse' has the same facilities as the superior except the bed is king-sized, the bath is a spa bath, the shower's a double and there's a fireplace.

Other facilities include a swimming pool, wireless hotspot, unique and private outdoor hot pool that you can hire for the evening, and they offer free use of kayaks. For the weary of body, they will arrange holistic treatments and massages; and for newly weds there are honeymoon packages. Breakfast is included in the price, but dinners should be reserved in advance; and meals are served either indoors in the spacious open-plan dining area or on the covered deck that looks straight into the tree tops. B&B rates for their standard rooms are from R550/ps, and for superior rooms from R690/ps. The honeymoon suite costs R1090/ps. To book tel 044-531-6663, e-mail info@tranquilitylodge.co.za or web www.tranquilitylodge.co.za.

LINEN

Nature's Valley Guest House has been offering comfy accommodation to hikers, birders and tourists for more than 20 years. It's a double-storey thatch house situated fairly close to beach and lagoon; and all rooms lead out onto the emerald lawn. Facilities include a separate kitchen and braai area for guests who wish to self-cater, and a garden that's alive with birds. B&B rates are from R225–R275/ps, and if you're lucky enough to be doing the Otter Trail, ask about their special for hikers. Tel 044-531-6805, e-mail reservations@naturesvalleyguesthouse.co.za or web www.naturesvalleyguesthouse.co.za.

CALICO

The nearest backpacker accommodation is **Bloukrans Backpacker's Lodge** that overlooks the stupendous Bloukrans gorge and Tsitsikamma mountains beyond. It's situated at the bungy site but it's rather isolated if you don't have your own wheels, although the Baz Bus does stop there. Dorms cost R100/p, doubles R200; tel 042-281-1450, e-mail juline@tsitsikamma.org.za or web www.tsitsikamma.org.za.

CANVAS

The **Nature's Valley Rest Camp**, De Vasselot, on the banks of the Groot River, is a few notches down from that with 45 sites (no electricity) set in the deep shade of indigenous trees, some of which are stately Outeniqua yellow-woods, and an additional 20 campsites on grass for use in busy times. There are also 10 A-frame forest huts, which are a little more luxurious than camping, but not to be confused with a chalet. What you get is a wooden hut that has 2 single beds, a table and chairs, and kitchen counter with toaster and kettle. There is no fridge or cooking facilities, apart from an outside braai place; no water; and no bathroom – just like camping but without the canvas. They're cosy and huts 1 to 4 have access from little front decks down to the water. You can hire canoes from the office for R25/

The rest camp's original name was De Vasselot, after the Cape's first forest conservator.

hour. Be aware of the dawn, dusk and any-time-of-day raiding parties in the form of monkeys and baboons that are adept at reducing unsuspecting visitors' larders. Here rates are R150 a site for 2 and the huts are R320 a unit. You can book directly with the rest camp on 044-531-6700 or e-mail naturesvalley@sanparks.org.

Eating Out in Nature's Valley

There is only 1 restaurant, and it serves a variety of the standard fast-food choices, plus a few wholesome options, and the odd special. The menu is fairly extensive and includes the ever-popular seafood and grills. The pub has Mitchell's beer on tap, plus bottled beers – just the thing for when you come off a hot beach with a hot bint. Check out the collection of unsavoury hiking boots hanging in the tree in their beer garden (you don't want to sit near them!). They also offer takeaways. The restaurant kitchen is open from 09h30–16h00, then again from 17h30–20h45, whereas the pub stays open even when the kitchen is closed. The restaurant and pub operate daily, except for Christmas Eve and Day; and it's also closed on New Year's Eve.

Tsitsikamma
Including Nature's Valley & Storms River

The first thing you need to get straight is the possible confusion between the names and areas that this chapter covers. Tsitsikamma is the region. For the purposes of this book we are writing about the following places that are within the Tsitsikamma region:

Nature's Valley village and surrounds, the Storms River village; Storms River bridge on the N2; and Storms River mouth, which is in the national park. What is also useful to know is that, when travelling from west to east on the N2, you will cross the Bloukrans Bridge first, then pass the turn-off to the Tsitsikamma National Park – where you'll find Storms River mouth, and you'll then reach the turn-off to Storms River village 4 km later. Continuing along the N2 for a further 5 km you'll cross the Storms River bridge.

Between Plett and the Storms River bridge lies approximately 65 km of N2 toll road, which is an attractive enough road considering its purpose, but is nothing like the original 'old' road, the R102. This was a narrow serpentine

A forest boardwalk leads you to the suspension bridge over the Storms River at its mouth.

waters', and is supposed to refer to the many rivers and mountain streams in the area. They cleave their way across the plateau in deep gorges as they make their way to the sea, creating impressive waterfalls en route. To the north, it's bordered by the Tsitsikamma mountains, and between them and the sea are large tracts of indigenous forest, fynbos, and commercial timber plantations, all of which are sustained by the high rainfall the region receives.

Out and About in Tsitsikamma

The year-round, mostly mild climate makes this area a favourite for outdoor activities and adrenaline sports. This section covers activities and attractions in an area that we can roughly describe as between Nature's Valley and Storms River bridge.

Heading from west to east, the first – and a hugely popular – attraction and activity is the **Bloukrans bridge** and its bungy jump. This is Africa's highest road bridge, and the world's highest single-span concrete arch bridge, with a central span of 272 m, and a total bridge length of 451 m. It was completed in 1983. Even if you don't want to bungy, there's a fabulous viewsite (and restaurant) at the bungy base called Face Adrenalin. At 216 m above the river gorge, this is advertised as the **world's highest bungy jump**. Forget about all the stuff there is to keep the kids amused, this is the top spot for parents to head to when the apples of your eye have driven you insane and your only release is to jump off a bridge. The guys at Face Adrenalin will happily urge you over the edge, having first strapped you

road that wound down through thick indigenous forest to the bottom of the valleys of first the Groot River, then Bloukrans River, and finally the Storms River. Today, spectacular bridges span these gorges, but only 1 of the passes remains open. The Storms River pass closed shortly after the bridge on the N2 opened; and the Bloukrans pass was recently closed due to rockslides after bad weather. The cost to repair the latter to a level safe enough for public access is so high it's unlikely to reopen, not soon anyway. However, the Groot River pass is still very much in daily use as this is the road, the R102, down to Nature's Valley.

The word 'tsitsikamma' is a Khoi one meaning something to the effect of 'place of abundant (or sparkling) into a harness, and then to a sturdy bungy cord, which will ensure your return to sanity.

It's an awesome experience – or as someone once described it, it's 7 seconds of absolute terror – and costs about R90 for each second (R620). Face Adrenalin also offers a 200 m zipline called the **Flying Fox** that takes you out onto the bridge arch and costs R170. It's like a foefie slide and again, you're in a harness, attached by various safety cables before whizzing out into the void, with a couple of hundred metres drop below you. If these don't grab you by the *cajones*, you can do the 400 m-return **Bridge Walk** for R90. The latter is on a metal-grid catwalk, also 216 m above ground, but it too is not for the faint hearted. Groups should pre-book jumps to enable the guys to process jumpers more timeously. They're open 7-days a week from 09h00–17h00. Tel 042-281-1458 or 083-231-3528, e-mail info@faceadrenalin. com or web www.faceadrenalin.com.

FORESTS OF THE GARDEN ROUTE

The real 'garden' of the Garden Route is the forest, yet many visitors know little about it. It is the largest continuous example of Afromontane forest in the country, and is scattered along the coastal strip, from the slopes of the Outeniqua and Tsitsikamma mountains down to the sea, between George and Storms River. This is where much of the region's history is written; and were it not for these forests, with their abundance of hard-wood trees and game, the pattern of settlement would have been quite different – black pastoralists probably would have reached CT before the *mzungus*! Certainly, before white settlers came to the area, it's thought that these forests remained virtually untouched. From the late 1700s, large-scale destruction ensued thanks to the timber trade, and today only 43 500 hectares of the original 250 000 that once grew in the southern Cape, remain. According to SANParks information, current-day harvesting is at a rate of no more than 1 tree a hectare, which in theory emulates the natural cycle of the forests.

DID YOU KNOW?

Tannins and humic acids that leach from leaf litter on the forest floor cause the brown colour of forest water, seen in streams and rivers of the region.

FOREST CODE

◆ Guard against all risk of fire.
◆ Protect trees, plants and wildlife.
◆ Leave things as you find them, take nothing away.
◆ When walking or cycling, never leave the marked route.
◆ Avoid damaging route-markers and signs on marked routes.
◆ Leave no litter.
◆ Observe signs and for your own safety keep clear of forestry operations.
◆ Respect the peace and quiet of the forest and avoid disturbing others.

Storms River village is the next destination on the N2 and lies less than 1 km off the national road. It's idyllically situated right on the edge of the Plaatbos indigenous forest, which offers many well marked trails for both hikers and mountain bikers. The village comprises 4 streets across, and 3 streets down, and apart from residential homes, there are a few accommodation establishments, a couple of tour operators, and the odd wee shop to keep you going. This is pretty much a hamlet, with quiet streets that are safe to walk at night, and it's a haven to small animals such as bush pigs, genet, bushbuck and porcupine, and birds. A resident bird enthusiast, Louise Reed, has been toting up her bird list since 1997 and has spotted 153 bird species in the forest,

It's not the rivers here that are so big, it's the gorges, and off them all Bloukrans is king.

fynbos, and her garden. If you like to have the knowledge of a local when exploring, join Bob and Louise Reed on 1 of their Forest and Fynbos guided walks, tel 082-787-1598.

Self-guided walks from the village are between 2 and 12 km long, and info is available from the SANParks (Tsitsikamma section) office in the village. The 22 km circular Storms River cycle route starts here too, and traverses indigenous forest, pine plantation and fynbos as it winds down the old Storms River Pass, along a plateau east of the gorge, and to the lookout point high above the river mouth.

This is also the area that a few famous, and less famous hiking trails start and finish. See The Big 6 of Hiking Trails on page 31 for info about the following 3 trails: the Otter Trail, which starts at Storms River mouth and ends on the beach at Nature's Valley; the Tsitsikamma Hiking Trail, which starts at the Nature's Valley rest camp and ends at either Storms River bridge or Storms River village (note, this trail cannot be done in reverse); and the Dolphin Trail, which is a portered slackpacking hike with upmarket accommodation.

The highlight of any visit to Storms River is the treetop tour. Tsitsikamma Canopy Tours was the first of its kind in Africa (although there are older canopy walkways in the forests of Ghana) and offers an unforgettable adventure and nature experience. It's a combination of an adrenalin activity; plus incredible views of the forest from a unique treetop perspective usually reserved for birds and monkeys; and you'll be educated by

It's called a foefie slide, but this is a rather special one ... 10 of them in fact, which make up the hour-long Tsitsikamma Canopy Tour eco-experience near Storms River village.

your guides who enthuse about the forest and its ecology. This treetop system is an engineering feat that allows you to glide through the canopy from giant forest tree to giant forest tree, stopping on platforms attached high up the trunks of towering yellowwoods – the big-shots of the Afromontane habitat. It's important to note here that the entire structure follows the highest safety standards, and is erected in such a way as to cause no harm to the environment. There are 10 slides in all and distances above the forest floor reach 30 m; but no need to fret as you are attached to the steel cables via the harness you're wearing and a series of safety ropes and clips.

While 30 m might not seem very high when you see it printed here, believe us, it is! The company is not only innovative in its activity, but it's also a member of Fair Trade in Tourism; they've won a long list of awards and they're involved in many community upliftment projects. Booking is essential and a maximum number of 8 people are taken on a tour. Departure times are every 30 minutes and are not restricted by inclement weather. Each tour takes 2½–3 hours and costs R450/p, which includes a light meal. To book, tel 042-281-1836, e-mail adventure@gardenroute.co.za or web either www.treetoptour.com or www.stormsriver.com.

Stormsriver Adventures offers a 2½–3 hour **Woodcutters Journey** in an open vehicle (an open vehicle or tractor with trailer, numbers depending) to the bottom of the Storms River pass and back. They follow the 'elephant trail' through the forest while a qualified guide relates the history of the area, and informs you about the flora and fauna. Lunch, or tea, is enjoyed at a picnic site alongside the golden-black waters of the river where ox wagons outspanned more than a century ago. The tours take a minimum of 6 people. The lunch trip costs R200/p, and the tea trips R140/p, and depart at 08h30, 11h30 (lunch) and 14h30 daily. To book, tel 042-281-1836, e-mail adventure@gardenroute.co.za or web www.stormsriver.com.

Tsitsikamma Falls Adventures offers a thrilling zipline (foefie slide) **over waterfalls**, with the longest glide being 211m. If you're into adrenalin activities, you'll love this one. Refreshments are enjoyed halfway on decks overlooking the waterfalls, and the cost is R300/p. You can also do an **abseil** 30m down a cliff into a fern cove with them at a cost of R80/p. They take all ages, from 3 years up, and do tours 365 days a year in all weather conditions. Tours start at 08h00 and depart every 30 minutes, with the last tour leaving at 16h00. For further info, tel 042-280-3770, e-mail tsitsikamma-falls@lantic.net or web www.tsitsikammaadventure.co.za.

Blackwater Tubing is done by Tube 'n Axe Backpackers about a 20-minute drive from the village on the Storms River, a 5-hour round trip that includes a lunch braai. Depending on the water level, you may be kloofing on low water, or 'white water' tubing on high water (the 'blackwater' part refers to the natural tannin-stained river water in the region). Kloofing entails about ½ walking/boulder hopping and ½ paddling, the latter is across pools, then you carry your tube over shallow sections, and leap off rock faces that may be as high as 8m into pools below. Black- (or white-) water tubing is what the guys call 'bounce, boink and scream blue murder on the roller coaster' and the high water can offer rapids of up to grade 3. Trips start at 07h00, and cost R495/p. To book tel 042-281-1757, e-mail info@tubenaxe.co.za or web www.blackwatertubing.co.za.

If all that frenetic and taxing activity makes you yearn for some treatment that's kinder to your body and soul, make an appointment at **Tsitsikamma Mountain Spa**, which is located at the Armagh Country Lodge, tel 042-281-1512, e-mail armagh@mweb.co.za or web www.thearmagh.com.

The **Tsitsikamma National Park** is a 10-minute drive west of the Storms River village. It's a spectacular marine reserve offering camping and chalets, but **day visitors** are welcome to swim, do the walks, snorkel, refresh at a restaurant, curio shop; there's a tiny but sheltered cove beach with floating platform, and the famous suspension bridge over the Storms River mouth. For details, see Calls to the Wild on page 15.

The **Storms River bridge**, as it's

commonly known, is actually called the **Paul Sauer Bridge** and carries the N2 over the Storms River. The original Storms River pass still lies far below but is no longer open to the general public and may be visited only on a tour (see previous page). Storms River bridge should not to be confused with the suspension foot bridge at Storms River mouth in the Tsitsikamma National Park. The road was completed in 1954 and was a landmark for the long-standing residents of the Garden Route who needed to do shopping forays to Port Elizabeth back in the 70s and early 80s, when retail therapy did not exist in Plett and Knysna. Storms River bridge was a stopover for those of us heading east, and also for those travelling west onto the Garden Route. The bridge is probably better known today because there's a petrol station, restaurant, take-aways and info centre there now.

For those interested in engineering feats of the 50s (it was quite awesome in its day: 2 concrete half arches were lowered from each side and the crowd held its breath to see if they would meet exactly as planned!), there's a walkway from the front of the restaurant complex to a viewsite. If it's a rainy day, be content to look at the display of photos documenting its construction. The other icon of this section of N2 is the **Big Tree**. This 800-year-old, 36 m tall Outeniqua yellowwood stands on the left not far off the N2. At the time of writing, the long-awaited and much dreaded 'upgrading' and therefore widening of this section of N2

Point of no return: it's 216 metres down to the Bloukrans River, reputedly the world's highest commercial bungy jump. The 451 metre single-span concrete arch bridge is also a world beater.

was taking place, and this 'big tree' was inaccessible. For years, locals and nature lovers petitioned the Department of Environment Affairs and Tourism and the National Roads Agency, to retain the narrow 'green tunnel' through this section of forest. It was the last remaining natural tunnel of its kind on the N2. The theory is that the Big Tree will once again be open to the public once road works are completed, so get the latest info from tourism – but alas the road planners won and the green tunnel is gone forever.

The Fernery offers a **nursery**, **restaurant**, **hiking** and **mountain biking trails** through the forest, a **lodge**, and **chalets**. If you're interested in ferns, you'll appreciate their large displays of indigenous ferns and it'll give you the chance to identify that particular specimen seen on a forest walk that you couldn't remember the name of…. Their accommodation is in a magnificent cliff-top setting near a 30 m waterfall, with views over the river gorge and out to sea. This establishment is part of the portered Dolphin Trail. If you want to visit The Fernery, continue with the N2 for 4 km past the Storms River bridge, and turn right onto the Blueliliesbush road, and travel to the T-junction, then follow their signs for another 7 km. Tel 042-280-3588, e-mail reservations@forestferns.co.za or web www.forestferns.co.za.

If you're heading to Port Elizabeth, or have travelled as far as Storms River bridge, it's worth the extra 8 km to turn into **Fine Bush Farm Stall**. It's great for a bite to eat, and offers light 'slow food' lunches with homegrown garden

salad, that can be enjoyed on the farm in warm weather. They also bake bread daily, and have an indigenous nursery. Opening hours are 09h00–17h00 daily (kitchen closes at 16h00). Tel 042-280-3503, e-mail finebush@iafrica.com or web www.finebush.co.za.

Overnight in Tsitsikamma
LINEN

There are quite a few options when it comes to accommodation in the area. Our recommendation on where to stay in the Storms River village is at **The Woods Guest House**. It's owned by the delightful Marco and Bev Coetzee, who are both hands-on hosts and will ensure you have everything you need. Marco has done a fabulous job of renovating and extending what was once a forlorn building into an attractive guesthouse. Finishes are wood, reclaimed where possible; rooms are spacious and bright and have king-sized extra-length beds;

Tsitsikamma is indeed the area where nature's garden is still mostly intact.

Storms River village, smallest and most colourful of 'towns' on the Garden Route.

linen is crisp; showers are walk-in; and the views are alluring. Depending on your room, you'll have a private deck or patio – ours had a fabulous mountain view; all have TV, tea/coffee trays, bar fridge, wall safes and ceiling fans. The earthy colours used complement the wooden balconies and stairways on the outside, and the grounds have sufficient room for the kids to race around. The Coetzees have small children of their own – not that you'll see or hear them – so the pool area is fenced off; there's a paddling pool adjoining the larger one; littlies of all ages are welcome. Breakfast is served in a large, airy room that leads onto a deck overlooking the pool and Storms River peak (dinners are available on request only); and there's an honesty bar and 2 lounges to relax in, plus internet facilities. Bev is an excellent source of info on the Garden Route, having worked at Knysna Tourism for years; and they're

both clued up on activities in the Tsitsikamma area. To book, tel 042-281-1446, e-mail info@atthewoods.co.za or web www.atthewoods.co.za.

The **Protea Hotel Tsitsikamma Village Inn** has 49 elegant rooms and is popular for its old-world charm that is enhanced by a 'village' reflecting various period styles of the old Cape. Among these are a drostdy (courthouse), Victorian-style cottage, Cape Dutch house, forester's cottage, Karoo pastor's home and quaint fisherman's cottage. Each is decorated according to its period, and has its own matching garden from its era. The main building dates back to 1845 and includes a spacious dining room, **De Oude Martha Restaurant**, and the **Hunter's Inn Pub** and Guest Lounge. Due to the scale of this establishment, it is popular with tour groups. The interesting owner, Jan du Rand, has a large **Cadillac collection**, so if you're keen on old cars have a chat and he might open up his displays for you. To book, tel 042-281-1711, e-mail info@village-inn.co.za or web www.village-inn.co.za.

Tsitsikamma Lodge is 8 km east of Storms River bridge and clearly visible from the N2. It's a collection of free-standing timber cabins, each with lovely mountain or forest views. Facilities include spa bath, braai, private deck, TV, telephone, mini fridge, and tea/coffee trays; and you can be assured of a most comfortable stay. The immaculate garden is in itself the kind of place you want to while away the hours. Look out for their winter weekend specials that include meals. See Eating Out in Tsitsikamma for info about their on-site restaurant. Rates are R415–R850/ps and include a scrumptious buffet breakfast. Tel 042-280-3802, e-mail tsitsikamma@riverhotels.co.za or web www.tsitsikammalodge.com. An attraction of the lodge is its 'striptease trail' past several natural pools on the Kruis River; the original idea of lodge founder Vossie Vorster was that you should remove 1 item of clothing at each successive pool.

CALICO & CANVAS

Tube 'n Axe Backpackers Lodge is the original Storms River backpackers and the most popular around. Apart from standard rooms and dorms, they also offer cosy, elevated forest tents and double rooms in the main building. Their main lounge chill area has an African-themed bar complete with timber finishes and African décor with good atmosphere and a pool table. Check out the big mural in their second lounge – it was done by a visiting backpacker some years ago and is a classic skit on the Tsitsikamma region and what it has to offer. Dorms cost R110/p; doubles, twins and triples from R140/p; forest tents from R200; camping R70. This is a Baz Bus stop; and these are the guys that offer the blackwater tubing (see Out and About in Tsitsikamma). To book, tel 042-281-1757, e-mail info@tubenaxe.co.za or web www.tubenaxe.co.za.

The 4-star **Tsitsikamma Backpackers** is the place to stay if you're an environmentally conscious traveller. They buy local produce whenever possible, use alien-tree firewood, recycle wastewater and supply biodegradable soap. Dorms cost R100/p, doubles R260, en-suite doubles R350. There are also tents set away from the main building on the 1-acre plot, doubles cost R210. Meals are available daily if you reserve one before 15h00. It's also a Baz Bus stop and has a shuttle to local activities. Tel 042-281-1868, e-mail stay@tsitsikammabackpackers.com or web www.tsitsikammabackpackers.com.

CALICO & CANVAS

Outside the village, Tsitsikamma National Park has an awesome location on the rugged coastline, and offers camping and chalets at **Storms River mouth**. The campsite – which includes built accommodation – stretches for 2 km along the rocky shore. It includes camping and caravan sites close to where the waves crash into the rocks, some with and others without electrical connections, and ablutions right on the rocks. The formal accommodation consists of 2-, 3- and 4-bed self-catering chalets and cottages, to suit just about every need, including those of honeymooners, all looking out at the crashing breakers. Rates are from R330–R695 a unit for 2 people, and R1050–R2100 a unit for 4 people; camping R210–R250 for 2 people depending on position of site. To contact Storms River mouth direct tel 042-281-1607.

Eating Out in Tsitsikamma

Rafters Restaurant is at the Armagh Country Lodge in Storms River village, offering 'true South African cuisine' (read: local produce). They're at pains to explain that their dishes are unpretentious, and they serve wholesome fare prepared with the freshest, local produce. Vegetables are grown locally in the village using organic techniques

Tsitsikamma's is an emerged coastline: the 200-metre cliffs above Storms River rest camp end on a narrow coastal plateau called a wave-cut platform, which represents a former sea level.

and delivered daily; their seafood is sourced in Plett and their meat comes from Kareedouw over the mountain. Most preserves are made locally by *Ouma*, the owner's mother. When it comes to wine, they personally select and purchase directly from the wine estates, and each complements the dishes on their menu. Meals are served in a relaxed atmosphere with friendly service. Enquire about their speciality evenings, such as braais, traditional buffets and seafood. To book, tel 042-281-1587, e-mail armagh@mweb.co.za or web www.thearmagh.com.

The Tsitsikamma Village Inn has 2 restaurants where you can sit outdoors, alongside the pool, or inside next to a fire in winter. **Café Bacchus** is a Victorian-style tea garden serving good cakes, breakfast all day, light lunches and dinners depending on time of year – open 09h00–21h00. **De Oude Martha Restaurant** is in the main building and serves traditional South African fare. They're open for breakfast 07h00–10h00 and supper 18h00–21h00. To book, tel 042-281-1711, e-mail info@village-inn.co.za or web www.village-inn.co.za.

If you're keen to just have a drink, the **Hunter's Inn Pub** is also at the Tsitsikamma Village Inn and is located in the original hunting lodge of Lieutenant Duthie, the son-in-law of George Rex, founder of Knysna. The original yellowwood ceiling remains, and the décor is in keeping with the

And finally, the suspension footbridge over the Storms River near its mouth that marks the eastern extent of the Garden Route and the end of our journey together: a 'must see'.

era and name of the pub, with trophies, skins and horns adorning the walls. Open 09h00 till late.

Fynboshoek Cheese has become very popular in recent years and offers a farm lunch of simple, but far from ordinary, fare. It is owner-run by cheese-maker Alje van Deemter, who's won international awards for his cheeses. Lunches are served either on the farm-house veranda, or in the sloping back garden and consist of a selection of cheeses (Alje's Formosa goat's milk cheese is a favourite), salads, and freshly baked bread, most of which is produced on the farm.

Be prepared to enjoy the peaceful surroundings while you wait for him to prepare and serve your lunch, which we can assure you will be fabulous; and take your own wine. Booking is essential – you cannot just pitch up – and you will get directions when you phone. Lunch is served every day except Tuesdays. The price per head is around R90 and includes dessert and coffee. To book, tel 042-280-3879.

Tsitsikamma Lodge restaurant offers a 5-course evening buffet in a cosy, but large log cabin with exposed wooden trusses and décor that includes wood-cutting paraphernalia from the old days. Dishes are more along the lines of home cooked than typical hotel fare, and their wine list is extensive but not overpriced. There is seating on 2 levels and, in win-ter, there's a welcoming fire to snuggle around. Price a head is R145–R165, and it is essential to book, preferably early in the day. Tel 042-280-3802, e-mail: tsitsikamma@riverhotels.co.za or web www.tsitsikammalodge.com.

Index

Abseiling
    Plettenberg Bay 175
    Storms River 216
Accommodation pricing 29
Airport & airlines 26, 67
Backpackers, Knysna 155
Backroad Safari, Mossel Bay 49
Banking/money 27
Beaches
    Glentana 64
    Knysna 141, 143
    Mossel Bay 44
    Nature's Valley 206, 208
    Plettenberg Bay 172
    Sedgefield 99
    Wilderness 87
Belvidere 126
    Eating out & accommodation
    127
Bendigo Gold Mine 121
Big Trees 70, 73, 91, 115, 119, 217
Birds of Eden bird sanctuary 198
Bird sanctuary, Lake Brenton 127
Birds & birding 16
    Knysna 145, 149
    Nature's Valley 208
    Sedgefield 101
Bloukrans Bridge 212
Boating
    Plettenberg Bay 174, 194
Boat/sea trips
    Mossel Bay 48
    Storms River 19
Brenton on Sea 128
    Accommodation 129
Brenton blue butterfly 129
Brewery tours, Knysna 147
Bridge catwalk, Bloukrans Bridge
213
Buffalo Bay & Goukamma 114
    Accommodation 115
    Eating out 114
Bungy jumping, Tsitsikamma 212
Bus services 26, 67
Canoeing & kayaking
    Buffalo Bay 114
    Keurbooms 194
    Knysna 143
    Nature's Valley 206

Plettenberg Bay 194
    Sedgefield 100
    Groot River, Storms River 20
Cape Nature 20
Car hire 27
Cities & towns 12
Climate 12
The Crags 196
    Accommodation & eating out
    201
Cycling
    Sedgefield 102
Diepwalle forest 138
Dolphins & whales 184
Eagle Encounters, Plettenberg
    Bay 187
Elephants (wild, forest) 14, 122
Elephant Sanctuary, Plettenberg
    Bay 199
Featherbed Nature Reserve 142
Feeding baboons and wild
    animals 24
Fishing
    Buffalo Bay 114
    Mossel Bay 46
    Nature's Valley 208
    Knysna 144
    Plettenberg Bay 175, 195
    Tsitsikamma 208
Forest canopy tours, Storms
    River 214
Forests of the Garden Route 213
Fuel 28
Fynbos 107
Game reserves
    Botlierskop Private Game
    Reserve 50
    Buffalo Hills 192
    Steenbok Nature Reserve,
    Knysna 145
Garden of Eden forest 140
Garden Route Botanical Garden,
    George 74
Garden Route National Park 17
George 65
    Accommodation 75, 80, 83
    Eating out 77, 80
George Motor Show 69
George Museum 74

Golf
    George 67
    Knysna 148
    Mossel Bay 51
    Plettenberg Bay 177
Goudveld forest 137
Gouna forest 138
Groenvlei & Lake Pleasant 110
    Accommodation 110
    Eating out 112
Great Brak River 62
Harkerville 188
    Accommodation 190
Health 28
Herold's Bay 79
Hiking trails & walks 31
    Brown Hooded Kingfisher Trail
    18
    Cape Dune Molerat Trail 18
    Circles in the Forest Trail
    (Rheenendal) 120
    Dolphin Trail 39
    Drupkelders (Rheenendal) 119
    The Fernery (Tsitsikamma) 218
    Garden Route Trail 37
    Groeneweide Nature Walk
    (George) 70
    Half-Collared Kingfisher Trail 18
    Harkerville Hiking Trail 189
    Nature's Valley 207
    Millwood Mine (Rheenendal)
    122
    Nature's Valley 207
    Otter Trail 33
    Outeniqua Trail 34
    Oystercatcher Trail 38
    Pied Kingfisher Trail 18
    Plaatbos (Storms River) 214
    Plettenberg Bay & surrounds
    175, 191, 193
    Sedgefield 101
    St Blaize Trail 50
    Tsitsikamma Trail 36
    Wilderness 91
Horse riding
    Forest horse rides,
    Rheenendal 117
    Goukamma Nature Reserve 22
    Sedgefield 104

Houseboat accommodation & cruises 124
Jukani Wildlife Predator Park 50
Keurbooms River 193
Keurbooms Nature Reserve 24
Keurboomstrand 195
Kite surfing, Sedgefield 101
Kloofing, Wilderness 18, 89
Knysna 131
    Accommodation 150, 154, 158, 165
    Eating out 160
Knysna Elephant Park 188
Knysna Fort 146
Knysna Heads 141
Knysna lagoon (estuary) 140
Knysna National Lake Area 20
Knysna oyster 149
    Festival 137
Knysna seahorse 142, 148
Kranshoek 191
Lake Brenton 128
    Accommodation 128
Lakes District 89
Language 13
Lawnwood Snake Sanctuary, Plettenberg Bay 200
Leisure Isle 133, 144
Little Brak River 61
Monkeyland, Plettenberg Bay 198
Mossel Bay 41
    Accommodation 52, 57, 62
    Eating out 54, 61, 63
Mountain biking & hire
    Karatara 113
    Knysna 139, 150
    Harkerville 189
    Nature's Valley 207
    Millwood Mine (Rheenendal) 122
    Montagu Pass 69
    Homtini (Rheenendal) 120
    Storms River 214
    Tsitsikamma 218
    Wilderness National Park 18
Nature reserves & wildlife 15
Nature's Valley 204
    Accommodation 209
    Eating out 211
Noetzie 143, 164
Old Gaol Museum, Knysna 145
Outeniqua Choo-Tjoe 68

Outeniqua Country Hop, George 73
Outeniqua mountain range 11
Outeniqua Nature Reserve 20, 70
Outeniqua Power Van, George 69
Paragliding
    Brenton on Sea 129
    Sedgefield 104
    Wilderness 90
Petro SA 43
Photography 30
Plettenberg Bay 167
    Accommodation 178, 180, 190, 193, 196, 201
    Eating out 183, 187, 196, 202
Plett Puzzle Park maze 200
Polo, Plettenberg Bay 177
Population 12
Prince Alfred's Pass 165
Rheenendal 116
    Accommodation 117
River ferry, Keurbooms River 193
River tubing, Storms River 216
Roads & driving 29
Robberg Nature Reserve 22
Ruigtevlei & Karatara 112
    Accommodation 112
Safety 27
Sandboarding, Mossel Bay 51
Scenic drives
    George 70
    Groot River Pass 204
    Montagu Pass 72
    Phantom Pass 122
    Prince Alfred's Pass 165
    Seven Passes Road 73
Scenic lookout points
    Four Passes, George 72
    Wilderness 89, 90
Scuba diving
    Knysna 142
    Tsitsikamma National Park 19
    Mossel Bay 47
    Plettenberg Bay 175
Sedgefield 97
    Accommodation 104
    Eating out 103, 107
Shark cage diving, Mossel Bay 46
Shell Museum, Mossel Bay 49
Shops & shopping 30
Size 10
Skydiving, Plettenberg Bay 175

Slackpacking 37
Snorkelling
    Tsitsikamma National Park 19
South African National Parks (SANParks) 17, 147
St Blaize Lighthouse, Mossel Bay 50
Storms River 211
    Accommodation 218
    Eating out 218, 220
Surfing
    Buffalo Bay 114
    Herold's Bay 79
    Plettenberg Bay 175
    Mossel Bay 47
    Sedgefield 101
    Victoria Bay 83
Surfboard hire 83
Tenikwa Wildlife Awareness Centre, Plettenberg Bay 199
Topography 10
Tourist highlights 13
Tourist seasons 29
Tsitsikamma mountain range 11
Tsitsikamma National Park 19
Tsitsikamma Region 203
Victoria Bay 81
Waterskiing 100
Western Head & Phantom Pass 122
    Accommodation 124
Whale-watching
    Knysna 143
    Mossel Bay 48
    Wilderness 89
    Plettenberg Bay 173
White Bridge 124
    Eating out 125
Wild Card 17
Wilderness 85
    Accommodation 91, 92, 94
    Eating out 94, 96
Wilderness National Park 18
Windsurfing
    Sedgefield 100
    Nature's Valley 206
Wittedrift 192
Yachting 100
Yellowwood Park Bird Sanctuary 127
Zipline gliding, Tsitsikamma 213, 216